Scott Foresman

CALIFORNIA
MATHEMATICS

Authors and Advisors

Jennie Bennett	Charles Calhoun	Mary Cavanagh
Lucille Croom	Stephen Krulik	Robert A. Laing
Donna J. Long	Stuart J. Murphy	Jesse A Rudnick
Clementine Sherman	Marian Small	William Tate
Randall I. Charles	Alma B. Ramirez	Jeanne F. Ramos

Scott
Foresman

Editorial Offices: Glenview, Illinois • Parsippany, New Jersey • New York, New York
Sales Offices: Reading, Massachusetts • Duluth, Georgia • Glenview, Illinois
Carrollton, Texas • Ontario, California

ISBN: 0-328-00466-9

19 20 21 22 23-V064-12 11 10 09 08

Contents

CHAPTER 1 — Using Addition and Subtraction Strategies

Place Value and Adding Two-Digit Numbers

CHAPTER 3

Subtracting Two-Digit Numbers

CHAPTER 4 Money

CHAPTER 5 Time

Patterns and Numbers to 1,000

CHAPTER 7

Adding and Subtracting Three-Digit Numbers

CHAPTER 8

Measurement

CHAPTER 9

Geometry

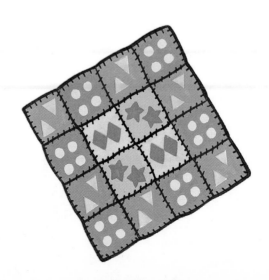

CHAPTER 10 Fractions and Probability

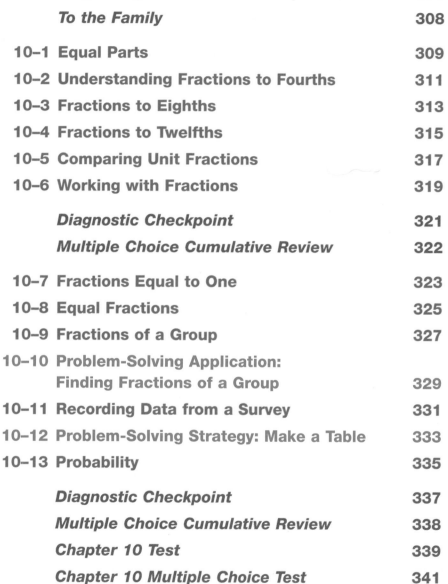

CHAPTER 11

Multiplication

CHAPTER 12 Division

California Mathematics Content Standards

Grade 2

Reproduced from the Mathematics Content Standards for California Public Schools. The symbol (🔑) indicates a key standard as designated by a green oval in the Mathematics Framework for California Public Schools.

By the end of grade two, students understand place value and number relationships in addition and subtraction, and they use simple concepts of multiplication. They measure quantities with appropriate units. They classify shapes and see relationships among them by paying attention to their geometric attributes. They collect and analyze data and verify the answers.

Number Sense

1.0 Students understand the relationship between numbers, quantities, and place value in whole numbers up to 1,000:

1.1 (🔑) Count, read, and write whole numbers to 1,000 and identify the place value for each digit.

1.2 Use words, models, and expanded forms (e.g., 45 = 4 tens + 5) to represent numbers (to 1,000).

1.3 (🔑) Order and compare whole numbers to 1,000 by using the symbols <, =, >.

2.0 Students estimate, calculate, and solve problems involving addition and subtraction of two- and three-digit numbers:

2.1 (🔑) Understand and use the inverse relationship between addition and subtraction (e.g., an opposite number sentence for 8 + 6 = 14 is 14 − 6 = 8) to solve problems and check solutions.

2.2 (🔑) Find the sum or difference of two whole numbers up to three digits long.

2.3 Use mental arithmetic to find the sum or difference of two two-digit numbers.

3.0 (🔑) Students model and solve simple problems involving multiplication and division:

3.1 (🔑) Use repeated addition, arrays, and counting by multiples to do multiplication.

3.2 (🔑) Use repeated subtraction, equal sharing, and forming equal groups with remainders to do division.

3.3 (🔑) Know the multiplication tables of 2s, 5s, and 10s (to "times 10") and commit them to memory.

4.0 Students understand that fractions and decimals may refer to parts of a set and parts of a whole:

4.1 (🔑) Recognize, name, and compare unit fractions from 1/12 to 1/2.

4.2 (🔑) Recognize fractions of a whole and parts of a group (e.g., one-fourth of a pie, two-thirds of 15 balls).

4.3 (🔑) Know that when all fractional parts are included, such as four-fourths, the result is equal to the whole and to one.

5.0 Students model and solve problems by representing, adding, and subtracting amounts of money:

5.1 (🔑) Solve problems using combinations of coins and bills.

5.2 (🔑) Know and use the decimal notation and the dollar and cent symbols for money.

6.0 Students use estimation strategies in computation and problem solving that involve numbers that use the ones, tens, hundreds, and thousands places:

6.1 Recognize when an estimate is reasonable in measurements (e.g., closest inch).

Algebra and Functions

1.0 Students model, represent, and interpret number relationships to create and solve problems involving addition and subtraction:

1.1 (🔑) Use the commutative and associative rules to simplify mental calculations and to check results.

1.2 Relate problem situations to number sentences involving addition and subtraction.

1.3 Solve addition and subtraction problems by using data from simple charts, picture graphs, and number sentences.

Measurement and Geometry

1.0 Students understand that measurement is accomplished by identifying a unit of measure, iterating (repeating) that unit, and comparing it to the item to be measured:

1.1 Measure the length of objects by iterating (repeating) a nonstandard or standard unit.

1.2 Use different units to measure the same object and predict whether the measure will be greater or smaller when a different unit is used.

1.3 (🔑) Measure the length of an object to the nearest inch and/or centimeter.

1.4 Tell time to the nearest quarter hour and know relationships of time (e.g., minutes in an hour, days in a month, weeks in a year).

1.5 Determine the duration of intervals of time in hours (e.g., 11:00 A.M. to 4:00 P.M.).

2.0 (🔑) Students identify and describe the attributes of common figures in the plane and of common objects in space:

2.1 (🔑) Describe and classify plane and solid geometric shapes (e.g., circle, triangle, square, rectangle, sphere, pyramid, cube, rectangular prism) according to the number and shape of faces, edges, and vertices.

2.2 (🔑) Put shapes together and take them apart to form other shapes (e.g., two congruent right triangles can be arranged to form a rectangle).

Statistics, Data Analysis, and Probability

1.0 (🔑) Students collect numerical data and record, organize, display, and interpret the data on bar graphs and other representations:

1.1 Record numerical data in systematic ways, keeping track of what has been counted.

1.2 Represent the same data set in more than one way (e.g., bar graphs and charts with tallies).

1.3 Identify features of data sets (range and mode).

1.4 Ask and answer simple questions related to data representations.

2.0 (🔑) Students demonstrate an understanding of patterns and how patterns grow and describe them in general ways:

2.1 Recognize, describe, and extend patterns and determine a next term in linear patterns (e.g., 4, 8, 12...; the number of ears on one horse, two horses, three horses, four horses).

2.2 Solve problems involving simple number patterns.

Mathematical Reasoning

1.0 Students make decisions about how to set up a problem:

1.1 Determine the approach, materials, and strategies to be used.

1.2 Use tools, such as manipulatives or sketches, to model problems.

2.0 Students solve problems and justify their reasoning:

2.1 Defend the reasoning used and justify the procedures selected.

2.2 Make precise calculations and check the validity of the results in the context of the problem.

3.0 Students note connections between one problem and another.

Using Addition and Subtraction Strategies

Diagnosing Readiness
for Chapter 1

1. What number comes just before 15? _____

2. 7 − 5 = _____

3. 3 + 6 = _____

4. Fill in +, −, or = to make the sentence true.

5 ◯ 3 ▢ 8

5. How many carrots are left in the garden? Write a number sentence.

_____

To the Family

In Grade 1 children learned addition and subtraction concepts and strategies to help them add and subtract.

Using Addition and Subtraction Strategies

Children review the meanings of addition and subtraction and the basic facts. Fact strategies include using doubles and using addition to subtract.

By the end of Grade 2 children will add and subtract two- and three-digit numbers.

Page 1 Your child solved problems that review math skills from Grade 1 and will help your child with the skills in Chapter 1.

Math at Home The chapter theme is gardens. Use index cards to make flash cards of basic facts. Children can illustrate facts by drawing garden vegetables.

Math Literature Read math or theme-related stories with your child. Look for the following books in your local library.
Twelve Ways to Get to Eleven by Eve Merriam (Simon & Schuster, 1996)
Seven Blind Mice by Ed Young (Penguin Putnam, 1992)

California Content Standards in Chapter 1 Lessons*

	Teach and Practice	Practice		Teach and Practice	Practice
Number Sense			1.2 Relate problem situations to number sentences involving addition and subtraction.	1, 2, 5 6, 9	7, 8
2.1 (🔑), Grade 1, Know the addition facts (sums to 20) and the corresponding subtraction facts and commit them to memory.	2, 3, 11		1.3 Solve addition and subtraction problems by using data from simple charts, picture graphs, and number sentences.	12	
2.5 (🔑), Grade 1, Show the meaning of addition (putting together, increasing) and subtraction (taking away, comparing, finding the difference).	1, 6		**Statistics, Data Analysis, and Probability**		
2.7, Grade 1, Find the sum of three one-digit numbers.		4	1.4 Ask and answer simple questions related to data representations.	12	
2.1 (🔑) Understand and use the inverse relationship between addition and subtraction to solve problems and check solutions.	7, 8, 10		2.1 Recognize, describe, and extend patterns and determine the next term in linear patterns (e.g., 4, 8, 12, . . . ; the number of ears on one horse, two horses, three horses, four horses).		2, 5
Algebra and Functions			**Mathematical Reasoning**		
1.0 Students model, represent, and interpret number relationships to create and solve problems involving addition and subtraction.	11		1.0 Students make decisions about how to set up a problem.		8
1.1 (🔑) Use the commutative and associative rules to simplify mental calculations and to check results.	4, 10 –		1.1 Determine the approach, materials, and strategies to be used.		1, 3, 6, 9
			3.0 Students note connections between one problem and another.		2, 10

* The symbol (🔑) indicates a key standard as designated in the Mathematics Framework for California Public Schools.
Full statements of the California Content Standards are found at the beginning of this book following the Table of Contents.

Name_____ **Meanings of Addition**

When you **put together** groups, you can add to find the total.

7 crows are on a fence.
5 robins are in a tree.
How many birds are there in all?

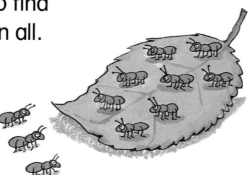

$7 + 5 = 12$

When you **increase** the number in a group, you add to find how many there are in all.

8 ants are on a leaf.
3 more ants come.
How many ants are there in all?

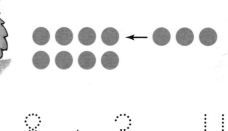

$8 + 3 = 11$

Write the number sentence.
Circle whether you put together or increased to add.

Word Bank

put together
increase
number sentence

1. 6 carrots are in a basket.
    7 more carrots are added.
    How many carrots are there in all?

    ____ + ____ = ____

    put together   increase

2. 9 children are playing.
    5 other children are eating.
    How many children are there in all?

    ____ + ____ = ____

    put together   increase

California Content Standards *Number Sense 2.5 (＊),
Grade 1, Show the meaning of addition. Algebra and Functions
1.2. Also Mathematical Reasoning 1.1.*

three **3**

Write the number sentence. Solve.
Use counters if you like.

3. 4 ants are near the food.
9 more ants come.
How many ants are there
in all?

$\underline{4} + \underline{9} = \underline{13}$

4. 8 boys are eating hot dogs.
4 other boys are eating
corn. How many boys
are eating something?

___ + ___ = ___

5. Dan found 9 shells.
He finds 2 more shells.
How many shells does
he have now?

___ + ___ = ___

6. Jamal ate 6 cherries.
He then ate 4 more cherries.
How many cherries did he
eat in all?

___ + ___ = ___

7. 8 dogs are playing.
7 dogs are sleeping.
How many dogs are
there in all?

___ + ___ = ___

8. 7 people play catch.
9 other people play tag.
How many people
are playing?

___ + ___ = ___

Math Reasoning

Number Sense

9. Write your own addition story.
Write the number sentence.
Tell whether you put together or increased.

Home Activity Tell an addition story to your child. Have him
or her use objects to show whether the story is putting together
or increasing. Homework Workbook 1-1

Name_____ **Using Doubles and Near Doubles**

Doubles facts help you learn other facts.

Think 6 + 6 and I more.

___6___ + ___6___ = _12_   ___6___ + ___7___ = _13_

Write the doubles fact. Then draw one more ○.
Write the new fact. Look for patterns.

Word Bank
double
fact

1. ● ● ● ● | ● ● ● ●
    ● ● ● ● | ● ● ● ●

____ + ____ = ____

____ + ____ = ____

2. ● ● ● | ● ● ●

____ + ____ = ____

____ + ____ = ____

3. ● ● ● | ● ● ●
    ● ● ● | ● ● ●
    ● | ●

____ + ____ = ____

____ + ____ = ____

4. ● ● ● | ● ● ●
    ● ● | ● ●

____ + ____ = ____

____ + ____ = ____

5. ● ● | ● ●
    ● ● | ● ●

____ + ____ = ____

____ + ____ = ____

California Content Standards *Number Sense 2.1 (🔑),
Grade 1, Know the addition facts. Algebra and Functions 1.2.
Also Statistics, Data Analysis, and Probability 2.1, Mathematical
Reasoning 3.0.*

five **5**

Add.

6.

7	7	4	5	8	9
+ 7	+ 8	+ 4	+ 4	+ 8	+ 8
14	15				

7.

6	7	5	6	7	8
+ 6	+ 6	+ 5	+ 5	+ 7	+ 7

8.

3	7	0	6	8	2
+ 5	+ 8	+ 0	+ 5	+ 9	+ 2

9.

9	6	8	3	4	8
+ 9	+ 7	+ 8	+ 3	+ 3	+ 7

 Math Reasoning

Patterns

Add. Look for a pattern.

10. $1 + 1 =$ _____

$1 + 2 =$ _____

$2 + 2 =$ _____

11. $2 + 3 =$ _____

$3 + 3 =$ _____

$3 + 4 =$ _____

12. $4 + 4 =$ _____

$4 + 5 =$ _____

$5 + 5 =$ _____

Tell how number patterns can help you.

Home Activity Ask your child to solve near-doubles facts like 7 + 8. Encourage him or her to use patterns to find the sum.
Homework Workbook 1-2

Name_____ **Using 10 to Add 7, 8, and 9**

Find 8 + 5. 8 is close to 10.
Make a 10 to help you add.

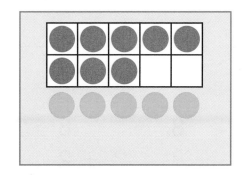 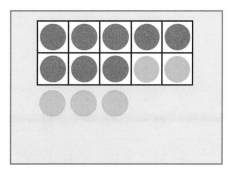 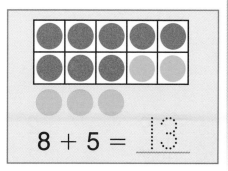

8 + 5 = 13

Show 8. Show 5.   Make a ten.   How many?

Use counters and Workmat 1.
Find each sum.

> **Word Bank**
>
> sum

1. Find 9 + 3.   Make a ten.   How many?

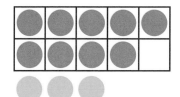 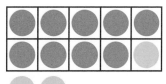

9 + 3 = _____

2. Find 7 + 4.   Make a ten.   How many?

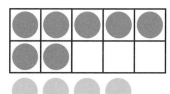 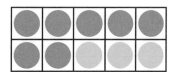

7 + 4 = _____

3.
$$\begin{array}{cccccc} 7 & 3 & 6 & 8 & 5 & 4 \\ +5 & +8 & +7 & +6 & +7 & +8 \end{array}$$

4.
$$\begin{array}{cccccc} 9 & 7 & 8 & 9 & 2 & 7 \\ +5 & +6 & +4 & +8 & +7 & +8 \end{array}$$

California Content Standards *Number Sense 2.1 (🔑),*
Grade 1, Know the addition facts. Also Mathematical Reasoning 1.1.

seven **7**

Find each sum.

5.
9 + 6	2 + 8	1 + 9	8 + 3	2 + 9	7 + 3
15					

6.
9 + 7	2 + 7	9 + 4	4 + 8	8 + 8	8 + 2

7. 9 + 1 = _____   8 + 9 = _____   6 + 9 = _____

8. 3 + 9 = _____   9 + 5 = _____   7 + 4 = _____

9. 7 + 5 = _____   3 + 8 = _____   1 + 8 = _____

 Problem Solving

Solve.

10. Pam picked 6 carrots and 8 turnips. How many vegetables did she pick in all?

_____ vegetables

11. Bill picked 6 onions before lunch and 7 onions after lunch. How many onions did he pick in all?

_____ onions

Home Activity Ask your child to use 10 to explain how to add facts like 8 + 5. Homework Workbook 1-3

Name_____ **Three Addends**

Add. Try different ways.

Word Bank

addend

sum

1.
```
   2      5      6      2
   8      3      0      2
 + 3    + 5    + 4    + 8
 ----   ----   ----   ----
  13
```

2.
```
   2      5      7      4      5      7
   8      2      3      2      3      3
 + 5    + 2    + 2    + 4    + 7    + 1
 ----   ----   ----   ----   ----   ----
```

3.
```
   3      1      6      8      4      5
   5      2      4      4      4      5
 + 4    + 8    + 4    + 2    + 4    + 4
 ----   ----   ----   ----   ----   ----
```

California Content Standards *Algebra and Functions 1.1* (🔑)
*Use the commutative and associative rules to simplify mental
calculations. Also Number Sense 2.7, Grade 1.*

Add. Try different ways.

4.
$$
\begin{array}{r} 1 \\ 8 \\ +5 \\ \hline 14 \end{array}
\qquad
\begin{array}{r} 5 \\ 4 \\ +2 \\ \hline \end{array}
\qquad
\begin{array}{r} 6 \\ 3 \\ +4 \\ \hline \end{array}
\qquad
\begin{array}{r} 8 \\ 2 \\ +2 \\ \hline \end{array}
\qquad
\begin{array}{r} 5 \\ 3 \\ +3 \\ \hline \end{array}
\qquad
\begin{array}{r} 7 \\ 3 \\ +6 \\ \hline \end{array}
$$

5.
$$
\begin{array}{r} 3 \\ 5 \\ +4 \\ \hline \end{array}
\qquad
\begin{array}{r} 1 \\ 2 \\ +8 \\ \hline \end{array}
\qquad
\begin{array}{r} 6 \\ 4 \\ +4 \\ \hline \end{array}
\qquad
\begin{array}{r} 8 \\ 4 \\ +1 \\ \hline \end{array}
\qquad
\begin{array}{r} 4 \\ 4 \\ +4 \\ \hline \end{array}
\qquad
\begin{array}{r} 2 \\ 5 \\ +4 \\ \hline \end{array}
$$

6.
$$
\begin{array}{r} 5 \\ 5 \\ +5 \\ \hline \end{array}
\qquad
\begin{array}{r} 1 \\ 3 \\ +7 \\ \hline \end{array}
\qquad
\begin{array}{r} 6 \\ 1 \\ +6 \\ \hline \end{array}
\qquad
\begin{array}{r} 9 \\ 0 \\ +1 \\ \hline \end{array}
\qquad
\begin{array}{r} 2 \\ 8 \\ +7 \\ \hline \end{array}
\qquad
\begin{array}{r} 3 \\ 3 \\ +3 \\ \hline \end{array}
$$

7. $6 + 5 + 4 = $ _____ $\quad 2 + 4 + 6 = $ _____ $\quad 6 + 3 + 3 = $ _____

8. $8 + 0 + 2 = $ _____ $\quad 5 + 5 + 9 = $ _____ $\quad 5 + 4 + 7 = $ _____

Math Reasoning

Number Sense

9. Write your own number sentence.
Tell which numbers you would add first. Explain.

_____ + _____ + _____ = _____

Home Activity Write an addition problem with 3 numbers.
Have your child tell you different ways to solve the problem.
Homework Workbook 1-4

Name_____ **Missing Addends**

Use counters to find how many
vegetables are in the basket.

9 in all

 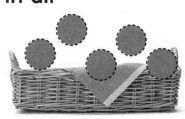 

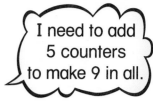 I need to add 5 counters to make 9 in all.

$4 + \underline{5} = 9$ $\underline{5}$ are in the basket.

Find how many vegetables there are in each basket.
Use counters to act out the problems.

1.   **15 in all**

$6 + \underline{} = 15$

_____ are in the basket.

2.   **14 in all**

$6 + \underline{} = 14$

_____ are in the basket.

3.   **12 in all**

$4 + \underline{} = 12$

_____ are in the basket.

California Content Standards *Algebra and Functions 1.2*
Relate problem situations to number sentences involving addition.
Also Statistics, Data Analysis, and Probability 2.1.

eleven **11**

Find how many vegetables there are in each basket.
Use counters to act out the problems.

4. **13 in all**

5 + _____ = 13

_____ are in the basket.

---

5. **8 in all**

8 + _____ = 8

_____ are in the basket.

---

6. **11 in all**

6 + _____ = 11

_____ are in the basket.

 **Problem Solving**

7. Find the missing numbers. Use patterns.
Write the next fact.

				☐
5	5	5	5	
+ ☐	+ ☐	+ ☐	+ ☐	+ ☐
6	8	10	12	☐

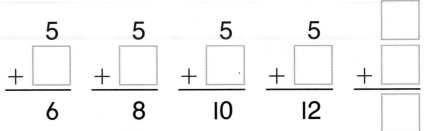

Home Activity Give your child a problem with a missing addend. Have him or her use small objects, such as pennies, to show how to find the missing addend. Homework Workbook 1-5

Write each addition sentence.
Circle whether you put together or increased to add.

1. 5 mice hide in a hole.   put together
    6 more mice join them.
    How many mice are in the hole?   increase

    _____ + _____ = _____

2. 5 horses are eating grass.   put together
    8 cows are eating grass.
    How many animals are eating grass?   increase

    _____ + _____ = _____

---

3. Use doubles to add.

7	7	6	7	8	9
+ 7	+ 8	+ 6	+ 6	+ 8	+ 8

---

4. Add. Make 10 when you can.

9	4	7	8	6	4
+ 7	+ 9	+ 5	+ 3	+ 8	+ 7

---

5. Add. Try different ways.

5	4	5	2	3	6
4	2	5	5	7	5
+ 6	+ 4	+ 5	+ 4	+ 3	+ 6

1. **22, 24, 26, 28, 30, _____**

29	30	31	32
○	○	○	○

2.

9	3	6	NH
○	○	○	○

3. **5 + 5 + 2 = ☐**

10	12	14	NH
○	○	○	○

4. **5 + 6 = ☐**

5 + 5 = 10	7 + 7 = 14	4 + 4 = 8	NH
○	○	○	○

5. **32**

33	42	43	NH
○	○	○	○

6.

20 > 10	15 < 16	9 > 10	11 < 13
○	○	○	○

Oral Directions *Mark the correct answer. NH means "Not here." Mark it whenever the answer is not given.*

#1. Look at the pattern. Which item is most likely to come next?
#2. Mark the number that shows how many more yellow counters there are than red counters.
#3. Add.

#4. Which doubles fact helps you solve 5 + 6 =?
#5. Which number is 10 more than 32?
#6. Mark the greater than/less than statement that is NOT true.

Name________________________________

Meanings of Subtraction

Algebra

When you **take away** from a group, you subtract to find how many are left.

Jose had 12 grapes.
He ate 5 of the grapes.
How many grapes are left?

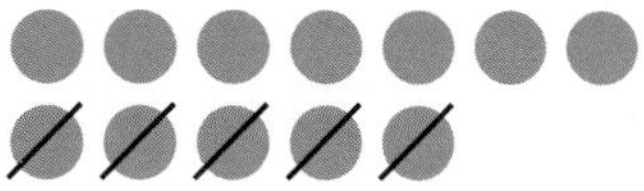

12 − 5 = 7

When you **compare** two groups, you subtract to find how many more are in the bigger group.

Pat picked 10 apples.
Jim picked 7 apples.
How many more apples did Pat pick?

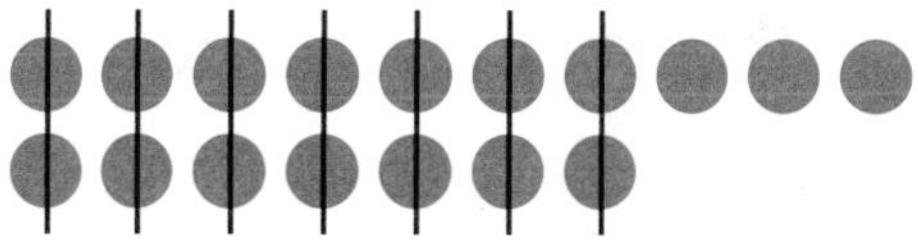

10 − 7 = 3

Write the number sentence.
Circle whether you subtract to take away or compare.

Word Bank
take away
compare

1. Maria saw 12 birds.
   3 of the birds flew away.
   How many birds are left?

   ____ − ____ = ____

   take away   compare

2. Tony found 11 acorns.
   Max found 8 acorns.
   How many more acorns did Tony find?

   ____ − ____ = ____

   take away   compare

California Content Standards *Number Sense 2.5 (key), Grade 1, Show the meaning of subtraction. Algebra and Functions 1.2. Also Mathematical Reasoning 1.1.*

Write the number sentence. Solve.
Use counters if you like.

3. 14 rabbits are by a tree.
6 of the rabbits hop away.
How many rabbits are still
by the tree?

$$14 - 6 = 8$$

4. Jon has 10 marbles.
Mary has 6 marbles.
How many more marbles
does Jon have?

____ – ____ = ____

5. Dan finds 11 leaves.
He later finds 2 rocks.
How many more leaves
than rocks did he find?

____ – ____ = ____

6. Terrell has 16 berries.
He eats 8 of the berries.
How many berries does
he have left?

____ – ____ = ____

7. 12 carrots are on a plate.
Jo takes 4 carrots away.
How many carrots are left
on the plate?

____ – ____ = ____

8. Lisa plays for 14 minutes.
Hal plays for 9 minutes.
How many more minutes
did Lisa play?

____ – ____ = ____

Math Reasoning

Number Sense

9. Write your own subtraction story.
Write the number sentence.
Tell whether you subtract to take away or compare.

Home Activity Tell a subtraction story to your child. Have him or her use objects to show whether the story is taking away or comparing. Homework Workbook 1-6

Name_____ **Using Doubles to Subtract**

Use the doubles fact to help you subtract.

$$5 + 5 = \underline{10}$$

$$10 - 5 = \underline{5}$$

Complete each number sentence.

1. $7 + 7 = \underline{}$ $3 + 3 = \underline{}$ $8 + 8 = \underline{}$

   $14 - 7 = \underline{}$ $6 - 3 = \underline{}$ $16 - 8 = \underline{}$

2. $2 + 2 = \underline{}$ $9 + 9 = \underline{}$ $6 + 6 = \underline{}$

   $4 - 2 = \underline{}$ $18 - 9 = \underline{}$ $12 - 6 = \underline{}$

3. $0 + 0 = \underline{}$ $4 + 4 = \underline{}$ $10 + 10 = \underline{}$

   $0 - 0 = \underline{}$ $8 - 4 = \underline{}$ $20 - 10 = \underline{}$

4.
$$\begin{array}{cc} 8 & 16 \\ +\ 8 & -\ 8 \end{array} \quad \begin{array}{cc} 6 & 12 \\ +\ 6 & -\ 6 \end{array} \quad \begin{array}{cc} 9 & 18 \\ +\ 9 & -\ 9 \end{array}$$

California Content Standards *Number Sense 2.1 (🔑) Use the inverse relationship between addition and subtraction to solve problems and check solutions. Also Algebra and Functions 1.2.*

Complete the doubles fact.
Use the double to help you subtract.

5.
$\begin{array}{r} 6 \\ + \boxed{6} \\ \hline 12 \end{array}$
$\begin{array}{r} 12 \\ - 6 \\ \hline 6 \end{array}$

$\begin{array}{r} 4 \\ + \boxed{} \\ \hline 8 \end{array}$
$\begin{array}{r} 8 \\ - 4 \\ \hline \end{array}$

$\begin{array}{r} 3 \\ + \boxed{} \\ \hline 6 \end{array}$
$\begin{array}{r} 6 \\ - 3 \\ \hline \end{array}$

6.
$\begin{array}{r} 9 \\ + \boxed{} \\ \hline 18 \end{array}$
$\begin{array}{r} 18 \\ - 9 \\ \hline \end{array}$

$\begin{array}{r} 7 \\ + \boxed{} \\ \hline 14 \end{array}$
$\begin{array}{r} 14 \\ - 7 \\ \hline \end{array}$

$\begin{array}{r} 2 \\ + \boxed{} \\ \hline 4 \end{array}$
$\begin{array}{r} 4 \\ - 2 \\ \hline \end{array}$

7.
$\begin{array}{r} 8 \\ + \boxed{} \\ \hline 16 \end{array}$
$\begin{array}{r} 16 \\ - 8 \\ \hline \end{array}$

$\begin{array}{r} 5 \\ + \boxed{} \\ \hline 10 \end{array}$
$\begin{array}{r} 10 \\ - 5 \\ \hline \end{array}$

$\begin{array}{r} 10 \\ + \boxed{} \\ \hline 20 \end{array}$
$\begin{array}{r} 20 \\ - 10 \\ \hline \end{array}$

Problem Solving **Algebra**

Solve. Write the number sentence.

8. What if there were 4 fewer onions?
How many would there be?

_____ ◯ _____ = _____

9. What if there were double the
number of onions? How many
would there be?

_____ ◯ _____ = _____

Home Activity Children often find it easy to remember
doubles facts. Ask your child how knowing $5 + 5 = 10$ helps
find $10 - 5$. Homework Workbook 1-7

Name_____ **Using Addition to Subtract**

You can use an addition fact
to help find a subtraction fact.
$12 - 3 = 9$ and $3 + 9 = 12$ are **related facts**.

See.

$$\begin{array}{r} 12 \\ -3 \\ \hline \end{array}$$

Think.

$$\begin{array}{r} 3 \\ +9 \\ \hline 12 \end{array}$$

Write.

$$\begin{array}{r} 12 \\ -3 \\ \hline 9 \end{array}$$

Use addition to help you subtract.

Word Bank

related facts

1.
$$\begin{array}{r} 13 \\ -7 \\ \hline \square \end{array} \qquad \begin{array}{r} 7 \\ +\square \\ \hline 13 \end{array}$$
$$\begin{array}{r} 10 \\ -6 \\ \hline \square \end{array} \qquad \begin{array}{r} 6 \\ +\square \\ \hline 10 \end{array}$$

2.
$$\begin{array}{r} 14 \\ -8 \\ \hline \square \end{array} \qquad \begin{array}{r} 8 \\ +\square \\ \hline 14 \end{array}$$
$$\begin{array}{r} 12 \\ -4 \\ \hline \square \end{array} \qquad \begin{array}{r} 4 \\ +\square \\ \hline 12 \end{array}$$
$$\begin{array}{r} 15 \\ -9 \\ \hline \square \end{array} \qquad \begin{array}{r} 9 \\ +\square \\ \hline 15 \end{array}$$

3.
$$\begin{array}{r} 16 \\ -9 \\ \hline \square \end{array} \qquad \begin{array}{r} 9 \\ +\square \\ \hline 16 \end{array}$$
$$\begin{array}{r} 11 \\ -5 \\ \hline \square \end{array} \qquad \begin{array}{r} 5 \\ +\square \\ \hline 11 \end{array}$$
$$\begin{array}{r} 17 \\ -8 \\ \hline \square \end{array} \qquad \begin{array}{r} 8 \\ +\square \\ \hline 17 \end{array}$$

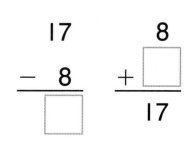

California Content Standards *Number Sense 2.1 (🔑) Use the inverse relationship between addition and subtraction to solve problems and check solutions. Also Algebra and Functions 1.2, Mathematical Reasoning 1.0.*

nineteen **19**

Use addition to help you subtract.

4.
$$
\begin{array}{r} 12 \\ -\ 7 \\ \hline 5 \end{array}
\qquad
\begin{array}{r} 7 \\ +\ 5 \\ \hline 12 \end{array}
$$

5.
$$
\begin{array}{r} 10 \\ -\ 4 \\ \hline \square \end{array}
\qquad
\begin{array}{r} 4 \\ +\ \square \\ \hline 10 \end{array}
$$

6.
$$
\begin{array}{r} 9 \\ -\ 0 \\ \hline \square \end{array}
\qquad
\begin{array}{r} 0 \\ +\ \square \\ \hline 9 \end{array}
$$

Add or subtract.
Draw lines to match related facts.

7.
$$
\begin{array}{r} 7 \\ +\ 7 \\ \hline 14 \end{array}
\qquad
\begin{array}{r} 3 \\ +\ 8 \\ \hline \end{array}
\qquad
\begin{array}{r} 6 \\ +\ 5 \\ \hline \end{array}
$$

8.
$$
\begin{array}{r} 3 \\ +\ 7 \\ \hline \end{array}
\qquad
\begin{array}{r} 6 \\ +\ 7 \\ \hline \end{array}
\qquad
\begin{array}{r} 9 \\ +\ 5 \\ \hline \end{array}
$$

9.
$$
\begin{array}{r} 11 \\ -\ 3 \\ \hline \end{array}
\qquad
\begin{array}{r} 14 \\ -\ 7 \\ \hline \end{array}
\qquad
\begin{array}{r} 11 \\ -\ 6 \\ \hline \end{array}
$$

10.
$$
\begin{array}{r} 14 \\ -\ 9 \\ \hline \end{array}
\qquad
\begin{array}{r} 10 \\ -\ 3 \\ \hline \end{array}
\qquad
\begin{array}{r} 13 \\ -\ 6 \\ \hline \end{array}
$$

 **Problem Solving** **Algebra**

Write the number sentence.

11. Liz sees 7 hares. Then she sees 5 more. How many hares does she see in all?

_____ ◯ _____ = _____

12. Earl has 12 fish. Joe has 5 fewer. How many fish does Joe have?

_____ ◯ _____ = _____

20 twenty

Home Activity Tell your child a subtraction fact. Then ask him or her to name a related addition fact. Homework Workbook 1-8

Name_____

8 rabbits are in the hole.
5 rabbits join them.
How many rabbits are in the hole now?

Understand

You need to find how many rabbits in all.

Plan

You can write a number sentence.

Solve

$$\underline{8} + \underline{5} = \underline{13} \text{ rabbits}$$

Look Back

Did you answer the question?

Write the number sentence.

1. 10 raccoons sit in a tree.
   3 raccoons leave the tree.
   How many raccoons are in the tree now?

   _____ _____ _____ raccoons

---

2. 5 bees fly in the field.
   8 bees join them.
   How many bees are there altogether?

   _____ + _____ = _____ bees

California Content Standards *Algebra and Functions 1.2*
*Relate problem situations to number sentences involving addition
and subtraction. Also Mathematical Reasoning 1.1.*

twenty-one **21**

Write the number sentence to solve.

3. 12 ants are digging.
   9 other ants are walking.
   How many more ants are digging?

   _____ ⫶ _____ ⫶ _____ ants

4. 5 squirrels bury pine cones.
   Another 9 squirrels bury nuts.
   How many squirrels are burying
   pine cones and nuts?

   _____ + _____ ⫶ _____ squirrels

5. A mouse finds 11 acorns on the ground.
   It eats 2 acorns.
   How many acorns are left?

   _____ acorns

6. 6 rabbits are eating.
   8 more rabbits join them.
   How many rabbits are eating now?

   _____ rabbits

 Math Reasoning

Number Sense

7. Tell a story for this number sentence:

   $4 + 5 = 9$

Home Activity Have your child write number sentences for stories you tell. Homework Workbook 1-9

Name_____ **Fact Families**

If you know one fact, you can find the
other facts in the fact family.

Word Bank

fact family

Algebra

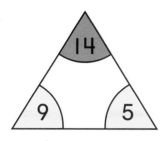

$$\begin{array}{r} 9 \\ + 5 \\ \hline 14 \end{array}$$

$$\begin{array}{r} 5 \\ + 9 \\ \hline 14 \end{array}$$

$$\begin{array}{r} 14 \\ - 5 \\ \hline 9 \end{array}$$

$$\begin{array}{r} 14 \\ - 9 \\ \hline 5 \end{array}$$

Add and subtract. Use counters if you like.

1.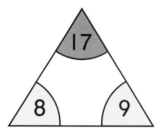

$$\begin{array}{r} 8 \\ + 9 \\ \hline \end{array}$$
$$\begin{array}{r} 9 \\ + 8 \\ \hline \end{array}$$
$$\begin{array}{r} 17 \\ - 9 \\ \hline \end{array}$$
$$\begin{array}{r} 17 \\ - 8 \\ \hline \end{array}$$

2.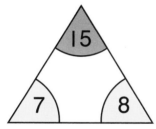

$$\begin{array}{r} 7 \\ + 8 \\ \hline \end{array}$$
$$\begin{array}{r} 8 \\ + 7 \\ \hline \end{array}$$
$$\begin{array}{r} 15 \\ - 8 \\ \hline \end{array}$$
$$\begin{array}{r} 15 \\ - 7 \\ \hline \end{array}$$

3.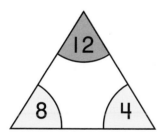

$$\begin{array}{r} 8 \\ + 4 \\ \hline \end{array}$$
$$\begin{array}{r} 4 \\ + 8 \\ \hline \end{array}$$
$$\begin{array}{r} 12 \\ - 4 \\ \hline \end{array}$$
$$\begin{array}{r} 12 \\ - 8 \\ \hline \end{array}$$

4.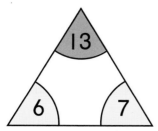

$$\begin{array}{r} 6 \\ + 7 \\ \hline \end{array}$$
$$\begin{array}{r} 7 \\ + 6 \\ \hline \end{array}$$
$$\begin{array}{r} 13 \\ - 7 \\ \hline \end{array}$$
$$\begin{array}{r} 13 \\ - 6 \\ \hline \end{array}$$

California Content Standards *Number Sense 2.1 (◦—)
Use the inverse relationship between addition and subtraction
to solve problems and check solutions. Algebra and Functions
1.1 (◦—). Also Mathematical Reasoning 3.0.*

Write each fact family.

5.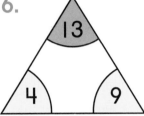

$8 + 6 = 14$ $14 - 6 = 8$

$6 + 8 = 14$ $14 - 8 = 6$

6.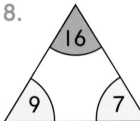

_____ + _____ = _____   _____ − _____ = _____

_____ + _____ = _____   _____ − _____ = _____

7.

_____ + _____ = _____   _____ − _____ = _____

_____ + _____ = _____   _____ − _____ = _____

8.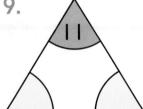

_____ + _____ = _____   _____ − _____ = _____

_____ + _____ = _____   _____ − _____ = _____

Math Reasoning

Complete the fact family.

9.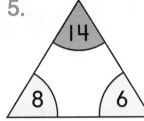

_____ + _____ = _____   _____ − _____ = _____

_____ + _____ = _____   _____ − _____ = _____

Home Activity Ask your child to tell you the fact family for 7, 8, and 15. Homework Workbook 1-10

Name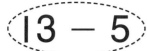_____ **Names for Numbers**

Which facts are names for 8?

(13 − 5)   7 + 7   (4 + 4)   (12 − 4)

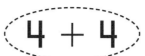

Circle the names for each number.

1.  **9**   8 + 1   17 − 8   14 − 4   16 − 7

2.  **7**   15 − 8   12 − 4   4 + 3   11 − 4

3.  **10**   17 − 8   5 + 5   3 + 7   6 + 4

4. **4**   13 − 9   11 − 9   12 − 8   11 − 7

5.  **8**   5 + 2   14 − 6   13 − 7   16 − 8

6. **6**   17 − 9   12 − 6   14 − 8   15 − 9

7. **12**   5 + 7   18 − 9   6 + 6   13 − 8

California Content Standards Number Sense 2.1 (🔑), Grade 1, Know the addition facts and corresponding subtraction facts. Algebra and Functions 1.0.

Match the names for each number.

8. $10 - 1$ $2 + 4$ $9 - 2$

    7   9   6

   $9 + 0$ $8 - 2$ $11 - 4$

9. $0 + 5$ $10 - 2$ $20 - 10$

    8   10   5

   $1 + 7$ $8 - 3$ $0 + 10$

10. $0 + 4$ $11 - 5$ $7 + 1$

    8   6   4

   $7 - 1$ $2 + 6$ $11 - 7$

11. $2 + 5$ $16 - 6$ $13 - 4$

    9   7   10

   $7 + 0$ $3 + 7$ $12 - 3$

Write your own names for each number.

12.

8   _____

     _____

13.

9   _____

     _____

 Math Reasoning   **Algebra**

Number Sense

Fill in the box so the number names match.

14. $7 + 1 = 2 + \boxed{6}$

    $5 + 8 = 6 + \boxed{}$

15. $9 - 1 = 12 - \boxed{}$

    $13 - 4 = 16 - \boxed{}$

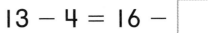 **Home Activity** Give your child 18 small objects, such as dried beans. Ask your child to show 3 ways to get a sum of 8 and 3 ways to show a difference of 8. Homework Workbook 1-11

Name_____

A graph can help you compare numbers. The graph below shows the number of animals at the park.

Park Animals

	0	1	2	3	4	5	6	7	8	9	10	11	12
Rabbit													
Squirrel													
Bird													

Use the graph to answer each question.

Think: What do you need to find out?

1. How many more rabbits are there than squirrels? _____ more

2. How many rabbits and squirrels are there altogether? _____ altogether

3. How many rabbits and birds are there altogether? _____ altogether

4. How many more rabbits are there than birds? _____ more

5. Which animal is there the most of in the park? _____

California Content Standards *Statistics, Data Analysis, and Probability 1.4 Ask and answer simple questions related to data representations. Algebra and Functions 1.3.*

18 classmates chose which animal they liked best.
This is the graph they made.

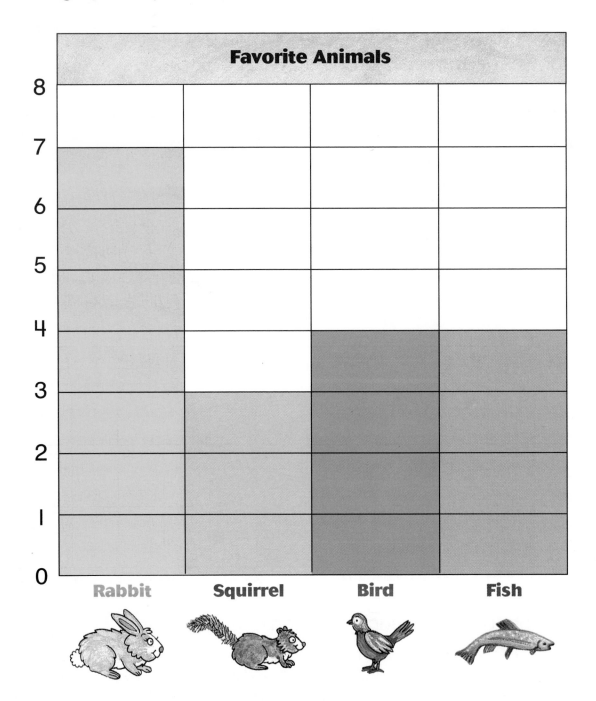

Favorite Animals

6. How many classmates like either birds or fish? _____

7. Which animal is liked the most? _____

8. Which animal is liked the least? _____

9. How many more classmates like the animal
   picked most than the animal picked least? _____

Home Activity Ask your child to explain how he or she used the graph to answer each question. Homework Workbook 1-12

Subtract.

1.

12	15	12	11	16	14
$-\ 6$	$-\ 7$	$-\ 9$	$-\ 7$	$-\ 8$	$-\ 9$

Complete each fact family.

2. $\quad 5\ +\ 9\ =\ $ _____

$\qquad$ _____ $+$ _____ $=$ _____

$\qquad$ _____ $-$ _____ $=$ _____

$\qquad$ _____ $-$ _____ $=$ _____

3. $\quad 7\ +\ 6\ =\ $ _____

$\qquad$ _____ $+$ _____ $=$ _____

$\qquad$ _____ $-$ _____ $=$ _____

$\qquad$ _____ $-$ _____ $=$ _____

Circle the names for each number.

4.

6	$14-8$	$15-9$	$10-4$	$13-8$
8	$15-7$	$13-6$	$14-6$	$18-9$

Use the chart to solve. Write the number sentence.

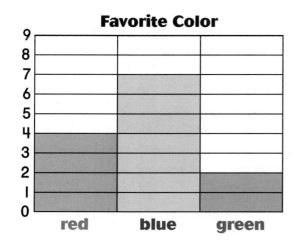

Favorite Color

5. How many more people chose red than green?

_____ $\bigcirc$ _____ $=$ _____

6. How many people chose blue or red?

_____ $\bigcirc$ _____ $=$ _____

Name_____

---

1. $9 + 4 = \square$

13	8	0	4
○	○	○	○

2. $6 - 0 = \square$

0	10	1	6
○	○	○	○

3.
$$\begin{array}{r} 8 \\ + 0 \\ \hline \end{array}$$

10	8	12	9
○	○	○	○

4.
$$\begin{array}{r} 12 \\ - 3 \\ \hline \end{array}$$

9	6	1	3
○	○	○	○

5.

6¢	7¢	11¢	NH
○	○	○	○

6.

3¢	16¢	13¢	NH
○	○	○	○

---

7. _____, 15, 16

17	14	10	NH
○	○	○	○

8. 11, _____, 13

10	12	14	15
○	○	○	○

---

9. 9 5

- ○ $9 + 5 = 14$
- ○ $9 - 5 = 4$
- ○ $9 + 4 = 13$
- ○ NH

10. 8 3

- ○ 11 apples
- ○ 3 apples
- ○ 5 apples
- ○ NH

Oral Directions *Mark the correct answer. NH means "Not here." Mark it whenever the answer is not given.*

#1–#4. Add or subtract.
#5–#6. Count the coins.

#7–#8. Mark the number that is missing.
#9. Ann has nine acorns. She gives five away. How many acorns does Ann have left?
#10. Tim had eight apples. He buys three more. How many apples does he have all together?

Circle the names for the number.

1. 9 | 14 − 6   4 + 5   16 − 7   1 + 8

Use doubles to add.

2. 3 + 3 = _____   5 + 5 = _____   8 + 8 = _____

    3 + 4 = _____   6 + 5 = _____   8 + 9 = _____

Write the fact family.

3. _____ + _____ = _____   _____ − _____ = _____

    _____ + _____ = _____   _____ − _____ = _____

Add.

4.   7   9   6   1   7   9
  + 8   + 4   + 9   + 5   + 6   + 0

Use the data to solve the problems.

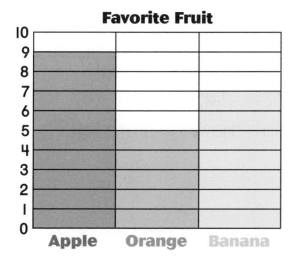

5. Which fruit is the favorite?

_____

6. How many more liked apples than liked oranges?

_____ more

Find each sum or difference.

7.
$$
\begin{array}{r} 8 \\ + 4 \\ \hline \end{array}
\qquad
\begin{array}{r} 12 \\ - 4 \\ \hline \end{array}
\qquad
\begin{array}{r} 12 \\ - 8 \\ \hline \end{array}
$$

8.
$$
\begin{array}{r} 8 \\ + 9 \\ \hline \end{array}
\qquad
\begin{array}{r} 17 \\ - 9 \\ \hline \end{array}
\qquad
\begin{array}{r} 17 \\ - 8 \\ \hline \end{array}
$$

Add.

9.
$$
\begin{array}{r} 3 \\ 4 \\ + 6 \\ \hline \end{array}
\qquad
\begin{array}{r} 5 \\ 1 \\ + 5 \\ \hline \end{array}
\qquad
\begin{array}{r} 7 \\ 1 \\ + 6 \\ \hline \end{array}
\qquad
\begin{array}{r} 8 \\ 5 \\ + 3 \\ \hline \end{array}
\qquad
\begin{array}{r} 4 \\ 7 \\ + 4 \\ \hline \end{array}
\qquad
\begin{array}{r} 9 \\ 0 \\ + 6 \\ \hline \end{array}
$$

Find each difference.

10. $14 - 8 = \underline{\quad}$ $\qquad$ $16 - 7 = \underline{\quad}$ $\qquad$ $12 - 5 = \underline{\quad}$

Fill in the missing addend.

11.
$$
\begin{array}{r} 6 \\ + \square \\ \hline 15 \end{array}
\qquad
\begin{array}{r} 8 \\ + \square \\ \hline 10 \end{array}
\qquad
\begin{array}{r} \square \\ + 4 \\ \hline 11 \end{array}
\qquad
\begin{array}{r} 9 \\ + \square \\ \hline 17 \end{array}
\qquad
\begin{array}{r} \square \\ + 7 \\ \hline 14 \end{array}
\qquad
\begin{array}{r} 8 \\ + \square \\ \hline 13 \end{array}
$$

Write the number sentence.

12. 2 rabbits ate lettuce.
9 rabbits did not eat.
How many rabbits are there in all?

$\underline{\quad} \bigcirc \underline{\quad} = \underline{\quad}$

13. 15 ants are on a leaf.
7 ants leave.
How many ants are left?

$\underline{\quad} \bigcirc \underline{\quad} = \underline{\quad}$

Name_____

1. 5

| 13 − 8 | 1 + 4 | 11 − 6 | 3 + 3 |
| ○ | ○ | ○ | ○ |

_____

2. 16 − 8 = ☐

| 8 | 9 | 10 | 11 |
| ○ | ○ | ○ | ○ |

_____

3. 7 + 4 = 11   4 + 7 = 11   11 − 4 = 7

| 7 − 4 = 3 | 7 + 7 = 14 | 11 − 7 = 4 | 7 − 7 = 0 |
| ○ | ○ | ○ | ○ |

_____

4. 8 + 7 = 15

| 7 + 7 = 14 | 4 + 4 = 8 | 6 + 6 = 12 | NH |
| ○ | ○ | ○ | ○ |

_____

5. **Favorite Food**

(bar graph with y-axis 0–10, bars for Hamburger, Hot Dog, Pizza)

| 3 | 4 | 6 | 8 |
| ○ | ○ | ○ | ○ |

_____

Oral Directions *Mark the correct answer. NH means "Not here." Mark it whenever the answer is not given.*

#1. Which is NOT a name for the number 5?
#2. Subtract.
#3. Which fact belongs to the fact family?
#4. Which doubles fact helps you add 8 + 7 = 15?
#5. How many more liked hot dogs than pizza?

6. 13 − 6 = 7

6 + 5 = 11	6 + 7 = 13	5 + 5 = 10	NH
○	○	○	○

---

7. 5 + 3 + 7 = ☐

15	13	8	17
○	○	○	○

---

8. 12
− 6

7	6	8	NH
○	○	○	○

---

9. 9
+ 9

0	16	17	18
○	○	○	○

---

10. 14 − ☐ = 5

10	9	12	NH
○	○	○	○

---

11. 7   3

7 + 7 = 14	7 − 3 = 4	7 + 3 = 10	3 − 3 = 0
○	○	○	○

---

12. 12 🍅   5 🍅

6 tomatoes	7 tomatoes	8 tomatoes	NH
○	○	○	○

Oral Directions *Mark the correct answer. NH means "Not here." Mark it whenever the answer is not given.*

#6. Which addition fact could you use to help subtract 6 from 13?
#7–9. Add or subtract.
#10. What is the missing addend?
#11. There are seven acorns on the ground. Three more acorns fall on the ground. How many acorns are on the ground?
#12. Mark had twelve tomatoes. He lost five tomatoes. How many tomatoes does Mark have left?

Diagnosing Readiness
for Chapter 2

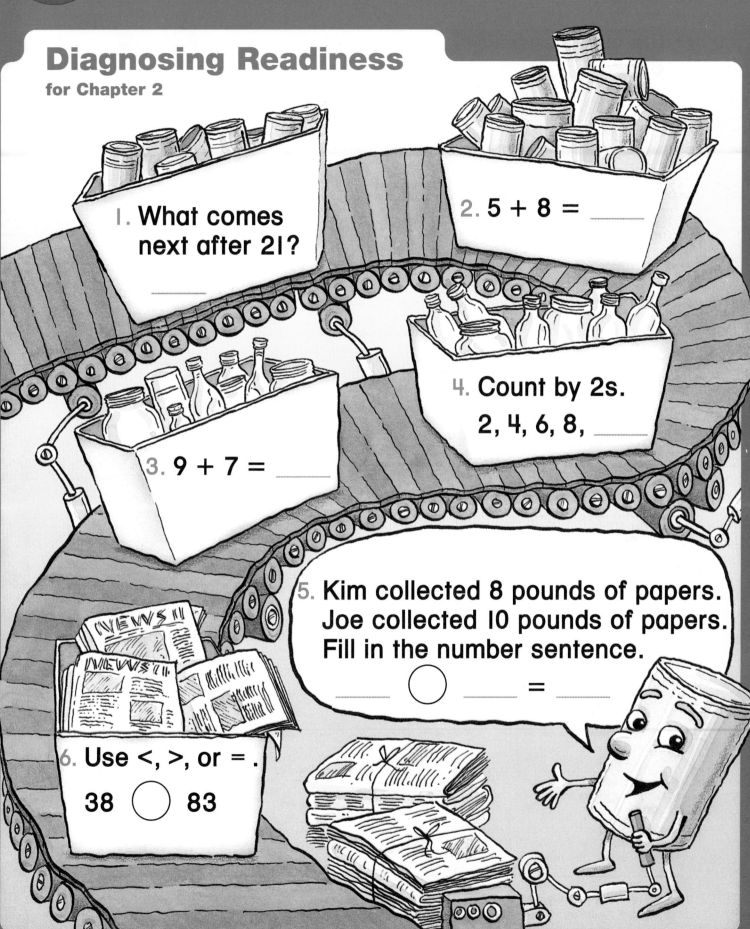

1. What comes next after 21?

2. $5 + 8 =$ _____

3. $9 + 7 =$ _____

4. Count by 2s.
2, 4, 6, 8, _____

5. Kim collected 8 pounds of papers. Joe collected 10 pounds of papers. Fill in the number sentence.

_____ ◯ _____ = _____

6. Use <, >, or = .

38 ◯ 83

To the Family

Looking Back

In Chapter 1 children reviewed the meanings of addition and subtraction and the basic facts.

Chapter 2

Place Value and Adding Two-Digit Numbers

Children review place value of numbers to 100. Then children add two-digit numbers using mental math and paper and pencil.

Looking Ahead

By the end of Grade 2, children will add and subtract two- and three-digit numbers.

Page 35 Your child solved problems that review math skills from Grade 1 and Chapter 1 and will help your child with the skills in Chapter 2.

Math at Home The chapter theme is recycling. Keep track of the number of items recycled in your home. Make and solve addition problems related to the items you recycle.

Math Literature Read math or theme-related stories with your child. Look for the following books in your local library.
From One to One Hundred by Teri Sloat (Puffin, 1995)
Earth Book for Kids by Linda Schwartz (The Learning Works, 1990)

California Content Standards in Chapter 2 Lessons*

	Teach and Practice	Practice
Number Sense		
1.1 (🔑), Grade 1, Count, read, and write whole numbers to 100.	1	
1.4 (🔑), Grade 1, Count and group objects in ones and tens.	6	1
2.2 (🔑) Find the sum of two whole numbers up to three digits long.	3, 4, 7–10, 12, 13	14
2.3 Use mental arithmetic to find the sum or difference of two two-digit numbers.	5, 12	13
5.1 (🔑) Solve problems using combinations of coins and bills.		6, 7
Algebra and Functions		
1.1 (🔑) Use the commutative and associative rules to simplify mental calculations and to check results.		5, 9
1.2 Relate problem situations to number sentences involving addition and subtraction.		10
1.3 Solve addition and subtraction problems by using data from simple charts, picture graphs, and number sentences.	14	

	Teach and Practice	Practice
Statistics, Data Analysis, and Probability		
2.0 (🔑) Students demonstrate an understanding of patterns and how patterns grow and describe them in general ways.		2, 12
2.1 Recognize, describe, and extend patterns and determine the next term in linear patterns.	2, 11	12
2.2 Solve problems involving simple number patterns.		2
Mathematical Reasoning		
1.1 Determine the approach, materials, and strategies to be used.	12	
2.1 Defend the reasoning used and justify the procedures selected.		3, 4
3.0 Students note connections between one problem and another.	11	

* The symbol (🔑) indicates a key standard as designated in the Mathematics Framework for California Public Schools.
Full statements of the California Content Standards are found at the beginning of this book following the Table of Contents.

Name_____ **Ways to Show Numbers**

You can show 36 in different ways.

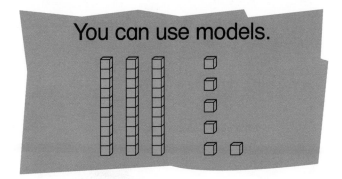

You can use models.

You can use pictures.

10   10   10

You can write tens and ones.

3 tens 6 ones

You can write the number.

36

Write tens and ones.

1.

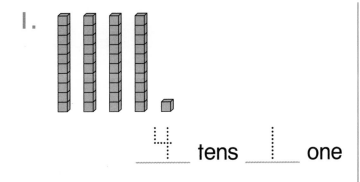

____ tens ____ one

2.

____ tens ____ ones

3.

29   ____ tens ____ ones

4.

65   ____ tens ____ ones

Write the number.

5.

10   10

_____

6.

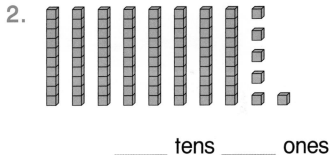

10   10
10   10   10
10   10

_____

California Content Standards *Number Sense 1.1( ), Grade 1, Count, read, and write whole numbers to 100. Also Number Sense 1.4, Grade 1.*

Match.

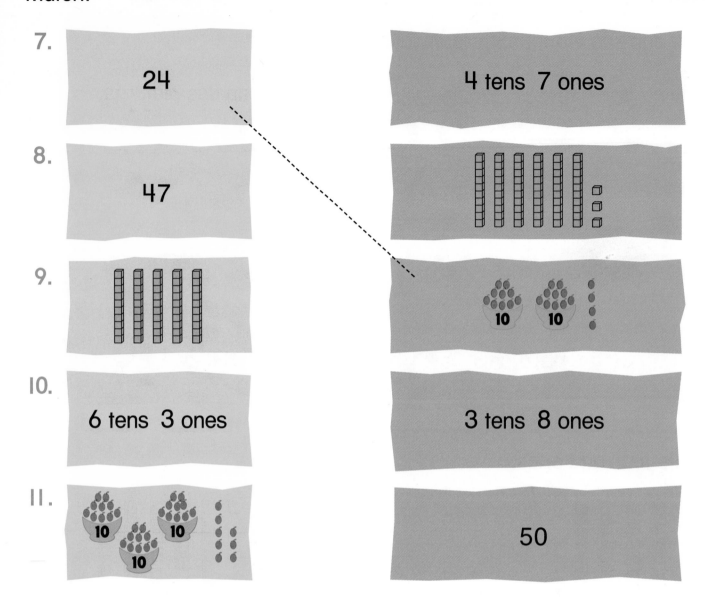

7. 24

8. 47

9. (five tens rods)

10. 6 tens 3 ones

11. (bowls of 10 and ones)

4 tens 7 ones

(four tens rods, three ones)

(two bowls of 10 and ones)

3 tens 8 ones

50

Math Reasoning

Number Sense

12. Cross out the one that does not show 28.

| | 2 tens 8 ones | | 28 |

Name_____ **Number Patterns**

1. Write the missing numbers.

0	1	2		4	5	6	7	8	
	11	12	13	14	15		17	18	19
20	21		23	24	25	26	27		29
30	31	32	33		35	36		38	39
40	41	42	43	44		46		48	49
		52	53	54	55	56	57	58	
	61	62	63	64	65		67	68	69
70	71	72		74	75	76	77	78	
	81	82	83		85	86	87	88	89
90	91		93	94	95	96	97		99

2. Color the squares that have 5 in the ones place. Tell about the pattern you see.

3. Circle the numbers that have 5 in the tens place. Tell about the pattern you see.

4. Which number is circled and colored? _____

California Content Standards *Statistics, Data Analysis, and Probability 2.1 Recognize and describe patterns. Also Statistics, Data Analysis, and Probability 2.0 (🔑), 2.2.*

5. Write the missing numbers.

0	1	2		4	5	6	7	8	9
10	11	12							
20	21	22							
						36			
40									
				54					
								68	
	71								
					85				
									99

6. Color the squares that have 7
   in the tens place.
   Tell about the pattern you see.

7. Circle the number 2. Then circle
   the numbers that have two more
   ones than they have tens.
   Tell about the pattern you see.

8. Which number is circled and colored? _____

Home Activity Ask your child to look at the chart and tell about different patterns he or she sees. Homework Workbook 2-2

Name_____ **Adding Tens**

You can use basic facts to help add tens.

 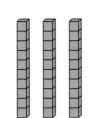 4 tens + 3 tens = __7__ tens   Think 4+3=7.

40 + 30 = 70

Find each sum.
Use tens models if you like.

1. 2 tens + 4 tens = _____ tens

   20 + 40 = _____

2. 8 tens + 1 ten = _____ tens

   80 + 10 = _____

3. 3 tens + 4 tens = _____ tens

   30 + 40 = _____

4. 6 tens + 2 tens = _____ tens

   60 + 20 = _____

5. 3 tens + 5 tens = _____ tens

   30 + 50 = _____

6. 2 tens + 3 tens = _____ tens

   20 + 30 = _____

7. 7 tens + 2 tens = _____ tens

   70 + 20 = _____

8. 5 tens + 2 tens = _____ tens

   50 + 20 = _____

9. 1 ten + 3 tens = _____ tens

   10 + 30 = _____

10. 3 tens + 6 tens = _____ tens

    30 + 60 = _____

11. 7 tens + 1 ten = _____ tens

    70 + 10 = _____

12. 3 tens + 3 tens = _____ tens

    30 + 30 = _____

California Content Standards *Number Sense 2.2 (🔑) Find the sum of two whole numbers up to three digits long. Also Mathematical Reasoning 2.1.*

Find each sum. Write the missing numbers.
Use tens models if you like.

13. 1 ten + 4 tens = __5__ tens

__10__ + __40__ = __50__

14. 4 tens + 4 tens = _____ tens

_____ + _____ = _____

15. 5 tens + 1 ten = _____ tens

_____ + _____ = _____

16. 2 tens + 6 tens = _____ tens

_____ + _____ = _____

17. 1 ten + 8 tens = _____ tens

_____ + _____ = _____

18. 2 tens + 2 tens = _____ tens

_____ + _____ = _____

19. 3 tens + 4 tens = _____ tens

_____ + _____ = _____

20. 2 tens + 0 tens = _____ tens

_____ + _____ = _____

21. 4 tens + 5 tens = _____ tens

_____ + _____ = _____

22. 1 ten + 6 tens = _____ tens

_____ + _____ = _____

 Problem Solving

Number Sense

Write **yes** or **no**.

23. The school is having a used toy sale.
Jesse has 4 dimes. Kristen has 3 dimes.
If they add their money together,
do they have enough to buy a ball? _____
Tell how you know.

65¢ EACH

🏠 **Home Activity** Children can use basic facts to help them add tens. Ask your child to add numbers like these.
Homework Workbook 2-3

Name_____ **Counting On Tens**

You can count by tens to add.

$27 + 20 = $ 47

Start at 27.
Count on 2 tens.
27, 37, 47

0	1	2	3	4	5	6	7	8	9
10	11	12	13	14	15	16	17	18	19
20	21	22	23	24	25	26	27	28	29
30	31	32	33	34	35	36	37	38	39
40	41	42	43	44	45	46	47	48	49

Use the chart or Workmat 5.
Count by tens to add.

1. $14 + 30 = $ 44 $20 + 10 = $ ____ $26 + 20 = $ ____

2. $24 + 20 = $ ____ $10 + 18 = $ ____ $20 + 21 = $ ____

3. $10 + 30 = $ ____ $5 + 20 = $ ____ $20 + 29 = $ ____

4. $20 + 16 = $ ____ $10 + 33 = $ ____ $10 + 7 = $ ____

5. $15 + 20 = $ ____ $12 + 30 = $ ____ $18 + 20 = $ ____

6. $40 + 7 = $ ____ $14 + 10 = $ ____ $17 + 20 = $ ____

California Content Standards *Number Sense 2.2 (⟡) Find the sum of two whole numbers up to three digits long. Also Mathematical Reasoning 2.1.*

forty-three **43**

Count by tens to add.
Use Workmat 5 if you like.

7. $66 + 10 = \underline{76}$ $54 + 30 = \underline{\hspace{1cm}}$ $20 + 22 = \underline{\hspace{1cm}}$

8. $10 + 84 = \underline{\hspace{1cm}}$ $37 + 20 = \underline{\hspace{1cm}}$ $32 + 30 = \underline{\hspace{1cm}}$

9. $30 + 56 = \underline{\hspace{1cm}}$ $72 + 10 = \underline{\hspace{1cm}}$ $39 + 20 = \underline{\hspace{1cm}}$

10. $35 + 20 = \underline{\hspace{1cm}}$ $30 + 35 = \underline{\hspace{1cm}}$ $43 + 10 = \underline{\hspace{1cm}}$

11. $52 + 20 = \underline{\hspace{1cm}}$ $11 + 10 = \underline{\hspace{1cm}}$ $30 + 13 = \underline{\hspace{1cm}}$

12. $64 + 30 = \underline{\hspace{1cm}}$ $10 + 34 = \underline{\hspace{1cm}}$ $77 + 20 = \underline{\hspace{1cm}}$

13. $26 + 10 = \underline{\hspace{1cm}}$ $45 + 30 = \underline{\hspace{1cm}}$ $64 + 10 = \underline{\hspace{1cm}}$

14. $20 + 34 = \underline{\hspace{1cm}}$ $41 + 10 = \underline{\hspace{1cm}}$ $57 + 20 = \underline{\hspace{1cm}}$

Math Reasoning

Mental Math

15. Circle the row of numbers
that shows counting on
to find $48 + 30$.
Tell how you know.

 48   49, 50, 51

 48   58, 68, 78

Home Activity Choose a number from the chart on page 47.
Ask your child to add 10, 20, or 30 to that number.
Homework Workbook 2-4

Name_____ **Breaking Apart to Add**

Find 30 + 24.

You can break apart numbers to add by using **mental math**.

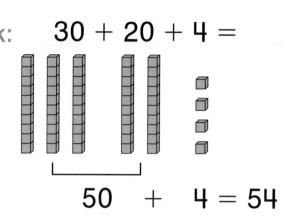

30 + 24 =

I broke apart 24 into 20 + 4.

Think: 30 + 20 + 4 =

50 + 4 = 54

Break apart numbers to add.
Use tens and ones models if you like.

Word Bank

mental math

1. 40 + 32 =

Think:

$40 + 30 + 2 =$
$70 + 2 = 72$

2. 20 + 15 =

Think:

___ + ___ + ___ =

___ + ___ = ___

3. 30 + 33 =

Think:

___ + ___ + ___ =

___ + ___ = ___

4. 50 + 37 =

Think:

___ + ___ + ___ =

___ + ___ = ___

California Content Standards *Number Sense 2.3 Use mental arithmetic to find the sum of two two-digit numbers. Also Algebra and Functions 1.1 ( ).*

forty-five **45**

Break apart numbers to add.
Use tens and ones models if you like.

5. 20 + 12 = 20 + 10 + 2 = 30 + 2 = 32

6. 40 + 27 = _____

7. 30 + 55 = _____

Use mental math to add.

8. 34 + 30 = ____   53 + 30 = ____   20 + 72 = ____

9. 46 + 30 = ____   40 + 27 = ____   56 + 30 = ____

10. 24 + 20 = ____   64 + 30 = ____   50 + 42 = ____

 Math Reasoning

Number Sense

11. Kim filled in the boxes with the number slips 0, 1, 2, and 3 to make the greatest sum. Did Kim make the greatest sum?

Use the numbers 0, 1, 2, and 3 to make the greatest sum.

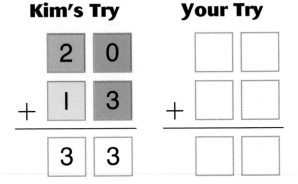

Kim's Try

```
    2  0
+   1  3
-------
    3  3
```

Your Try

0   1   2   3

Name_____ **Regrouping**

We can show 24 in different ways.

0 tens   24 ones

1 ten   14 ones

2 tens   4 ones

Use tens and ones models to show each number.
Then regroup to show the number another way. Record.

1. 17   _0_ tens _17_ ones
           _1_ tens _7_ ones

Word Bank

regroup

2. 12   ___ tens ___ ones
           ___ tens ___ ones

3. 19   ___ tens ___ ones
           ___ tens ___ ones

4. 28   ___ tens ___ ones
           ___ tens ___ ones
           ___ tens ___ ones

5. 26   ___ tens ___ ones
           ___ tens ___ ones
           ___ tens ___ ones

California Content Standards *Number Sense 1.4, Grade 1, Count and group objects in ones and tens. Also Number Sense 5.1 (🔑).*

Use tens and ones.
Write different ways to show each number.

6. 25   __0__ tens   __25__ ones | 7. 31   _____ tens   _____ ones

            __1__ tens   __15__ ones   _____ tens   _____ ones

            __2__ tens   __5__ ones   _____ tens   _____ ones

                                                  _____ tens   _____ ones

8. 38   _____ tens   _____ ones | 9. 27   _____ tens   _____ ones

          _____ tens   _____ ones   _____ tens   _____ ones

          _____ tens   _____ ones   _____ tens   _____ ones

          _____ tens   _____ ones

10. 35   _____ tens   _____ ones | 11. 33   _____ tens   _____ ones

          _____ tens   _____ ones   _____ tens   _____ ones

          _____ tens   _____ ones   _____ tens   _____ ones

          _____ tens   _____ ones   _____ tens   _____ ones

 **Problem Solving**

Solve.

12. Tom has 2 dimes and 5 pennies. Emma has 1 dime and 18 pennies. Who has more money?

    _____

13. Lisa has 37 pennies. Filipe has 2 dimes and 16 pennies. Who has more money?

    _____

Home Activity Ask your child to show two-digit numbers like 12 or 24 in two different ways. Homework Workbook 2-6

Name _____ **Diagnostic Checkpoint**

Write tens and ones.

1.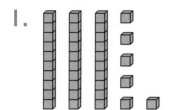

_____ tens _____ ones

2.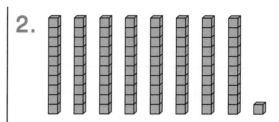

_____ tens _____ ones

3. 46 _____ tens _____ ones

4. 72 _____ tens _____ ones

Write the missing numbers.

5. 85, _____, 87, 88, _____

6. 50, _____, 52, 53, _____

7. 39, _____, 41, 42, _____

8. 96, _____, 98, 99, _____

Find each sum.
Use tens and ones models or mental math.

9. 30 + 60 = _____   10 + 50 = _____   20 + 30 = _____

10. 40 + 36 = _____   12 + 80 = _____   50 + 21 = _____

Use tens and ones.
Write different ways to show each number.

11. 39 _____ tens _____ ones

_____ tens _____ ones

_____ tens _____ ones

_____ tens _____ ones

12. 24 _____ tens _____ ones

_____ tens _____ ones

_____ tens _____ ones

Name_____

1. $20 + 31 =$ ☐

15	50	51	NH
○	○	○	○

---

2. $8 + 2 = 10$ $2 + 8 = 10$ $10 - 2 = 8$

$8 - 2 = 6$	$8 + 8 = 16$	$8 - 8 = 0$	$10 - 8 = 2$
○	○	○	○

---

3. $8 + 8 = 16$
    so $16 - 8 =$ ☐

8	6	16	9
○	○	○	○

---

4. **35**

2 tens 15 ones	3 tens 5 ones	3 tens 15 ones	35 ones
○	○	○	○

5.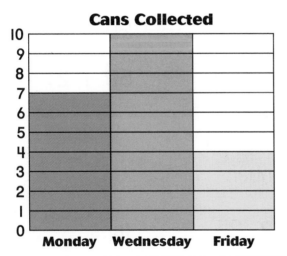

Cans Collected

Monday   Wednesday   Friday

3	6	14	NH
○	○	○	○

Oral Directions *Mark the correct answer. NH means "Not here." Mark it whenever the answer is not given.*

#1. Use mental math to add.
#2. Which fact is missing from the fact family?
#3. Use the doubles fact $8 + 8 = 16$ to solve $16 - 8$.
#4. Which is NOT equal to 35?
#5. How many more cans were collected on Wednesday than on Friday?

Name_____ **Deciding When to Regroup**

You have 3 tens and 4 ones.
How do you add 8 ones?

Sometimes you need to regroup.

1 Show 3 tens 4 ones.

Tens	Ones

2 Add 8 ones.

Tens	Ones

3 Regroup 10 ones as one ten.

Tens	Ones

4 tens 2 ones

Use tens and ones models and Workmat 3.
Complete the chart.

	Do you need to regroup?		How many in all?
1. Show 2 tens 7 ones. Add 6 ones.	(yes)	no	3 tens 3 ones
2. Show 5 tens 2 ones. Add 9 ones.	yes	no	____ tens ____ ones
3. Show 4 tens 7 ones. Add 2 ones.	yes	no	____ tens ____ ones
4. Show 3 tens 8 ones. Add 4 ones.	yes	no	____ tens ____ ones
5. Show 6 tens 5 ones. Add 5 ones.	yes	no	____ tens ____ ones

California Content Standards Number Sense 2.2 (🔑) Find the sum of two whole numbers up to three digits long. Also Number Sense 5.1 (🔑).

Use tens and ones models and Workmat 3.
Complete the chart.

	Do you need to regroup?	How many in all?
6. Show 5 tens 7 ones. Add 5 ones.	(yes) no	6 tens 2 ones
7. Show 4 tens 2 ones. Add 8 ones.	yes no	___ tens ___ ones
8. Show 7 tens 4 ones. Add 3 ones.	yes no	___ tens ___ ones
9. Show 3 tens 9 ones. Add 6 ones.	yes no	___ tens ___ ones
10. Show 1 ten 7 ones. Add 6 ones.	yes no	___ tens ___ ones
11. Show 4 tens 6 ones. Add 2 ones.	yes no	___ tens ___ ones
12. Show 2 tens 8 ones. Add 5 ones.	yes no	___ tens ___ ones

 Problem Solving

Solve.

13. Raul has 3 dimes and 5 pennies.
His grandmother gives him
a nickel and a penny.
How much money does he have?

 _____

Home Activity Ask your child to explain his or her decision about regrouping in each exercise on this page. Homework Workbook 2-7

Name_____ **Adding with Regrouping**

Find 34 + 8. Regroup if necessary.

1 Add the ones. Regroup.
Record 1 ten in the tens place.

2 Add the tens.

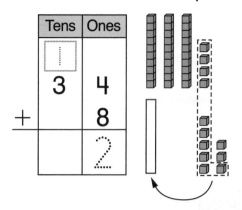

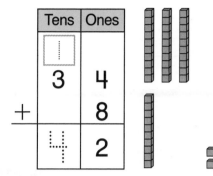

Regroup 10 ones
for 1 ten.

Add. Use tens and ones models and Workmat 3.
Did you need to regroup? Circle **yes** or **no**.

1.

Tens	Ones
2	7
+	4

yes

no

2.

Tens	Ones
	3
+ 2	6

yes

no

3.

Tens	Ones
	8
+ 4	1

yes

no

4.

Tens	Ones
5	9
+	5

yes

no

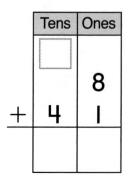

California Content Standards *Number Sense 2.2 (▶━) Find the sum of two whole numbers up to three digits long.*

Use tens and ones models and Workmat 3.
Add. Circle problems if you regroup.

5.

Tens	Ones
[1]	
7	4
+	9
8	3

Tens	Ones
[ ]	
4	6
+	3

Tens	Ones
[ ]	
	1
+ 4	2

Tens	Ones
[ ]	
2	4
+	7

6.

Tens	Ones
[ ]	
3	0
+	8

Tens	Ones
[ ]	
	2
+ 3	9

Tens	Ones
[ ]	
6	5
+	3

Tens	Ones
[ ]	
	8
+ 2	2

7.

Tens	Ones
[ ]	
3	5
+	9

Tens	Ones
[ ]	
	4
+ 7	4

Tens	Ones
[ ]	
5	5
+	5

Tens	Ones
[ ]	
8	3
+	9

Problem Solving

Which two boxes will make each total?
Write the numbers.

8. Total of 43 books _____ and _____

9. Total of 34 books _____ and _____

10. Least total _____ and _____

54 fifty-four

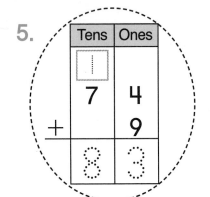

Home Activity Have your child show you the exercises on
this page that required regrouping 10 ones as 1 ten.
Homework Workbook 2-8

Name_____ **Adding Two-Digit Numbers**

Add. Regroup if necessary.

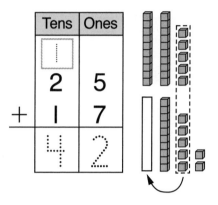

Tens	Ones
□	
2	5
+ 1	7
4	2

Tens	Ones
□	
3	4
+ 2	4
5	8

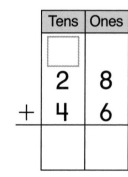

Add. Use tens and ones models and Workmat 3.
Did you need to regroup? Circle **yes** or **no**.

1.

Tens	Ones
□	
5	3
+ 4	5

yes

no

2.

Tens	Ones
□	
2	8
+ 4	6

yes

no

3.

Tens	Ones
□	
1	9
+ 6	2

yes

no

4.

Tens	Ones
□	
3	1
+ 5	5

yes

no

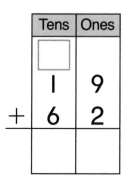 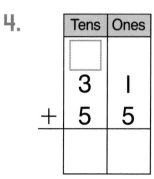

California Content Standards *Number Sense 2.2 (🔑) Find the sum of two whole numbers up to three digits long. Also Algebra and Functions 1.1 (🔑).*

fifty-five **55**

Use tens and ones models and Workmat 3.
Add. Circle problems if you regroup.

5.

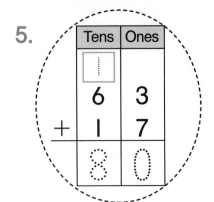

Tens	Ones
☐	
6	3
+ 1	7
8	0

Tens	Ones
☐	
1	9
+ 7	6

Tens	Ones
☐	
4	7
+ 2	6

Tens	Ones
☐	
3	0
+ 3	9

6.

Tens	Ones
☐	
2	1
+ 1	8

Tens	Ones
☐	
5	4
+ 3	7

Tens	Ones
☐	
4	2
+ 5	3

Tens	Ones
☐	
1	8
+ 7	8

7.

Tens	Ones
☐	
2	4
+ 3	4

Tens	Ones
☐	
3	3
+ 1	7

Tens	Ones
☐	
7	1
+ 1	9

Tens	Ones
☐	
3	6
+ 1	5

Math Reasoning

Algebra

Number Sense

8. If you know 63 + 17 = 80,
how much is 17 + 63?
Explain.

Tens	Ones
☐	
6	3
+ 1	7
8	0

Tens	Ones
☐	
1	7
+ 6	3

 Home Activity Ask your child to explain how he or she knows that regrouping is necessary. Homework Workbook 2-9

Name_____ **Two-Digit Addition**

Cans Collected	
Class	**Number of cans**
Mr. Carrera	58
Ms. Earl	36

How many cans did the classes collect altogether?

 Add the ones. Regroup.

Tens	Ones
☐	
5	8
+ 3	6
	4

 Add the tens.

Tens	Ones
☐	
5	8
+ 3	6
9	4

94 cans

Add. Use tens and ones models if you like.

1.
```
  34      54      68      45      18      20
+ 29    +  7    + 12    + 43    + 59    + 34
  63
```

2.
```
  21      27      42       8      26      13
+ 36    + 63    + 30    + 84    + 16    + 25
```

3.
```
  24      52      39      16      19      64
+  9    + 25    + 37    + 16    + 11    + 15
```

4.
```
  36      28      15      87      18      48
+ 45    + 14    + 58    + 11    + 38    + 19
```

California Content Standards *Number Sense 2.2 (🔑) Find the sum of two whole numbers up to three digits long. Also Algebra and Functions 1.2.*

Add. Use tens and ones models if you like.

5.
$$\begin{array}{r} 34 \\ + 24 \\ \hline \end{array}$$
58

$$\begin{array}{r} 19 \\ + 45 \\ \hline \end{array}$$

$$\begin{array}{r} 23 \\ + 62 \\ \hline \end{array}$$

$$\begin{array}{r} 34 \\ + 56 \\ \hline \end{array}$$

$$\begin{array}{r} 70 \\ + 18 \\ \hline \end{array}$$

$$\begin{array}{r} 53 \\ + 29 \\ \hline \end{array}$$

6.
$$\begin{array}{r} 25 \\ + 25 \\ \hline \end{array}$$

$$\begin{array}{r} 47 \\ + 40 \\ \hline \end{array}$$

$$\begin{array}{r} 38 \\ + 27 \\ \hline \end{array}$$

$$\begin{array}{r} 20 \\ + 60 \\ \hline \end{array}$$

$$\begin{array}{r} 84 \\ + 7 \\ \hline \end{array}$$

$$\begin{array}{r} 63 \\ + 27 \\ \hline \end{array}$$

7.
$$\begin{array}{r} 28 \\ + 58 \\ \hline \end{array}$$

$$\begin{array}{r} 32 \\ + 49 \\ \hline \end{array}$$

$$\begin{array}{r} 48 \\ + 12 \\ \hline \end{array}$$

$$\begin{array}{r} 9 \\ + 36 \\ \hline \end{array}$$

$$\begin{array}{r} 17 \\ + 35 \\ \hline \end{array}$$

$$\begin{array}{r} 24 \\ + 56 \\ \hline \end{array}$$

8.
$$\begin{array}{r} 32 \\ + 26 \\ \hline \end{array}$$

$$\begin{array}{r} 46 \\ + 35 \\ \hline \end{array}$$

$$\begin{array}{r} 42 \\ + 39 \\ \hline \end{array}$$

$$\begin{array}{r} 26 \\ + 8 \\ \hline \end{array}$$

$$\begin{array}{r} 50 \\ + 14 \\ \hline \end{array}$$

$$\begin{array}{r} 77 \\ + 13 \\ \hline \end{array}$$

 Problem Solving

Solve the problem.
Write the answer.
Estimate to check your answer.

9. Dillon collected 33 cans
    on Monday and 31 cans
    on Tuesday. How many
    cans did he collect in all?

    _____ cans

Solve	Check

Home Activity Ask your child to explain how he or she found each sum. Homework Workbook 2-10

Name_____ **Problem-Solving Strategy**

Find a Pattern

On Monday, Alicia read 5 pages.
On Tuesday, she read 10 pages.
On Wednesday, she read 15 pages.
If she continues this pattern, how
many pages will she read on Friday?

Understand

You need to find out how many
pages Alicia will read on Friday.

Plan

Look for a pattern.

The pattern
is to add 5
each day.

Monday	5
Tuesday	10
Wednesday	15
Thursday	20
Friday	25

Solve

Continue the pattern.
On Friday, Alicia will
read 25 pages.

Look Back

Does your answer make sense?

Find each pattern. Solve.

1. Mike collected 3 cans in Week 1 and 6 cans
   in Week 2. He collected 12 cans in Week 3
   and 24 cans in Week 4. Look at the number of
   cans he collected. What is the pattern?

   _____

2. Look back at 1. If Mike continues the pattern,
   how many cans will he collect in Week 5?   _____ cans

 California Content Standards *Statistics, Data Analysis, and
Probability 2.1 Recognize, describe, and extend patterns and
determine the next term in linear patterns. Mathematical
Reasoning 3.0.*

Find the pattern. Solve.

3. Danny wants to make a tower of boxes.
He will put 1 box in the top row,
2 boxes in the second row, and
3 boxes in the third row. Look at the
number of boxes in each row.
What is the pattern?

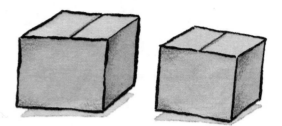

_____

4. Look back at 3. If Danny continues this
pattern, how many boxes will he need
for the sixth row?   _____ boxes

5. Carolyn rode her bike 3 miles the first day.
She rode 5 miles the next day and 7 miles
the day after that. Look at the number of miles
she rode each day. What is the pattern?

_____

6. Look back at 5. If Carolyn continues this
pattern, how many miles will she ride on
the tenth day?   _____ miles

7. Jenna made a necklace of red and blue
beads. She used the following pattern:
1 red, 1 blue, 2 red, 2 blue, 3 red, 3 blue.
If she continues this pattern until she has
21 beads, how many are red and how
many are blue? Color the beads.

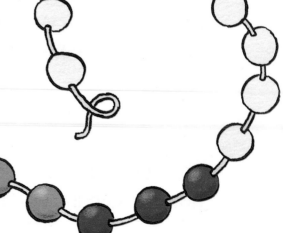

_____ red   _____ blue

Home Activity Ask your child to extend the pattern in each
problem. Homework Workbook 2-11

Name_____

Ways to Add

Find each sum.

Use models or paper and pencil.

1.
$$13 + 39 = 52$$ $$58 + 6$$ $$36 + 44$$ $$17 + 52$$ $$7 + 29$$ $$45 + 26$$

2.
$$54 + 29$$ $$23 + 68$$ $$72 + 8$$ $$36 + 36$$ $$63 + 18$$ $$16 + 7$$

Use a hundred chart or mental math.

3. 15 + 20 = _____   19 + 30 = _____   76 + 10 = _____

4. 44 + 30 = _____   57 + 10 = _____   38 + 20 = _____

5. 26 + 10 = _____   72 + 20 = _____   35 + 30 = _____

California Content Standards Number Sense 2.2 (🔑) Find the sum of two whole numbers up to three digits long. Number Sense 2.3, Mathematical Reasoning 1.1. Also Statistics, Data Analysis, and Probability 2.0 (🔑), 2.1.

Look at each problem.
Choose one of the ways to solve it.
Circle your choice. Then solve.

Sometimes one way
is easier than another.

6.
26
+ 16
a. tens and ones
b. hundred chart
c. paper and pencil
d. mental math

7.
53
+ 30
a. tens and ones
b. hundred chart
c. paper and pencil
d. mental math

8.
18
+ 3
a. tens and ones
b. hundred chart
c. paper and pencil
d. mental math

9.
17
+ 30
a. tens and ones
b. hundred chart
c. paper and pencil
d. mental math

10.
40
+ 50
a. tens and ones
b. hundred chart
c. paper and pencil
d. mental math

11.
18
+ 65
a. tens and ones
b. hundred chart
c. paper and pencil
d. mental math

 Problem Solving

Solve.

12. Bobby collected 25 newspapers on Monday.
What if each day he collects 10 more newspapers
than the day before? How many would he collect on

Tuesday? _____

Wednesday? _____

Thursday? _____

Friday? _____

Home Activity Encourage your child to explain the different
ways to add two-digit numbers. Ask: What are different ways
to find 22 + 19? Homework Workbook 2-12

Name_____

Adding Three Numbers

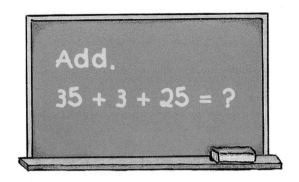

Add.

35 + 3 + 25 = ?

I can line up numbers to make adding easier.

① Line up the numbers by tens and ones.

```
  35
   3
+ 25
```

② Add the ones. Regroup if you can.

```
   |
  35
   3
+ 25
   3
```

③ Add the tens.

```
 |
  35
   3
+ 25
  63
```

Add. Line up numbers by tens and ones to make adding easier.

1. 7 + 16 + 54 = _____

```
   7
  16
+ 54
```

2. 42 + 33 + 19 = _____

3. 3 + 40 + 25 = _____

4. 34 + 6 + 11 = _____

California Content Standards *Number Sense 2.2 (🔑) Find the sum of two whole numbers up to three digits long. Also Number Sense 2.3.*

Find each sum.

5. 26 + 13 + 4 = _____   6. 32 + 37 + 13 = _____

7. 29 + 6 + 40 = _____   8. 45 + 13 + 25 = _____

9.
53	9	13	20	35	22
8	25	42	30	18	12
+ 24	+ 41	+ 25	+ 18	+ 25	+ 62

10.
43	34	13	12	7	25
27	12	38	52	20	12
+ 16	+ 44	+ 42	+ 32	+ 37	+ 40

11.
19	37	61	42	6	24
21	12	16	3	21	34
+ 20	+ 5	+ 14	+ 34	+ 19	+ 9

Math Reasoning

12. Is it easy for you to add these numbers in
your head? Think of a way. Explain how.

20 + 31 + 10 = _____

Home Activity Discuss with your child how he or she added
the numbers above. Homework Workbook 2-13

Name_____ **Problem-Solving Application**

Getting Data from a Table

Every day for one week, Ms. Taylor's class collected cans to recycle. The table shows how many cans they collected.

Cans Collected					
Day	Mon.	Tues.	Wed.	Thurs.	Fri.
Number of cans	9	14	20	17	24

Use the table to solve each problem.

Think: Do you need to add or subtract?

Show your work.

1. How many cans did the class collect on Monday and Tuesday?

   23 cans

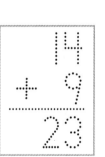

2. How many cans did the class collect on Wednesday and Thursday?

   _____ cans

3. How many more cans did the class collect on Tuesday than on Monday?

   _____ cans

4. How many cans did the class collect on Monday, Tuesday, and Wednesday?

   _____ cans

California Content Standards Algebra and Functions 1.3 Solve addition and subtraction problems by using data from simple charts. Also Number Sense 2.2 (🔑).

The children collected cans for six weeks. The table shows how many pounds of cans they collected to recycle.

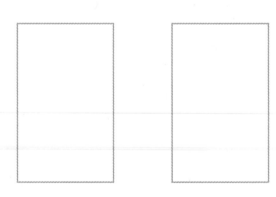

Pounds Collected						
Week	1	2	3	4	5	6
Pounds	9	16	7	13	11	18

Use the table to solve each problem. Show your work.

5. During which two weeks did the class collect the most pounds?

   Week _____ and Week _____

   How many pounds did they collect those weeks?

   _____ pounds

6. How many more pounds were collected during Week 6 than during Week 1?

   _____ pounds

Circle the answer. Add.

7. Were more cans collected in Weeks 1, 2, and 3 or Weeks 4, 5, and 6?

   Weeks 1, 2, and 3

   Weeks 4, 5, and 6

Home Activity To help your child organize data, ask him or her to make a table that shows your weekly recycling.
Homework Workbook 2-14

Name_____ **Diagnostic Checkpoint**

Add. Circle problems if you regroup.

1.

Tens	Ones
2	6
+	8

Tens	Ones
4	6
+ 1	3

Tens	Ones
7	3
+	4

Tens	Ones
6	6
+ 2	5

Add.

2.
  48   63   37   59   71   32
 + 2   +21   +46   + 7   +19   +28

Add. Use tens and ones models if you like.

3.
  41   38   32   14   26   10
  16   21   7   24   9   50
 +24   +35   +25   +34   +12   +30

Find the pattern. Solve.

4. Pete collected 4 bags of paper in Week 1.
   He collected 8 bags in Week 2 and 12 bags
   in Week 3. Look at the number of bags
   collected. What is the pattern?

   _____

5. Look back at 4. If he continues the pattern,
   how many bags will Pete collect in Week 4?   _____ bags

Name_____

1. $9 + 7 = \boxed{}$

2	15	16	NH
○	○	○	○

2. $14 - 5 = \boxed{}$

10	9	8	7
○	○	○	○

3.
$$\begin{array}{r} 25 \\ + \ 7 \\ \hline \end{array}$$

22	26	31	32
○	○	○	○

4.
$$\begin{array}{r} 43 \\ + 15 \\ \hline \end{array}$$

58	52	28	NH
○	○	○	○

5.   78, 79, 80, ——, 82

83	81	79	77
○	○	○	○

6.   38, 39, ——, 41, 42

40	41	42	NH
○	○	○	○

7.

Day 1	Day 2	Day 3	Day 4
4	8	12	?

10	14	16	18
○	○	○	○

8.

Day 1	Day 2	Day 3	Day 4
1	4	7	?

10	9	8	7
○	○	○	○

9.   20   10

- ○ 20 + 10 = 30 stacks
- ○ 20 − 10 = 10 stacks
- ○ 10 + 10 = 20 stacks
- ○ NH

10.   14   30

- ○ 16 bottles
- ○ 34 bottles
- ○ 44 bottles
- ○ NH

Oral Directions *Mark the correct answer. NH means "Not here." Mark it whenever the answer is not given.*

#1–4. Add or subtract.
#5–6. Mark the number that is missing.
#7–8. If the pattern stays the same, what number is missing?

#9. Karen tied up 20 stacks of newspapers. Lois tied up 10 stacks of newspapers. How many more stacks did Karen tie up? Mark the number sentence.
#10. Team A drank 14 bottles of water during the game. Team B drank 30 bottles of water. How many bottles of water did they drink altogether?

Name_____ **Chapter 2 Test**

Write how many tens and ones. Write the number.

1.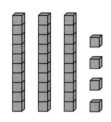

_____ tens _____ ones _____

2.

_____ tens _____ ones _____

Cross out the one that does not show 34.

3. | | 3 tens 4 ones

Write the missing numbers.

4. 43, _____, 45, 46, _____

5. 77, _____, 79, _____, 81

6. 50, _____, _____, 53, 54

7. 36, _____, 38, 39, _____

Find each sum.

8. 20 + 40 = _____   30 + 50 = _____   60 + 10 = _____

9. 70 + 14 = _____   33 + 30 = _____   40 + 34 = _____

Use tens and ones.
Write different ways to show each number.

10. 15 _____ tens _____ ones

_____ tens _____ ones

11. 28 _____ tens _____ ones

_____ tens _____ ones

_____ tens _____ ones

Add. Circle problems if you regroup.

12.

Tens	Ones
□	
5	4
+ 1	9

Tens	Ones
□	
5	8
+ 2	6

Tens	Ones
□	
3	7
+ 2	1

Tens	Ones
□	
8	9
+	2

Add.

13.
$$\begin{array}{r} 37 \\ + 13 \\ \hline \end{array} \qquad \begin{array}{r} 26 \\ + 37 \\ \hline \end{array} \qquad \begin{array}{r} 10 \\ + 79 \\ \hline \end{array} \qquad \begin{array}{r} 28 \\ + 4 \\ \hline \end{array} \qquad \begin{array}{r} 63 \\ + 30 \\ \hline \end{array} \qquad \begin{array}{r} 14 \\ + 27 \\ \hline \end{array}$$

14.
$$\begin{array}{r} 32 \\ 12 \\ + 20 \\ \hline \end{array} \qquad \begin{array}{r} 20 \\ 36 \\ + 30 \\ \hline \end{array} \qquad \begin{array}{r} 23 \\ 25 \\ + 7 \\ \hline \end{array} \qquad \begin{array}{r} 12 \\ 22 \\ + 32 \\ \hline \end{array} \qquad \begin{array}{r} 20 \\ 10 \\ + 40 \\ \hline \end{array} \qquad \begin{array}{r} 15 \\ 26 \\ + 36 \\ \hline \end{array}$$

Find the pattern. Solve.

15. Sara walked for 4 minutes on Monday and 8 minutes on Tuesday. On Wednesday she walked for 12 minutes. If the pattern continues, how long will she walk Thursday? _____ minutes

16. Use the table to solve. Show your work. Which group has the most cans?

Cans Collected		
	Group 1	Group 2	Group 3
Day 1	25	17	26
Day 2	23	34	18

Group _____

Name_____

1.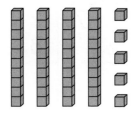

     54   45   9   NH
    ○   ○   ○   ○

2.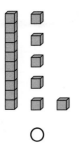

  ○   ○   6 tens 1 one   16
                      ○   ○

3. 47, 48, 49, ____, 51

  48   52   53   NH
  ○   ○   ○   ○

4. 40 + 30 = ☐   70   60   27   7
                        ○   ○   ○   ○

5. 24 + 30 = ☐   44   50   54   NH
                        ○   ○   ○   ○

6. 24

1 ten 4 ones   2 tens 14 ones   2 tens 4 ones   1 ten 24 ones
   ○   ○   ○   ○

Oral Directions *Mark the correct answer. NH means "Not here." Mark it whenever the answer is not given.*

#1. What number is shown by the tens and ones?
#2. Which does NOT show sixteen?
#3. What is the missing number?
#4–5. Add.
#6. Which shows twenty-four correctly?

7.

Tens	Ones
3	2
+	9

○

Tens	Ones
2	7
+	1	6

○

Tens	Ones
5	8
+ 3	1

○

Tens	Ones
7	2
+	8

○

8.
35
+ 18

43	53	413	NH
○	○	○	○

9.
59
+ 9

68	58	50	18
○	○	○	○

---

10. 34 + 27 + 6 = ☐

60	73	121	NH
○	○	○	○

11.

3   6   9   ?

10 cans	11 cans	12 cans	13 cans
○	○	○	○

12.

Cans Collected		
	Group 1	Group 2
Day 1	24	35
Day 2	36	23

58	59	60	NH
○	○	○	○

Oral Directions *Mark the correct answer. NH means "Not here." Mark it whenever the answer is not given.*

#7. Which problem does NOT need regrouping?
#8–10. Add or subtract.

#11. Susi collected 3 cans on Monday, 6 cans on Tuesday, and 9 cans on Wednesday. If this pattern continues, how many cans will she collect on Thursday?
#12. How many cans did Group 1 collect?

CHAPTER 3

Subtracting Two-Digit Numbers

Diagnosing Readiness

for Chapter 3

1. What number comes before 98?

   100, 99, 98, _____

2. $9 - 7 =$ _____

3. $\begin{array}{r} 36 \\ + 25 \\ \hline \end{array}$

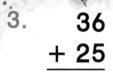

4. Use >, <, or = to make the statement true.

   86 ◯ 79

5. Beth has 18 shells. Dan has 6. Tom has 5 more shells than Dan. How many more shells does Beth have than Tom?

   _____ ◯ _____ = _____

To the Family

Looking Back

In Chapter 2 children reviewed place value to one hundred and added two-digit numbers.

Chapter 3

Subtracting Two-Digit Numbers

Children subtract two-digit numbers with and without regrouping. Children check subtraction by using addition.

Looking Ahead

Children will add and subtract two- and three-digit numbers in Chapter 7.

Page 73 Your child solved problems that review math skills from previous chapters and will help your child with the skills in Chapter 3.

Math at Home Collect about 25 small objects such as beads, pennies, or pasta pieces. Take turns removing some and finding out how many are left.

Math Literature Read math or theme-related stories with your child. Look for the following books in your local library.
Mike's Kite by Elizabeth MacDonald (HBJ School, 1993)
Wake Up, City! by Alvin Tresselt (Lothrop, 1990)

California Content Standards in Chapter 3 Lessons*

Number Sense	Teach and Practice	Practice
1.3 (🔑) Compare whole numbers by using the symbols <, =, >.		6
2.0 Estimate, calculate, and solve problems involving subtraction of two-digit numbers.		5
2.1 (🔑) Understand and use the inverse relationship between addition and subtraction to solve problems and check solutions.	10	
2.2 (🔑) Find the sum or difference of two whole numbers up to three digits long.	1–6, 8, 9, 11, 12	10
2.3 Use mental arithmetic to find the sum or difference of two two-digit numbers.	9	1, 2
5.1 (🔑) Solve problems by using combinations of coins.		1, 3
Algebra and Functions		
1.0 Students model, represent, and interpret number relationships to create and solve problems involving addition and subtraction.		6
1.2 Relate problem situations to number sentences involving addition and subtraction.	12	2
1.3 Solve addition and subtraction problems by using data from simple charts, picture graphs, and number sentences.	13	

Statistics, Data Analysis, and Probability	Teach and Practice	Practice
1.3 Identify features of data sets (range and mode).	13	
1.4 Ask and answer simple questions related to data representations.	13	
2.0 (🔑) Students demonstrate an understanding of patterns and how patterns grow and describe them in general ways.		7
2.1 Recognize, describe, and extend patterns and determine the next term in linear patterns.		7
2.2 Solve problems involving simple number patterns.	7	
Mathematical Reasoning		
1.1 Determine the approach, materials, and strategies to be used.		9
1.2 Use tools, such as manipulatives or sketches, to model problems.		5, 6, 11
2.1 Defend the reasoning used and justify the procedures selected.		4, 9, 10
2.2 Make precise calculations and check the validity of the results in the context of the problem.		10
3.0 Students note connections between one problem and another.		7, 8

* The symbol (🔑) indicates a key standard as designated in the Mathematics Framework for California Public Schools.
Full statements of the California Content Standards are found at the beginning of this book following the Table of Contents.

Name_____ **Subtracting Tens**

Just as with addition, you can use
basic facts to help subtract tens.

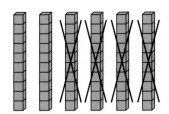

6 tens − 4 tens = __2__ tens

60 − 40 = 20

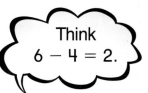

Think
6 − 4 = 2.

Find each difference.
Use tens models if you like.

1. 7 tens − 3 tens = _____ tens

   70 − 30 = _____

2. 9 tens − 6 tens = _____ tens

   90 − 60 = _____

3. 8 tens − 5 tens = _____ tens

   80 − 50 = _____

4. 6 tens − 1 ten = _____ tens

   60 − 10 = _____

5. 5 tens − 4 tens = _____ ten

   50 − 40 = _____

6. 9 tens − 5 tens = _____ tens

   90 − 50 = _____

7. 8 tens − 2 tens = _____ tens

   80 − 20 = _____

8. 7 tens − 5 tens = _____ tens

   70 − 50 = _____

9. 6 tens − 3 tens = _____ tens

   60 − 30 = _____

10. 4 tens − 3 tens = _____ ten

    40 − 30 = _____

California Content Standards *Number Sense 2.2 (🔑) Find
the difference of two whole numbers up to three digits long.
Also Number Sense 2.3, 5.1.*

seventy-five **75**

Find each difference. Write the missing numbers.
Use tens models if you like.

11. 5 tens − 3 tens = __2__ tens

50 − 30 = 20

12. 9 tens − 2 tens = _____ tens

_____ − _____ = _____

13. 8 tens − 4 tens = _____ tens

_____ − _____ = _____

14. 6 tens − 5 tens = _____ ten

_____ − _____ = _____

15. 6 tens − 2 tens = _____ tens

_____ − _____ = _____

16. 5 tens − 2 tens = _____ tens

_____ − _____ = _____

17. 8 tens − 7 tens = _____ ten

_____ − _____ = _____

18. 7 tens − 4 tens = _____ tens

_____ − _____ = _____

19. 9 tens − 3 tens = _____ tens

_____ − _____ = _____

20. 3 tens − 2 tens = _____ ten

_____ − _____ = _____

Math Reasoning

Number Sense

21. Write the numbers.

5 dimes − 2 dimes = _____ dimes

_____ ¢ − _____ ¢ = _____ ¢

Home Activity Ask your child to subtract numbers like the ones on this page. Homework Workbook 3-1

Name_____ **Counting Back by Tens**

You can count back by tens to subtract.

$35 - 20 = 15$

Start at 35.
Count back 2 tens.
35, 25, 15

0	1	2	3	4	5	6	7	8	9
10	11	12	13	14	15	16	17	18	19
20	21	22	23	24	25	26	27	28	29
30	31	32	33	34	35	36	37	38	39
40	41	42	43	44	45	46	47	48	49

Use the chart or Workmat 5.
Count back by tens to subtract.

1. $48 - 30 =$ _____ $42 - 20 =$ _____ $33 - 10 =$ _____

2. $40 - 30 =$ _____ $27 - 10 =$ _____ $31 - 30 =$ _____

3. $43 - 20 =$ _____ $37 - 20 =$ _____ $41 - 10 =$ _____

4. $22 - 10 =$ _____ $47 - 20 =$ _____ $49 - 10 =$ _____

5. $35 - 30 =$ _____ $34 - 20 =$ _____ $29 - 20 =$ _____

California Content Standards *Number Sense 2.2 (🔑) Find
the difference of two whole numbers up to three digits long. Also
Number Sense 2.3, Algebra and Functions 1.2.*

seventy-seven **77**

Count back by tens to subtract.
Use Workmat 5 if you like.

6. $86 - 30 = \underline{56}$ $45 - 30 = \underline{}$ $82 - 10 = \underline{}$

7. $40 - 20 = \underline{}$ $75 - 20 = \underline{}$ $32 - 30 = \underline{}$

8. $95 - 20 = \underline{}$ $91 - 30 = \underline{}$ $67 - 20 = \underline{}$

9. $53 - 30 = \underline{}$ $72 - 10 = \underline{}$ $84 - 30 = \underline{}$

10. $62 - 20 = \underline{}$ $56 - 30 = \underline{}$ $76 - 10 = \underline{}$

11. $26 - 10 = \underline{}$ $45 - 20 = \underline{}$ $74 - 30 = \underline{}$

12. $85 - 20 = \underline{}$ $58 - 30 = \underline{}$ $39 - 20 = \underline{}$

13. $98 - 10 = \underline{}$ $29 - 10 = \underline{}$ $64 - 30 = \underline{}$

Problem Solving

Solve.

14. 38 fish are in the cove. 20 fish swim out of the cove. How many fish are still in the cove?

_____ fish

15. 65 dolphins are in the bay. 30 dolphins are outside the bay. How many more dolphins are in the bay?

_____ dolphins

Home Activity Choose a number from the chart on page 77. Ask your child to subtract 10, 20, or 30 from that number.
Homework Workbook 3-2

Name_____ **Deciding When to Regroup**

You have 3 tens and 2 ones.
How do you subtract 7 ones?

Sometimes you need to regroup.

① Show 3 tens 2 ones.

Tens	Ones
|||	::

② Regroup 1 ten as 10 ones.

Tens	Ones
||	▭▭ ▭▭ ▭▭ ▭▭ ▭▭

③ Subtract 7 ones.

Tens	Ones
||	▭☒ ▭☒ ▭☒ ▭☒☒ ▭☒☒

2 tens 5 ones are left.

Use tens and ones models and Workmat 3.
Complete the chart.

	Do you need to regroup?		How many are left?
1. Show 3 tens 6 ones. Subtract 8 ones.	(yes)	no	_2_ tens _8_ ones
2. Show 2 tens 5 ones. Subtract 7 ones.	yes	no	_____ ten _____ ones
3. Show 4 tens 8 ones. Subtract 5 ones.	yes	no	_____ tens _____ ones
4. Show 5 tens 1 one. Subtract 3 ones.	yes	no	_____ tens _____ ones
5. Show 6 tens 2 ones. Subtract 5 ones.	yes	no	_____ tens _____ ones

California Content Standards *Number Sense 2.2 (🔑) Find the difference of two whole numbers up to three digits long. Also Number Sense 5.1 (🔑).*

seventy-nine **79**

Use tens and ones models and Workmat 3.
Complete the chart.

	Do you need to regroup?		How many are left?
6. Show 2 tens 3 ones. Subtract 6 ones.	(yes)	no	__1__ ten __7__ ones
7. Show 1 ten 9 ones. Subtract 7 ones.	yes	no	_____ ten _____ ones
8. Show 4 tens 6 ones. Subtract 8 ones.	yes	no	_____ tens _____ ones
9. Show 3 tens 2 ones. Subtract 9 ones.	yes	no	_____ tens _____ ones
10. Show 4 tens 2 ones. Subtract 6 ones.	yes	no	_____ tens _____ ones
11. Show 2 tens 9 ones. Subtract 2 ones.	yes	no	_____ tens _____ ones
12. Show 4 tens 1 one. Subtract 9 ones.	yes	no	_____ tens _____ ones

Problem Solving

Solve.

13. You have 2 dimes and 2 pennies.
You want to give 5 pennies to a friend.
What would you do first?

Name_____ **Subtracting with Regrouping**

Find 35 − 9.
Regroup if necessary.

There are not enough ones to subtract.

1 Show 35.
Do you need to regroup?

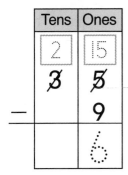

Tens	Ones
3	5
−	9

2 Regroup 1 ten as 10 ones.

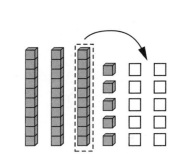

Tens	Ones
2	15
3	5
−	9

3 Subtract the ones.

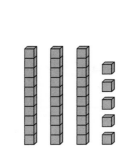

Tens	Ones
2	15
3	5
−	9
	6

4 Bring down the tens.

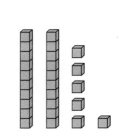

Tens	Ones
2	15
3	5
−	9
2	6

Subtract. Use tens and ones models and Workmat 3.
Did you need to regroup? Circle **yes** or **no**.

1.

Tens	Ones
7	3
−	8

yes

no

2.

Tens	Ones
4	8
−	8

yes

no

California Content Standards *Number Sense 2.2 (⚷) Find the difference of two whole numbers up to three digits long. Also Mathematical Reasoning 2.1.*

Use tens and ones models and Workmat 3.
Subtract. Circle problems if you regroup.

3.

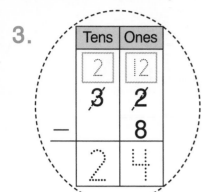

Tens	Ones
2	12
3̸	2̸
−	8
2	4

Tens	Ones
☐	☐
6	5
−	5

Tens	Ones
☐	☐
7	1
−	6

Tens	Ones
☐	☐
6	7
−	8

4.

Tens	Ones
☐	☐
5	4
−	6

Tens	Ones
☐	☐
2	7
−	9

Tens	Ones
☐	☐
8	5
−	6

Tens	Ones
☐	☐
7	4
−	3

5.

Tens	Ones
☐	☐
4	2
−	8

Tens	Ones
☐	☐
9	5
−	2

Tens	Ones
☐	☐
2	3
−	7

Tens	Ones
☐	☐
5	5
−	7

 Math Reasoning

Number Sense

6. Put an *X* on the wrong way
to show 42 − 9.
Tell why it is wrong.
Then find the answer.

$$\begin{array}{r} 42 \\ -\ 9 \\ \hline \end{array}$$ $$\begin{array}{r} 42 \\ -\ 9 \\ \hline \end{array}$$

Home Activity Ask your child to explain how he or she
would solve a problem like 29 − 4. Homework Workbook 3-4

Name_____ **Subtracting Two-Digit Numbers**

Use tens and ones to find 45 − 27.
Regroup if necessary.

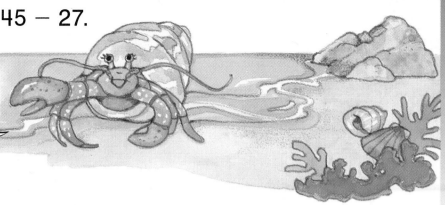

To subtract
7 ones, I will
need to regroup.

① There are not enough ones.
Record 1 ten as 10 ones.

Tens	Ones
3̷	15̷
4̷	5̷
− 2	7

② Cross out ones and tens to
subtract. Write the difference.

Tens	Ones
3̷	15̷
4̷	5̷
− 2	7
1	8

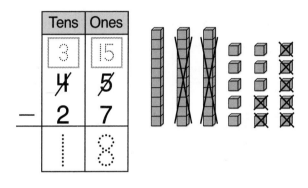

Subtract. Use tens and ones models and Workmat 3.
Did you need to regroup? Circle yes or no.

1.

Tens	Ones
5	1
− 3	4

yes

no

2.

Tens	Ones
3	4
− 1	6

yes

no

3.

Tens	Ones
6	5
− 3	5

yes

no

4.

Tens	Ones
4	5
− 3	6

yes

no

California Content Standards *Number Sense 2.2 (🔑) Find the
difference of two whole numbers up to three digits long. Also Number Sense
2.0, Mathematical Reasoning 1.2.*

eighty-three **83**

Use tens and ones models and Workmat 3.
Subtract. Circle problems if you need to regroup.

5.

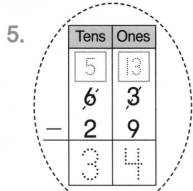

Tens	Ones
5	*13*
6́	3́
− 2	9
3	*4*

Tens	Ones
5	6
− 3	4

Tens	Ones
4	2
− 1	6

Tens	Ones
5	7
− 3	9

6.

Tens	Ones
3	5
− 1	8

Tens	Ones
3	7
− 1	8

Tens	Ones
8	1
− 5	2

Tens	Ones
8	6
− 2	6

7.

Tens	Ones
4	4
− 2	5

Tens	Ones
7	1
− 3	7

Tens	Ones
3	1
− 1	7

Tens	Ones
9	6
− 5	9

 **Problem Solving**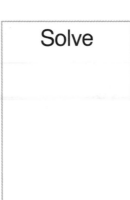

Solve the problem.
Estimate to check your answer.
Write the answer.

Solve	Check

8. 37 terns fly over the ocean.
18 terns dive into the water.
How many terns keep flying?

_____ terns

🏠 **Home Activity** Ask your child to explain why he or she
needed to regroup to solve one of the exercises above.
Homework Workbook 3-5

Name_____ **Subtracting with Zero**

There are 50 sea gulls on the rocks.
15 fly away.
How many are left?

① There are not any ones in 50.
Record 1 ten as 10 ones.

Tens	Ones
4	10
5̷	0̷
− 1	5

② Cross out ones and tens to
subtract. Write the difference.

Tens	Ones
4	10
5̷	0̷
− 1	5
3	5

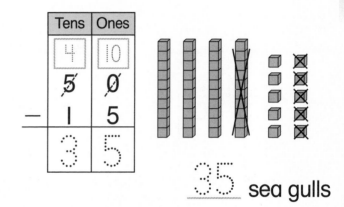

35 sea gulls

Use tens and ones models and Workmat 3.
Decide if you need to regroup. Then subtract.

1.

Tens	Ones
8	9
− 2	0

Tens	Ones
7	0
− 1	2

Tens	Ones
8	4
− 6	0

Tens	Ones
3	0
−	7

2.

Tens	Ones
9	0
− 3	8

Tens	Ones
4	7
− 1	0

Tens	Ones
5	3
− 2	0

Tens	Ones
7	6
− 5	6

California Content Standards *Number Sense 2.2 (🔑)*
Find the difference of two whole numbers up to three digits long.
Also Number Sense 1.3 (🔑), Algebra and Functions 1.0,
Mathematical Reasoning 1.2.

Use tens and ones models and Workmat 3.
Decide if you need to regroup. Subtract.

3.

Tens	Ones
6	7
− 2	0
4	7

Tens	Ones
7	4
− 3	4

Tens	Ones
3	0
− 1	6

Tens	Ones
5	1
− 3	9

4.

Tens	Ones
3	0
− 1	8

Tens	Ones
4	2
− 1	8

Tens	Ones
7	3
− 5	0

Tens	Ones
9	4
− 5	4

5.

Tens	Ones
5	0
− 2	5

Tens	Ones
7	7
− 3	7

Tens	Ones
5	0
− 2	8

Tens	Ones
6	3
− 5	9

Math Reasoning

Algebra

Mental Math

Write a number that makes each number sentence true.

6. $50 - 30 < 50 -$ _____

7. $80 - 20 > 80 -$ _____

8. $90 - 60 > 90 -$ _____

9. $70 - 40 < 70 -$ _____

Home Activity Ask your child to explain how he or she completed each of the exercises on this page.
Homework Workbook 3-6

Name_____ **Problem-Solving Strategy**

Find a Pattern

On Sunday, Max had 66 cars to paint.
On Monday, he had 60 cars left to paint.
On Tuesday, he had 54 cars left to paint.
If he continues this pattern, how many
cars will he have left to paint on Friday?

Understand

You need to find out how many
cars Max will have left to
paint on Friday.

Plan

Look for a pattern.

The pattern is
to subtract 6
each day.

Solve

Continue the pattern.
Max will have 36 cars
left to paint on Friday.

Sunday	66
Monday	60
Tuesday	54
Wednesday	48
Thursday	42
Friday	36

Look Back

Is your answer reasonable?

Find each pattern. Solve.

1. Ana has 32 paper flowers to make. After 1 hour
she has 28 flowers to make. After 2 hours she
has 24 flowers to make. Look at the number of
flowers she has left to make after each hour. What is the pattern?

_____

2. Look back at 1. If Ana continues the pattern,
how many flowers will she have left after 6 hours? _____ flowers

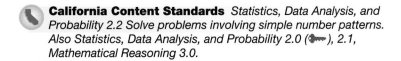

California Content Standards *Statistics, Data Analysis, and
Probability 2.2 Solve problems involving simple number patterns.
Also Statistics, Data Analysis, and Probability 2.0 (*), 2.1,
Mathematical Reasoning 3.0.*

Find each pattern. Solve.

3. Tony has 70 shells to give away. After the first day he has 67 left. After 2 days he has 62 left. After 3 days he has 55 left. Look at the number of shells Tony has left each day. What is the pattern?

_____

_____

4. Look back at 3. If Tony continues this pattern, how many shells will he have left after 7 days?   _____ shells

5. Kris has 90 pages to read. After 1 day she has 80 pages left. After 2 days she has 70 pages. Look at the number of pages she reads each day. What is the pattern?

_____

_____

6. Look back at 5. If Kris continues this pattern, how many days will it take her to read all the pages?   _____ days

 Math Reasoning

Number Sense

7. Look for a pattern. Write the missing numbers.

62	62	62	☐	62
− 9	− 19	− ☐	− 39	− ☐
53	43	33	23	13

 Home Activity Ask your child to extend the patterns for Exercises 3 and 5. Homework Workbook 3-7

Name_____

Find each difference.
Use tens and ones models or Workmat 3 if you like.

1. 80 − 50 = _____   60 − 20 = _____   90 − 20 = _____

2. 46 − 10 = _____   72 − 20 = _____   35 − 20 = _____

3.
Tens	Ones
☐	☐
6	8
−	9

Tens	Ones
☐	☐
5	0
−	6

Tens	Ones
☐	☐
6	7
− 3	4

Tens	Ones
☐	☐
3	6
− 1	7

4.
Tens	Ones
☐	☐
7	6
− 4	0

Tens	Ones
☐	☐
5	3
− 2	8

Tens	Ones
☐	☐
4	6
− 1	3

Tens	Ones
☐	☐
8	0
− 2	1

Find each pattern. Solve.

5. Tom wants to walk 40 laps around the playground.
After Day 1, he has 35 laps to walk. After Day 2,
he has 30 laps to walk. Look at the number of
laps he walks each day. What is the pattern?

_____

6. Look back at 5. If he continues this pattern, how
many days will it take Tom to walk 40 laps?   _____

Name_____

1.   13
    − 5

| 35
+ 5
18
○ | 8
+ 5
13
○ | 5
+ 5
10
○ | 8
+ 8
16
○ |

2.   57
    + 33

| 24
○ | 80
○ | 90
○ | NH
○ |

3.   12 + 28 = 40
    so 28 + 12 = ☐

| 16
○ | 30
○ | 39
○ | 40
○ |

4.   24 + 30 = ☐

| 54
○ | 44
○ | 27
○ | NH
○ |

5.

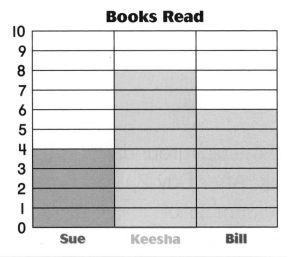

Books Read

10	12	19	NH
○	○	○	○

Oral Directions *Mark the correct answer. NH means "Not here." Mark it whenever the answer is not given.*

#1. Which addition sentence would best help you subtract 13 − 5?
#2. Add.

#3. Use the sentence 12 + 28 = 40 to help you add 28 + 12.
#4. Count on by tens to add.
#5. How many books did Sue, Keesha, and Bill read altogether?

Name_____   **Two-Digit Subtraction**

Harborside Aquarium rescued 72 seals
last year. It released 54 seals.
How many seals are still at the aquarium?

① Regroup 1 ten
as 10 ones.

Tens	Ones
6	12
7̸	2̸
– 5	4

② Subtract the ones.
Subtract the tens.

Tens	Ones
6	12
7̸	2̸
– 5	4
1	8

 seals

---

Subtract. Use tens and ones models if you like.

1.
```
   43        65        36        50        74        47
 – 15      – 48      – 24      – 32      –  9      – 25
```

2.
```
   64        28        62        41        90        53
 – 59      – 10      – 19      – 24      – 27      – 33
```

3.
```
   80        54        61        77        80        36
 – 46      – 28      – 40      – 69      –  8      – 17
```

California Content Standards *Number Sense 2.2 (🔑) Find
the difference of two whole numbers up to three digits long. Also
Mathematical Reasoning 3.0.*

Subtract. Use tens and ones models if you like.

4.

66	37	75	40	84	53
− 8	− 19	− 15	− 23	− 37	− 21

58

5.
58	90	27	89	60	35
− 39	− 56	− 9	− 38	− 25	− 27

6.
70	48	83	47	94	28
− 25	− 9	− 61	− 18	− 5	− 9

7.
98	60	83	35	60	37
− 25	− 35	− 51	− 17	− 6	− 18

Problem Solving

Solve. Show your work.

8. Jed had 38 shells. He gave 16 shells to his sister. How many did he have then?

_____ shells

9. What if Jed had given only 12 shells to his sister? How many shells would he have then?

_____ shells

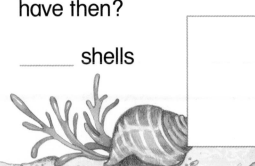

Home Activity Write two or three subtraction problems like the ones on this page. Ask your child to find each difference.
Homework Workbook 3-8

Name_____ **Ways to Subtract**

Find each difference.
Use tens and ones models or paper and pencil.

1.	53	45	70	72	23	93
	− 23	− 8	− 45	− 14	− 18	− 48
	30					

2.	85	50	34	91	88	76
	− 49	− 22	− 9	− 29	− 77	− 29

Use a hundred chart or mental math.

3. $90 - 30 =$ _____ $73 - 20 =$ _____ $38 - 30 =$ _____

4. $56 - 10 =$ _____ $80 - 10 =$ _____ $41 - 20 =$ _____

5. $67 - 20 =$ _____ $29 - 10 =$ _____ $70 - 30 =$ _____

California Content Standards *Number Sense 2.2 (✎) Find the difference of two whole numbers up to three digits long. Number Sense 2.3. Also Mathematical Reasoning 1.1, 2.1.*

Look at each problem.
Circle one of the ways to solve it.
Then solve.

Sometimes one way is easier than another.

6. 42   **a.** tens and ones
   − 16   **b.** hundred chart
         c. paper and pencil
         d. mental math

7. 63   **a.** tens and ones
   − 20   **b.** hundred chart
         c. paper and pencil
         d. mental math

8. 82   **a.** tens and ones
   − 3   **b.** hundred chart
         c. paper and pencil
         d. mental math

9. 50   **a.** tens and ones
   − 33   **b.** hundred chart
         c. paper and pencil
         d. mental math

10. 80   **a.** tens and ones
   − 30   **b.** hundred chart
         c. paper and pencil
         d. mental math

11. 34   **a.** tens and ones
   − 19   **b.** hundred chart
         c. paper and pencil
         d. mental math

 Problem Solving

Does the answer make sense? Circle **yes** or **no**.
Explain your choice.

12. Miguel found 53 shells on the beach.
    He kept 36. How many shells did he
    put back?

    89 shells   yes   no

Home Activity Ask your child to tell you about the different ways to subtract. Ask if she or he has a favorite way.
Homework Workbook 3-9

Name_____ **Checking Subtraction with Addition**

Keiko has 52 shells.
34 are scallop shells.
The rest are conch shells.
How many are conch shells?

conch shells   scallop shells

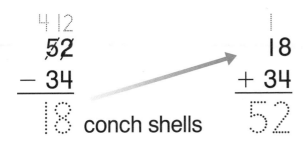

$$
\begin{array}{r} \overset{4\ 12}{\cancel{5}2} \\ -\ 34 \\ \hline 18 \end{array}
$$ conch shells

$$
\begin{array}{r} 18 \\ +\ 34 \\ \hline 52 \end{array}
$$

Start with the difference. Add 34.
Why should the sum be 52?

Subtract. Check by adding.
Use tens and ones models if you like.

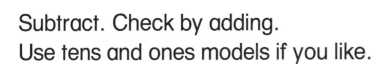

1. $\begin{array}{r} 35 \\ -\ 17 \\ \hline \end{array}$ $+\ \underline{}$

2. $\begin{array}{r} 86 \\ -\ 41 \\ \hline \end{array}$ $+\ \underline{}$

3. $\begin{array}{r} 40 \\ -\ 25 \\ \hline \end{array}$ $+\ \underline{}$

4. $\begin{array}{r} 63 \\ -\ 23 \\ \hline \end{array}$ $+\ \underline{}$

5. $\begin{array}{r} 50 \\ -\ 27 \\ \hline \end{array}$ $+\ \underline{}$

6. $\begin{array}{r} 91 \\ -\ \ 6 \\ \hline \end{array}$ $+\ \underline{}$

7. $\begin{array}{r} 37 \\ -\ 25 \\ \hline \end{array}$ $+\ \underline{}$

8. $\begin{array}{r} 72 \\ -\ 34 \\ \hline \end{array}$ $+\ \underline{}$

California Content Standards *Number Sense 2.1 (🔑)*
*Understand and use the inverse relationship between addition and
subtraction to solve problems and check solutions. Also Number
Sense 2.2 (🔑), Mathematical Reasoning 2.1, 2.2.*

Subtract. Check by adding.
Use tens and ones models if you like.

9.
$$\begin{array}{r} 35 \\ -\ 23 \\ \hline 12 \end{array}$$

$$\begin{array}{r} 12 \\ +\ 23 \\ \hline 35 \end{array}$$

10.
$$\begin{array}{r} 53 \\ -\ 28 \\ \hline \end{array}$$

$$+\ \underline{}$$

11.
$$\begin{array}{r} 82 \\ -\ 26 \\ \hline \end{array}$$

$$+\ \underline{}$$

12.
$$\begin{array}{r} 70 \\ -\ 18 \\ \hline \end{array}$$

$$+\ \underline{}$$

13.
$$\begin{array}{r} 38 \\ -\ \ 9 \\ \hline \end{array}$$

$$+\ \underline{}$$

14.
$$\begin{array}{r} 96 \\ -\ 10 \\ \hline \end{array}$$

$$+\ \underline{}$$

15.
$$\begin{array}{r} 62 \\ -\ 39 \\ \hline \end{array}$$

$$+\ \underline{}$$

16.
$$\begin{array}{r} 85 \\ -\ \ 8 \\ \hline \end{array}$$

$$+\ \underline{}$$

Math Reasoning

17. Sam solved this subtraction problem
and used addition to check his work.
What mistake did he make?

$$\begin{array}{r} {\scriptstyle 4\ 12} \\ 5\!\!\!/2 \\ -\ 38 \\ \hline 24 \end{array}$$

$$\begin{array}{r} {\scriptstyle 1} \\ 24 \\ +\ 38 \\ \hline 62 \end{array}$$

Home Activity Write two or three subtraction problems and ask your child to solve and check them. Ask why adding is a good way to check. Homework Workbook 3-10

Name_____ **Mixed Addition and Subtraction**

Line up the problems in boxes
by tens and ones.
Then add or subtract.

64 − 17

Tens	Ones
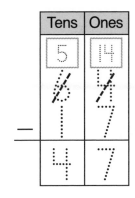

53 + 7

Tens	Ones
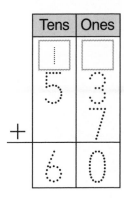

Rewrite the problems in the boxes.
Then add or subtract.

1.   24 − 8   45 + 8   70 + 21   32 − 10

Tens	Ones		Tens	Ones		Tens	Ones		Tens	Ones
------	------		------	------		------	------		------	------

2.   80 − 28   40 + 27   95 − 45   36 + 8

Tens	Ones		Tens	Ones		Tens	Ones		Tens	Ones
------	------		------	------		------	------		------	------
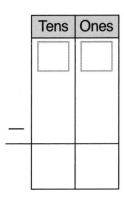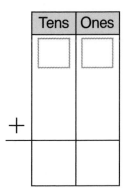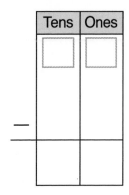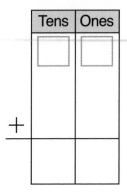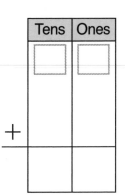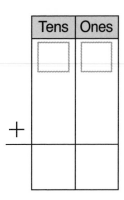

California Content Standards *Number Sense 2.2 (🔑) Find
the sum or difference of two whole numbers up to three digits long.
Also Mathematical Reasoning 1.2.*

Rewrite the problems below. Then add or subtract.

3. 35 − 6   46 + 13   80 − 21   53 + 28

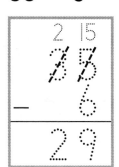

4. 90 − 25   60 + 35   35 + 17   60 − 6

5.
| 27 | 82 | 55 | 50 | 75 | 36 |
| + 19 | − 46 | − 17 | + 7 | − 46 | + 34 |

6.
| 30 | 99 | 85 | 44 | 66 | 51 |
| − 16 | − 39 | + 9 | + 28 | − 10 | + 48 |

 Math Reasoning

Visual Thinking

7. We started with this: | Now we have this: | Draw what was subtracted.

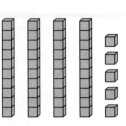 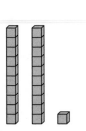

Home Activity Ask your child to explain how he or she lined up each problem on the page. Homework Workbook 3-11

Name_____ **Problem-Solving Application**

Choose the Operation

Algebra

Natalia has 36 shells. She uses 28 shells to make a necklace. How many loose shells does she have left?

Think: Do you add or subtract?

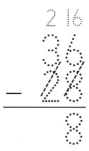

$$\begin{array}{r} \overset{2\ \ 16}{3\ 6} \\ -2\ 8 \\ \hline 8 \end{array}$$

_____8_____ shells

Circle **add** or **subtract**. Solve.

1. Tor has 42 shells. He buys 19 more shells. How many shells does he have now?

   add   subtract   _____ shells

2. Jessie has 51 shells. Mike has 28 shells. How many more shells does Jessie have than Mike?

   add   subtract   _____ shells

3. Ben had 64 shells. He used 18 shells to make a bracelet. How many loose shells does he have left?

   add   subtract   _____ shells

California Content Standards *Number Sense 2.2 (*🔑*) Find the sum or difference of two whole numbers up to three digits long. Algebra and Functions 1.2.*

Circle **add** or **subtract**. Solve.

4. Anna has 33 shells.
   She finds 19 more shells.
   How many shells does
   she have now?

   add   subtract   _____ shells

5. Peter finds 45 shells on the
   beach. He leaves 16 shells for
   someone else to find. How
   many does he take home?

   add   subtract   _____ shells

6. Lee has 25 shells. His
   cousin gives him 17 shells.
   How many shells does he
   have now?

   add   subtract   _____ shells

7. Katrina had 72 shells.
   She used 24 to make
   a belt. How many loose
   shells does she have left?

   add   subtract   _____ shells

Home Activity Ask your child to explain how he or she
decided whether to add or subtract to solve each problem
on this page. Homework Workbook 3-12

Name_____ **Range and Mode**

Ms. Shen's class made this graph to show
how many fish each child has at home.

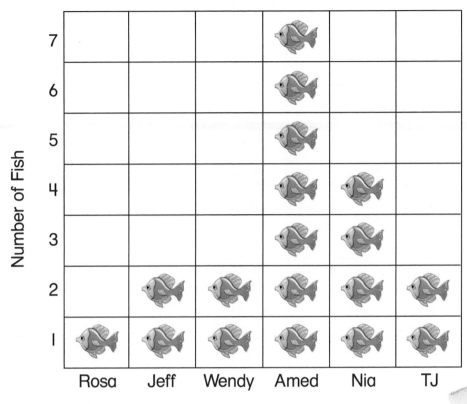

2 fish are above Jeff's name. That means Jeff has 2 fish.

Use the graph above to answer
each question below.

1. Who has the most fish?   _____

2. Who has the fewest fish?   _____

3. How many children have

   1 fish? _____   2 fish? _____   3 fish? _____

   4 fish? _____   6 fish? _____   7 fish? _____

4. What number of fish does the
   greatest number of children have?   _____

California Content Standards *Statistics, Data Analysis, and Probability 1.3 Identify features of data sets (range and mode). Statistics, Data Analysis, and Probability 1.4.*

one hundred one **101**

Mr. Lopez's class kept track of the number
of laps they walked at recess.

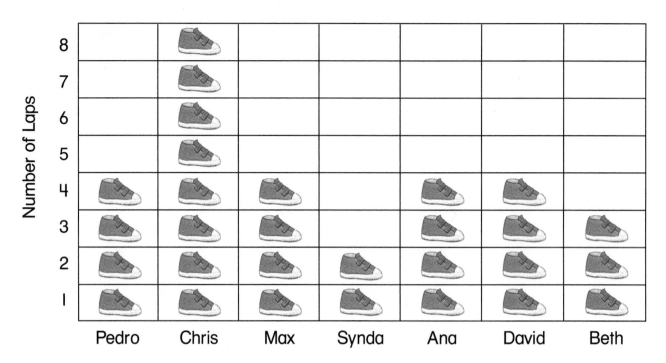

Use the graph to answer each question below.

5. Who walked the least number of laps? _____

6. Who walked the most number of laps? _____

7. How many children walked

2 laps? _____   3 laps? _____   4 laps? _____

6 laps? _____   7 laps? _____   8 laps? _____

8. What number of laps did the
   greatest number of children walk? _____

Math Reasoning

9. Write another question that can be answered
   if you use the graph above.

_____

Home Activity Ask your child to tell how many fish all the
children have on page 101 (18 fish) and how many laps all the
children walked on this page. (29 laps) Homework Workbook
3-13

Name_____

1. Rewrite the numbers in the boxes below.
   Then subtract.

   84 − 36   45 − 9   90 − 46   66 − 26

Tens	Ones
□	□

Tens	Ones
□	□

Tens	Ones
□	□

Tens	Ones
□	□

---

2. Subtract. Check by adding.
   Use tens and ones models if you like.

   ```
     32          40          65
   − 19        − 21        − 26
   ```

---

3. Add or subtract.

   ```
     16        59        70        46        83
   + 37      − 11      − 59      + 36      − 47
   ```

Circle **add** or **subtract**. Solve.

4. Lisa found 46 shells on Tuesday. She had
   found 18 shells on Monday. How many
   shells did she find altogether?

   add   subtract   _____ shells

Name_____

1.
$$\begin{array}{r} 25 \\ -\ 7 \\ \hline \end{array}$$

22	28	18	NH
○	○	○	○

2.
$$\begin{array}{r} 43 \\ -15 \\ \hline \end{array}$$

28	32	58	60
○	○	○	○

3.
$$\begin{array}{r} 60 \\ -34 \\ \hline \end{array}$$

36	34	26	NH
○	○	○	○

4.

Day 1	Day 2	Day 3	Day 4	Day 5
24	21	18	15	?

16	13	12	10
○	○	○	○

5.
$$\begin{array}{r} 52 \\ -41 \\ \hline 11 \end{array}$$

$\begin{array}{r} 11 \\ +41 \\ \hline \end{array}$	$\begin{array}{r} 11 \\ +52 \\ \hline \end{array}$	$\begin{array}{r} 52 \\ +11 \\ \hline \end{array}$	$\begin{array}{r} 41 \\ +52 \\ \hline \end{array}$
○	○	○	○

6.

Shells Collected	
Monday	24
Tuesday	12
Wednesday	9
Thursday	16
Friday	21

○ $16 + 9 = 25$

○ $21 - 16 = 5$

○ $16 + 21 = 37$

○ NH

Oral Directions *Mark the correct answer. NH means "Not here." Mark it whenever the answer is not given.*

#1–3. Subtract.
#4. Matt wanted to read a book in less than 8 days. On Day 1, he had 24 pages left to read. On Day 2, he had 21 pages left. On Day 3, he had 18 pages left. On Day 4, he had 15 pages left. If the pattern continues, how many pages will he have left on Day 5?

#5. Which addition can you use to check $52 - 41 = 11$?
#6. How many shells were collected on Thursday and Friday together? Mark which number sentence you would use to solve the problem.

Find each difference.

1. 30 − 10 = _____   60 − 20 = _____   80 − 70 = _____

2. 41 − 30 = _____   57 − 10 = _____   87 − 50 = _____

Subtract. Circle the problem if you regroup.

3.

Tens	Ones
☐	☐
3	8
−	6

Tens	Ones
☐	☐
4	1
−	3

Tens	Ones
☐	☐
4	7
− 3	0

Tens	Ones
☐	☐
4	8
− 1	9

4.

Tens	Ones
☐	☐
6	0
− 2	4

Tens	Ones
☐	☐
7	7
− 2	6

Tens	Ones
☐	☐
4	3
− 1	6

Tens	Ones
☐	☐
9	1
− 7	9

Find the pattern. Solve.

5. Cecy added 3 marbles to her fish tank in Week 1.
    She added 6 marbles in Week 2 and 9 marbles
    in Week 3. Look at the number of marbles she
    added each week. What is the pattern?

    _____

    _____

6. Look back at 5. If she continues this pattern, how
    many marbles will she add to the tank in Week 4?   _____ marbles

Subtract.

7.
$$\begin{array}{r} 50 \\ -30 \\ \hline \end{array}$$
$$\begin{array}{r} 63 \\ -35 \\ \hline \end{array}$$
$$\begin{array}{r} 37 \\ -20 \\ \hline \end{array}$$
$$\begin{array}{r} 44 \\ -8 \\ \hline \end{array}$$
$$\begin{array}{r} 77 \\ -48 \\ \hline \end{array}$$
$$\begin{array}{r} 88 \\ -18 \\ \hline \end{array}$$

Subtract. Check by adding.

8.
$$\begin{array}{r} 74 \\ -38 \\ \hline \end{array}$$
$$\begin{array}{r} 40 \\ -23 \\ \hline \end{array}$$
$$\begin{array}{r} 85 \\ -56 \\ \hline \end{array}$$

---

9. Add or subtract.

$$\begin{array}{r} 93 \\ -38 \\ \hline \end{array}$$
$$\begin{array}{r} 20 \\ +69 \\ \hline \end{array}$$
$$\begin{array}{r} 50 \\ -35 \\ \hline \end{array}$$
$$\begin{array}{r} 65 \\ -15 \\ \hline \end{array}$$
$$\begin{array}{r} 37 \\ +53 \\ \hline \end{array}$$

Circle **add** or **subtract**. Then solve.

10. Jen has 37 shells. Her friend Alexi has 63 shells. How many more shells does Alexi have than Jen?

add   subtract   _____ shells

---

11. Luis found 16 shells on Sunday. On Monday, he found 45 more. How many shells did he find altogether?

add   subtract   _____ shells

Name_____

1. 40 − 30 = ☐ | 70 ○   37 ○   10 ○   1 ○

2. 44 − 10 = ☐ | 34 ○   43 ○   45 ○   NH ○

3.
       45   30   94   55
     − 18   − 7   − 26   − 34
        ○   ○   ○   ○

4. 46
   − 5 | 39 ○   41 ○   51 ○   NH ○

5. 72
   − 17 | 65 ○   57 ○   55 ○   45 ○

6.

Monday	28
Tuesday	24
Wednesday	20
Thursday	16
Friday	?

17 ○   15 ○   14 ○   12 ○

Oral Directions *Mark the correct answer. NH means "Not here." Mark it whenever the answer is not given.*

#1–2: Subtract.
#3. Which problem does NOT need regrouping?

#4–5. Decide if you need to regroup. Subtract.
#6. On Monday, Sue had 28 stickers left. On Tuesday, she had 24 stickers left. On Wednesday, she had 20 stickers left. On Thursday, she had 16 stickers left. If she continues this pattern, how many stickers will she have left on Friday?

7.

$$\begin{array}{r} 35 \\ -\ 18 \\ \hline 17 \end{array}$$

$\begin{array}{r} 35 \\ +\ 18 \\ \hline \end{array}$	$\begin{array}{r} 23 \\ +\ 18 \\ \hline \end{array}$	$\begin{array}{r} 23 \\ +\ 35 \\ \hline \end{array}$	$\begin{array}{r} 17 \\ +\ 18 \\ \hline \end{array}$
○	○	○	○

8.

$$\begin{array}{r} 62 \\ -\ 18 \\ \hline \end{array}$$

34	44	56	NH
○	○	○	○

9.

$$\begin{array}{r} 48 \\ +\ 19 \\ \hline \end{array}$$

67	57	31	29
○	○	○	○

10.

34   23

34 + 23 = 57	57 − 23 = 34	34 − 23 = 11	NH
○	○	○	○

11.

41   16

41 + 16 = 57	57 − 16 = 41	41 − 16 = 25	16 + 25 = 41
○	○	○	○

Oral Directions *Mark the correct answer. NH means "Not here." Mark it whenever the answer is not given.*

#7. Which addition can you use to check 35 − 18 = 17?
#8−9. Add or subtract.
#10. Sam has 34 sea shells. His friend Jamal has 23 sea shells. How many more sea shells does Sam have? Mark which number sentence you would use to solve the problem.

#11. Luz found 41 shells in the morning and 16 shells in the afternoon. How many shells did she find in all? Mark which number sentence you would use to solve the problem.

Chapter 4 Money

Diagnosing Readiness
for Chapter 4

1. **Count on to find the total.**

_____ ¢   _____ ¢   _____ ¢   _____ ¢   _____ ¢   _____ ¢

total

2. **Write the amount.**

      total _____ ¢

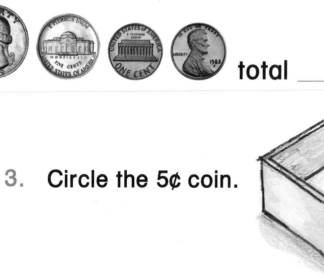

3. Circle the 5¢ coin.

4. **Add.**
   5¢
   + 6¢
   _____ ¢

5. **Subtract.**
   25¢
   − 13¢
   _____ ¢

To the Family

Looking Back	Chapter 4	Looking Ahead
In Grade 1 children learned the value of coins and to add and subtract amounts of money.	**Money** Children review the value of coins from a penny to a quarter and learn the value of a half dollar and dollar. They make change and add and subtract amounts of money under a dollar.	By Chapter 11 children will add and subtract money amounts over a dollar.

Page 109 Your child solved problems that review math skills from previous chapters and will help your child with the skills in Chapter 4.

Math at Home The chapter theme is ways to earn money. Give your child several dimes, nickels, and pennies. Name an amount of money. Ask your child to use the coins to show the exact amount.

Math Literature Read math or theme-related stories with your child. Look for the following books in your local library.
A Money Adventure: Earning, Saving, Spending, Sharing by Neale S. Godfrey (Silver Burdett Press, 1995)
Arthur's Pet Business by Marc Brown (Little, Brown and Company, 1993)

California Content Standards in Chapter 4 Lessons*

Number Sense	Teach and Practice	Practice
1.3 (🔑) Compare numbers by using the symbols <, =, >.		5
5.0 Students model and solve problems by representing, adding, and subtracting amounts of money.	8, 10, 11	9
5.1 (🔑) Solve problems using combinations of coins and bills.	1, 2, 4–10	3, 11
5.2 (🔑) Know and use the decimal notation and the dollar and cent symbols for money.	1, 2, 4–9	3, 10, 11
Statistics, Data Analysis, and Probability		
1.0 (🔑) Students record, organize, display, and interpret data.	3	6
1.1 Record numerical data in systematic ways, keeping track of what has been counted.	3	6

Mathematical Reasoning	Teach and Practice	Practice
1.0 Students make decisions about how to set up a problem.		1, 2, 8
2.0 Students solve problems and justify their reasoning.		9, 11
2.2 Make precise calculations and check the validity of the results in the context of the problem.	3	

* The symbol (🔑) indicates a key standard as designated in the Mathematics Framework for California Public Schools.
   Full statements of the California Content Standards are found at the beginning of this book following the Table of Contents.

Name_____ **Pennies, Nickels, and Dimes**

penny	nickel	dime
or	or	or
I¢	5¢	I0¢
one cent	five cents	ten cents

Count on to find the total value.

1.

   $\underline{10¢}$ $\underline{20¢}$ $\underline{25¢}$ $\underline{26¢}$ $\underline{27¢}$ $\qquad$ $\underline{27¢}$
   total

2.

   ___¢ ___¢ ___¢ ___¢ ___¢ ___¢ ___¢
   total

3.

   ___¢ ___¢ ___¢ ___¢ ___¢ ___¢ ___¢
   total

4.

   ___¢ ___¢ ___¢ ___¢ ___¢ ___¢ ___¢
   total

California Content Standards *Number Sense 5.1 (⚬) Solve problems using combinations of coins. Number Sense 5.2 (⚬). Also Mathematical Reasoning 1.0.*

one hundred eleven **111**

Find the value of each group.

5.   41¢

6.     ___ ¢

7.    ___ ¢

8.   ___ ¢

9.   ___ ¢

Problem Solving

Solve.

10. You have seven coins that total 28¢. How many of each coin do you have?

_____   _____   _____

Home Activity Give your child some pennies, nickels, and dimes. Ask him or her to find the total value. Homework Workbook 4-1

Name_____

Quarters and Half Dollars

Look at the money.
Each coin has a front and a back.

quarter

 or

25¢
twenty-five cents

half dollar

 or

50¢
fifty cents

Find the value of each group.
Circle the groups that are worth one quarter.
Draw a line under the groups that are worth
one half dollar.

Word Bank
quarter
half dollar
worth

1. 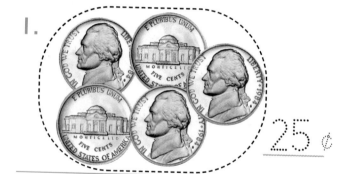 25 ¢

2.   50¢

3.  ____ ¢

4.  ____ ¢

5.  ____ ¢

6.  ____ ¢

California Content Standards *Number Sense 5.1 (🔑) Solve
problems using combinations of coins. Number Sense 5.2 (🔑).
Also Mathematical Reasoning 1.0.*

Count on to find the value of each group.

7.

50¢   75¢   80¢   81¢   81¢

_____ total

8.

_____¢   _____¢   _____¢   _____¢   _____¢   _____¢

total

9.

_____¢   _____¢   _____¢   _____¢   _____¢

total

10. 

_____¢   _____¢   _____¢   _____¢   _____¢   _____¢

total

Problem Solving

11. You have two dimes and
I penny in your pocket.
How many more pennies
do you need to make 25¢?

_____ more pennies

12. Rico has 4 dimes and
2 nickels. Mai has a quarter,
2 dimes, and 3 pennies. Who
has the same as a half dollar?

_____

Name_____ **Problem-Solving Strategy**

Make a List

Sean puts quarters and nickels in his bank.
He is adding 3 coins to his bank.
How much money could this be?

Understand

> There are 3 coins.
> The coins are quarters
> or nickels.

Plan

> You can make a list to show
> every combination of 3 coins.

Solve

Quarters	Nickels	Amount
3	0	75¢
		¢
		¢
		¢

1. What is the greatest amount Sean could add to the bank? _____ ¢

2. What is the least amount Sean could add to the bank? _____ ¢

   Sean could add 75¢, 55¢, 35¢, or 15¢.

Look Back

> Do your answers make sense?

 California Content Standards *Statistics, Data Analysis, and*
Probability 1.1 Record numerical data in systematic ways.
Mathematical Reasoning 2.2. Statistics, Data Analysis, and
Probability 1.0 (🔑). Also Number Sense 5.1 (🔑), 5.2 (🔑).

one hundred fifteen **115**

You have 3 coins.
No coin is worth more than 25¢.
No coin is worth less than 5¢.
How much money could you have?

Make a list to show every combination
of 3 coins.

Use coins
if you like.

Quarters	Dimes	Nickels	Amount
3	0	0	75¢
2	1	0	60¢
			¢
			¢
			¢
			¢
			¢
			¢
			¢
			¢

3. How many different amounts of money could you have? _____

4. What is the greatest amount you could have? _____¢

5. What is the least amount you could have? _____¢

116 one hundred sixteen

Home Activity Ask your child to tell you how he or she
solved the problem on this page. Homework Workbook 4-3

Name_____ **Finding Values**

Native American Crafts

Count by 25s when you count quarters.

25¢   50¢   75¢   75¢
                      total

Count on to find the total value.

1.

___¢   ___¢   ___¢   ___¢   ___¢   ___¢
                                          total

2.

___¢   ___¢   ___¢   ___¢   ___¢   ___¢
                                          total

3.

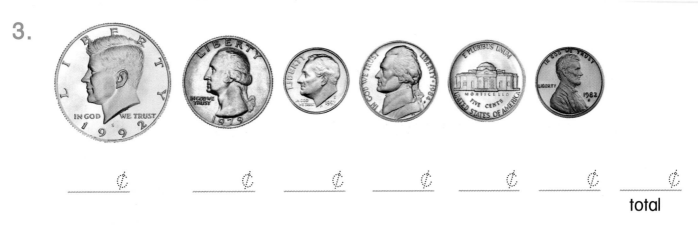

___¢   ___¢   ___¢   ___¢   ___¢   ___¢   ___¢
                                            total

California Content Standards *Number Sense 5.1 (🔑) Solve problems using combinations of coins. Number Sense 5.2 (🔑).*

one hundred seventeen **117**

Do you have enough money to buy each item?
Find the value of each group. Circle **yes** or **no**.

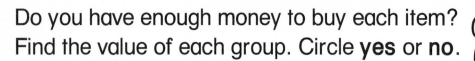

It helps to count coins of greatest value first.

4.

51¢

_51_ ¢ (yes) no

5.

71¢

_____ ¢ yes no

6.

85¢

_____ ¢ yes no

7.

65¢

_____ ¢ yes no

Math Reasoning

Number Sense

8. Circle the coins you would use to make 75¢.

75¢

Home Activity Give your child some coins to count. Remind him or her to start with the coin of greatest value. Homework Workbook 4-4

Name_____ **Comparing Sets of Coins**

Who earned more money?

Josh   Tanya

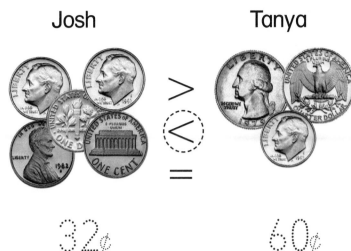

>
<
=

32¢   60¢

Find the value of each group.
Compare the values.
Circle <, >, or =.

1.

<
>
=

_____ ¢   _____ ¢

2.

<
>
=

_____ ¢   _____ ¢

3.

<
>
=

_____ ¢   _____ ¢

California Content Standards *Number Sense 5.1 (🔑) Solve problems using combinations of coins. Number Sense 5.2 (🔑). Also Number Sense 1.3 (🔑).*

one hundred nineteen **119**

Find the value of each group.
Compare the values.
Circle <, >, or =.

4.

    <
    >
    =

_____ ¢   _____ ¢

5.

    <
    >
    =

_____ ¢   _____ ¢

6.

    <
    >
    =

_____ ¢   _____ ¢

7.

    <
    >
    =

_____ ¢   _____ ¢

Home Activity Make cards with the symbols < (less than), > (greater than), or = (equal to). Write 2 amounts on a piece of paper. Ask your child to use the cards to compare the amounts. Homework Workbook 4-5

Name_____ **Ways to Show Amounts**

You can use different coins to make the same value.

half dollar

dime

nickel

quarter

penny

63¢

Write 2 ways to show how many of each coin you could use.

1.

63¢

_____ half dollars

2 quarters

1 dimes

_____ nickels

3 pennies

_____ half dollars

_____ quarters

_____ dimes

_____ nickels

_____ pennies

2.

85¢

_____ half dollars

_____ quarters

_____ dimes

_____ nickels

_____ pennies

_____ half dollars

_____ quarters

_____ dimes

_____ nickels

_____ pennies

California Content Standards *Number Sense 5.1 (🔑) Solve problems using combinations of coins. Number Sense 5.2 (🔑). Also Statistics, Data Analysis, and Probability 1.0 (🔑), 1.1.*

Use coins to show each value in different ways.
Use tally marks to record the coins you use.

3.

Ways to show 58¢				
half dollars	quarters	dimes	nickels	pennies
		⊥⊥⊥⊥⊥	I	III

4.

Ways to show 86¢				
half dollars	quarters	dimes	nickels	pennies

Math Reasoning

5. Find 3 ways to show 31¢. Explain.

1. Count on to find the total value.

_____ ¢   _____ ¢   _____ ¢   _____ ¢   _____ ¢   _____ ¢   _____ ¢

total

2. Write the value of each group.
Circle the group that
is worth 50¢.

   _____ ¢

_____ ¢

3. Find the value of each group.

   _____ ¢

   _____ ¢

4. Find the value of each group.
Compare the values.
Circle <, >, or =.

   <
                       >
                       =

_____ ¢   _____ ¢

1.	6 + 6	10 ○	11 ○	12 ○	NH ○
2.	16 − 7	9 ○	11 ○	23 ○	33 ○
3.	12 − 3	8 ○	9 ○	10 ○	11 ○
4.	3 9 + 3	13 ○	14 ○	15 ○	16 ○
5.	4 2 + 6	8 ○	10 ○	12 ○	NH ○
6.	4 7 + 4	11 ○	14 ○	17 ○	NH ○
7.	14 − 7	4 ○	5 ○	6 ○	7 ○

Oral Directions *Mark the correct answer. NH means "Not here." Mark it whenever the answer is not given.*

#1. Add.
#2–3. Subtract
#4–6. Use mental math to add.
#7. Use mental math to subtract.

Name_____ **Dollars**

100¢

one dollar

$1.00

Write how many more coins you need to make one dollar.
Write the total number of coins needed.
Write the value of the coins in cents.

1. Use quarters.

_____ more quarter

_____ quarters

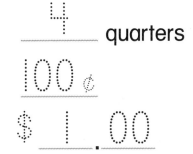100¢

$ 1.00

2. Use dimes.

_____ more dimes

_____ dimes

_____ ¢

$ 1.00

3. Use nickels.

_____ more nickels

_____ nickels

_____ ¢

$ 1.00

California Content Standards *Number Sense 5.2 (⟲) Use decimal notation and symbols for money. Number Sense 5.1 (⟲).*

one hundred twenty-five **125**

Write the value of each group in cents.
Then write the value in dollars.

4.

100¢

$ 1.00

5.

_____ ¢

$ _____ . _____

6.

_____ ¢

$ _____ . _____

7.

_____ ¢

$ _____ . _____

8.

_____ ¢

$ _____ . _____

Home Activity Give your child a dollar bill and coins. Ask your child to show you coins that equal one dollar. Homework Workbook 4-7

Name_____ **Using Dollars and Cents**

Martin earns $1.40 each week for
walking his neighbor's dog.
How much does Martin earn in two weeks?

To count the total value, I start with the dollars and then count the coins.

I can make two groups of $1.40 to find out!

$2.00, $2.25, $2.50,
        $2.60, $2.70,
                $2.75, $2.80

In two weeks, Martin earns $2.80!

Use dollar bills and coins to solve.

1. Kiyo buys paint for $1.35 and chalk for $2.22.
    What is the total cost for both? $ 3 .57

2. Aldo buys marbles for $1.67 and a hat for $3.10.
    How much money does he spend on both? $ ____ . ____

3. Wendy buys a jump rope for $3.14 and bean
    bags for $2.10. What is the total for both? $ ____ . ____

4. T.J. earns $2.50 each week for weeding a
    garden. How much does T.J. earn in three
    weeks? $ ____ . ____

California Content Standards *Number Sense 5.2 ( )*
Use decimal notation and symbols for money. Number Sense 5.0,
5.1 ( ).

one hundred twenty-seven **127**

$3.65

$1.32

$1.15

$1.50

Use dollar bills and coins to solve.

5. Ana wants to buy the boat and the doll.
   How much money does she need?

   $ 2 .65

6. Damir wants to buy the boat and the kite.
   How much money does he need?

   $ _____ . _____

7. Tomaz wants to buy the cup and ball game
   and the kite. How much do they cost together?

   $ _____ . _____

8. Iris wants to buy the cup and ball game
   and the doll. How much do they cost together?

   $ _____ . _____

Math Reasoning

Write how many of each coin it takes to make $2.50.

9.

	_____ pennies = $2.50
	_____ nickels = $2.50
	_____ dimes = $2.50
	_____ quarters = $2.50

Home Activity Use dollar bills and coins. Show your child an amount of money. Ask him or her to tell you the amount of money shown. Homework Workbook 4-8

Name_____

Use the picture to find the price.

Is there enough money? Write **yes** or **no**.

Think: Is the amount you have greater than the price of the toy?

You want to buy	You have	Do you have enough money?
1.		yes
2.		
3.		
4.		

California Content Standards *Number Sense 5.1 (🔑) Solve problems using combinations of coins and bills. Number Sense 5.2 (🔑). Also Number Sense 5.0, Mathematical Reasoning 2.0.*

one hundred twenty-nine **129**

Use the picture to find the price. Do you have enough money?
Write the amount of money. Then write **yes** or **no**.

$2.38 $4.29 $1.31 $4.42 $1.50

You want to buy	You have	Do you have enough money?
5.	4 dollar bills 2 dimes 1 nickel $4.25	
6.	1 dollar bill 2 half dollars 3 quarters 1 dime 1 nickel $____.____	_____
7.	2 half dollars 1 quarter 2 nickels $____.____	_____
8.	1 dollar bill 4 dimes 1 penny $____.____	_____
9.	3 dollar bills 4 quarters 3 dimes 3 nickels $____.____	_____

Home Activity Give your child some coins. Name an item and an amount under one dollar. Ask your child if he or she has enough money to buy the item. Homework Workbook 4-9

Name_____

Making Change

Use pennies.

Count up from the price.

Write how much change.

Price	You Pay	Your Change
1. 18¢		2 ¢
2. 26¢		¢
3. 32¢		¢

California Content Standards *Number Sense 5.1 ( ) Solve problems using combinations of coins and bills. Number Sense 5.0. Also Number Sense 5.2 ( ).*

one hundred thirty-one **131**

Use pennies.
Count up from the price.
Write how much change.

Price	You Pay	Your Change
4. $1.27		____ ¢
5. 31¢		____ ¢
6. 48¢		____ ¢
7. 74¢		____ ¢
8. $1.98		____ ¢

Home Activity Play store to help your child practice making change. Homework Workbook 4-10

Name_____ **Adding and Subtracting Money**

Adding and subtracting money
is just like adding and subtracting
two-digit numbers.

$$
\begin{array}{r}
^{1}\ \ \ \\
29¢ \\
+\ 38¢ \\
\hline
67¢
\end{array}
\qquad
\begin{array}{r}
^{6\ 15}\ \\
\cancel{75}¢ \\
-\ 67¢ \\
\hline
8¢
\end{array}
$$

Watch the +
and − signs.

1¢

Add or subtract.
Use dimes and pennies if you like.

1.
$$
\begin{array}{r} 36¢ \\ +28¢ \\ \hline \end{array}
\qquad
\begin{array}{r} 90¢ \\ +\ 8¢ \\ \hline \end{array}
\qquad
\begin{array}{r} 50¢ \\ -26¢ \\ \hline \end{array}
\qquad
\begin{array}{r} 77¢ \\ -27¢ \\ \hline \end{array}
\qquad
\begin{array}{r} 83¢ \\ -37¢ \\ \hline \end{array}
$$

2.
$$
\begin{array}{r} 60¢ \\ -41¢ \\ \hline \end{array}
\qquad
\begin{array}{r} 15¢ \\ +45¢ \\ \hline \end{array}
\qquad
\begin{array}{r} 45¢ \\ -20¢ \\ \hline \end{array}
\qquad
\begin{array}{r} 57¢ \\ +29¢ \\ \hline \end{array}
\qquad
\begin{array}{r} 63¢ \\ +27¢ \\ \hline \end{array}
$$

3.
$$
\begin{array}{r} 54¢ \\ -11¢ \\ \hline \end{array}
\qquad
\begin{array}{r} 95¢ \\ -36¢ \\ \hline \end{array}
\qquad
\begin{array}{r} 70¢ \\ -\ 7¢ \\ \hline \end{array}
\qquad
\begin{array}{r} 33¢ \\ +28¢ \\ \hline \end{array}
\qquad
\begin{array}{r} 65¢ \\ +15¢ \\ \hline \end{array}
$$

4.
$$
\begin{array}{r} 43¢ \\ -26¢ \\ \hline \end{array}
\qquad
\begin{array}{r} 94¢ \\ -20¢ \\ \hline \end{array}
\qquad
\begin{array}{r} 56¢ \\ +34¢ \\ \hline \end{array}
\qquad
\begin{array}{r} 70¢ \\ -32¢ \\ \hline \end{array}
\qquad
\begin{array}{r} 18¢ \\ +56¢ \\ \hline \end{array}
$$

California Content Standards *Number Sense 5.0 Students solve problems by adding and subtracting amounts of money. Also Number Sense 5.1 (⚷), 5.2 (⚷), Mathematical Reasoning 2.0.*

one hundred thirty-three **133**

Add or subtract.
Use dimes and pennies if you like.

5.
$$\begin{array}{r} \overset{3\ 13}{\cancel{4}3¢} \\ -\ 18¢ \\ \hline 25¢ \end{array}$$

$$\begin{array}{r} 39¢ \\ +\ 7¢ \\ \hline \end{array}$$

$$\begin{array}{r} 54¢ \\ -\ 30¢ \\ \hline \end{array}$$

$$\begin{array}{r} 62¢ \\ -\ 28¢ \\ \hline \end{array}$$

$$\begin{array}{r} 41¢ \\ +\ 36¢ \\ \hline \end{array}$$

6.
$$\begin{array}{r} 87¢ \\ -\ 42¢ \\ \hline \end{array}$$

$$\begin{array}{r} 60¢ \\ +\ 35¢ \\ \hline \end{array}$$

$$\begin{array}{r} 28¢ \\ +\ 9¢ \\ \hline \end{array}$$

$$\begin{array}{r} 13¢ \\ +\ 63¢ \\ \hline \end{array}$$

$$\begin{array}{r} 53¢ \\ -\ 25¢ \\ \hline \end{array}$$

Rewrite the numbers in the boxes below.
Then add or subtract.

7. 18¢ + 32¢

Tens	Ones
1	
1	8¢
+ 3	2¢
5	0¢

90¢ − 45¢

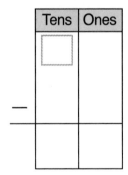

Tens	Ones
−	

44¢ + 27¢

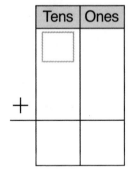

Tens	Ones
+	

 Problem Solving

Solve.

8. Nell has saved 57¢. Her dad
   gives her a dime. Her mom
   gives her 5¢ more than her
   dad. How much money does
   she have now?

9. Nell buys a shell for 69¢.
   She gives the store clerk
   3 quarters. How much
   change should she get?

Home Activity Ask your child to add and subtract money
while playing store. Homework Workbook 4-11

1. Find the value of each group.
   Circle the group that makes $1.00.

_____ ¢   _____ ¢

_____

2. Write the value of each group.

$ _____ . _____ $ _____ . _____

_____

3. Do you have enough money?
   Write **yes** or **no**.

$2.48

_____

_____

4. How much change will you get?

45¢

_____

_____

5. Add or subtract.

25¢	14¢	21¢	47¢	15¢	8¢
− 9¢	+ 14¢	− 10¢	+ 32¢	− 9¢	+ 41¢

Half Dollar	Nickels	Amount
3	0	$1.50
2	1	$1.05
1	2	$0.60
0	3	$0.15

1. $1.50 $1.05 $0.60 $0.15
       ○   ○   ○   ○
_____

2. $1.50 $1.05 $0.60 $0.15
       ○   ○   ○   ○
_____

3.

Price	You Pay
 29¢	

      5¢   4¢   2¢   1¢
       ○   ○   ○   ○
_____

4.

      61¢   36¢   56¢   70¢
       ○   ○   ○   ○
_____

5.

      $2.55 $2.50 $2.45 $2.40
       ○   ○   ○   ○
_____

Oral Directions *Mark the correct answer. NH means "Not here." Mark it whenever the answer is not given.*

#1. What is the greatest value on the chart?
#2. What is the least value shown on the chart?
#3. How much change do you get?
#4–5. How much money is shown?

1. Andre is adding 3 coins to his bank.
   The coins are dimes or nickels.
   How much money could he be adding?
   Make a list to show the combinations of coins.

Dimes	Nickels	Amount

What is the most money Andre could add to his bank? _____ ¢

Count on to find the total value.

2.

_____¢   _____¢   _____¢   _____¢   _____¢   _____¢

3.

$_____ $_____ $_____ $_____ $_____

4.

$_____ $_____ $_____ $_____ $_____

5. Find the value for each group.
   Compare the values.
   Circle <, >, or =.

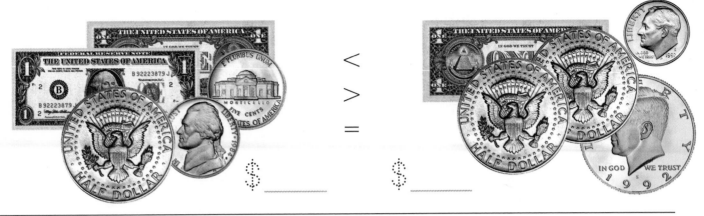

$<$

$>$

$=$

$ _____$ $ _____$

Write the value for each group.
Is there enough to buy the toy?
Circle **yes** or **no**.

55¢

6.

¢ _____   yes   no

7.

¢ _____   yes   no

---

8. Count up from the price to find your change.
   Write how much change.

Price	You Pay	Your Change
12¢		¢ _____

---

9. Add or subtract.

74¢	21¢	46¢	19¢	73¢
− 22¢	+ 34¢	− 14¢	+ 40¢	− 33¢

1.

42¢	47¢	52¢	57¢
○	○	○	○

Use the chart to answer questions 2 and 3.

Quarters	Dimes	Amount
3	0	75¢
2	1	60¢
1	2	45¢
0	3	30¢

2.

75¢	60¢	45¢	30¢
○	○	○	○

3.

75¢	60¢	45¢	30¢
○	○	○	○

4.

1 half dollar	4 quarters	9 dimes	25 nickels
○	○	○	○

5.

5¢	4¢	3¢	2¢
○	○	○	○

Oral Directions *Mark the correct answer. NH means "Not here." Mark it whenever the answer is not given.*

#1. What is the total value of the money shown?
#2. What is the greatest value of the money on the chart?

#3. What amount of money on the chart is more than 30¢ and less than 60¢?
#4. Which is the same as $1.00?
#5. How much change do you get if you pay 80¢?

6.

70¢

5¢   4¢   3¢   2¢
○   ○   ○   ○

7.

$1.85 $2.75 $3.75   NH
○   ○   ○   ○

8.

10¢ 20¢ 25¢ _____

35¢   26¢   30¢   50¢
○   ○   ○   ○

9.	45¢ − 23¢	12¢ ○	22¢ ○	68¢ ○	NH ○
10.	49¢ + 31¢	18¢ ○	70¢ ○	80¢ ○	NH ○
11.	73¢ +19¢	54¢ ○	64¢ ○	82¢ ○	92¢ ○

Oral Directions *Mark the correct answer. NH means "Not here." Mark it whenever the answer is not given.*

#6. How much change do you get if you pay 75¢?
#7. How much money is shown?
#8. Count on to find the total value.
#9–11. Add or subtract.

Diagnosing Readiness
for Chapter 5

1. What numbers are missing?

2. Count by 5s around the clock.

3. What time is it?

4. About how long does it take?

To the Family

Looking Back

In Grade 1 children learned to tell time to the hour and half hour and to use a calendar. They also learned how understanding time helps them organize their lives.

Chapter 5

Time

Children review how to tell time to the hour and half hour and learn to tell time to the quarter hour and 5-minute intervals. Children also learn how to analyze and solve time-related problems using logical reasoning and a calendar.

Looking Ahead

In Grade 3 children will solve problems involving time.

Page 141 Your child solved problems that review math skills from previous chapters and will help your child with the skills in Chapter 5.

Math at Home Work with your child to make a paper-plate clock. Help your child write the numbers on the clock face. Attach the long and the short hands with a paper fastener. Challenge your child to show times to the hour, half hour, quarter hour, and 5-minute intervals.

Math Literature Read stories about time with your child. Look for the following books in your local library.
Telling Time with Big Mama Cat by Dan Harper (Harcourt, 1998)
What Time Is It? by Judith Grey (Troll Communications, 1989)

California Content Standards in Chapter 5 Lessons*

	Teach and Practice	Practice
Number Sense		
6.0 Students use estimation strategies in computation and problem solving.		3
6.1 Recognize when an estimate is reasonable in measurements.	4	
Measurement and Geometry		
1.2, Grade 1, Tell time to the nearest half hour and relate time to events.	1	
1.4 Tell time to the nearest quarter hour and know relationships of time.	2–5, 9–10	
1.5 Determine the duration of intervals of time in hours.	6–8	

	Teach and Practice	Practice
Statistics, Data Analysis, and Probability		
1.0 (⚷) Students collect numerical data and record, organize, display, and interpret the data on bar graphs and other representations.		8–10
1.1 Record numerical data in systematic ways.		9
1.4 Ask and answer simple questions related to data representations.		9, 10
2.0 (⚷) Students demonstrate an understanding of patterns and how patterns grow and describe them in general ways.		2
Mathematical Reasoning		
1.0 Students make decisions about how to set up a problem.		6, 7
2.0 Students solve problems and justify their reasoning.		1, 4, 5

* The symbol (⚷) indicates a key standard as designated in the Mathematics Framework for California Public Schools.
Full statements of the California Content Standards are found at the beginning of this book following the Table of Contents.

Name_____ **Time to the Hour and Half Hour**

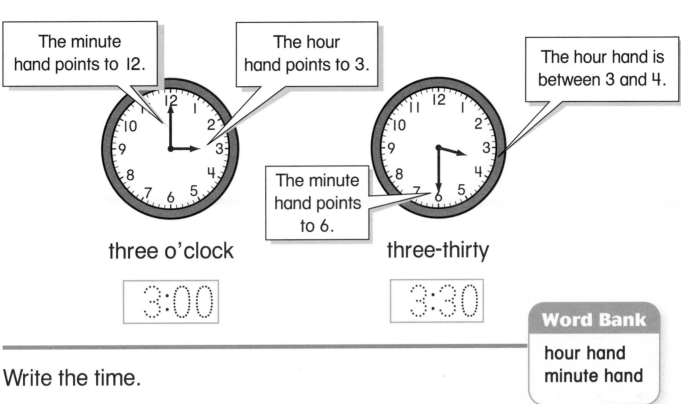

The minute hand points to 12.

The hour hand points to 3.

The hour hand is between 3 and 4.

The minute hand points to 6.

three o'clock

3:00

three-thirty

3:30

Word Bank

hour hand
minute hand

Write the time.

1.

:

:

2.

:

:

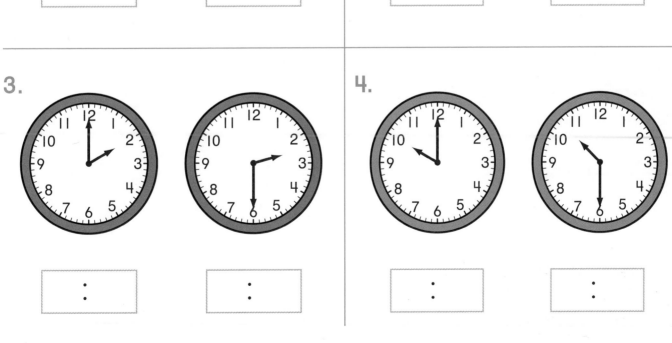

3.

:

:

4.

:

:

California Content Standards *Measurement and Geometry 1.2, Grade 1, Tell time to the nearest half hour and relate time to events. Also Mathematical Reasoning 2.0.*

one hundred forty-three **143**

Draw the clock hands. Write the time.

5. four o'clock   seven-thirty   one o'clock

 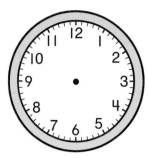 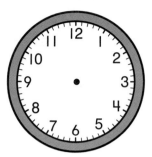

4:00   :   :

6. ten-thirty   twelve o'clock   nine-thirty

 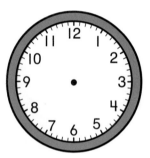 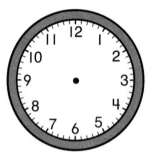

:   :   :

Problem Solving

Use the picture to solve. Write **early** or **late**.

7. Tanya arrived at 3:30.

Tanya was _____ .

8. Marta arrived at 2:30.

Marta was _____ .

Movie starts at

Home Activity Have your child tell you the times that are shown on the clocks above. Homework Workbook 5-1

Name_____ **Time to the Quarter Hour**

Races at the fair start every 15 minutes.

I see a pattern.

10:00   10:15   10:30   10:45

Draw the missing hands to complete each pattern.
Write each time. Use a clock if you like.

1.

    :   :   :   :

2.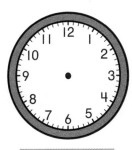

    :   :   :   :

3.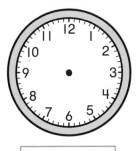

    :   :   :   :

California Content Standards *Measurement and Geometry 1.4 Tell time to the nearest quarter hour. Also Statistics, Data Analysis, and Probability 2.0 ( ).*

one hundred forty-five **145**

Write the time. Look for a pattern.

4.

5.

6.

Math Reasoning

Visual Thinking

7. Look for a pattern. What time would the last clock show? Write the time and draw the hands.

   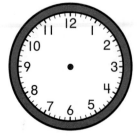

Home Activity Make up a pattern like the ones above. Challenge your child to complete the pattern. Homework Workbook 5-2

Name_____ **Time to Five Minutes**

Count by 5s to find the minutes after the hour.

| 10:00 | 10:20 | 20 minutes after 10 |

Find the minutes after the hour.
Write the time.

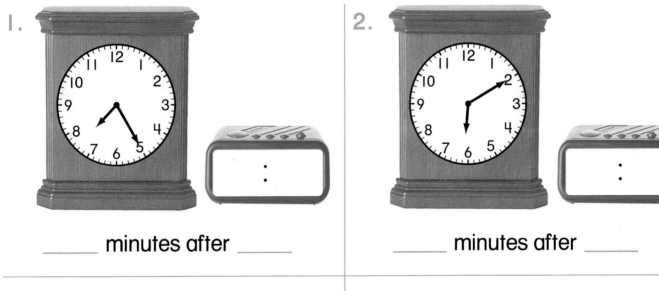

1. _____ minutes after _____

2. _____ minutes after _____

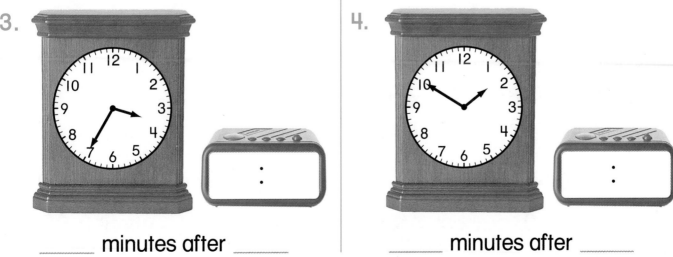

3. _____ minutes after _____

4. _____ minutes after _____

California Content Standards Measurement and Geometry 1.4
Tell time to the nearest quarter hour. Also Number Sense 6.0.

one hundred forty-seven **147**

Draw the clock hands. Write the time.

5. 5 minutes after 8

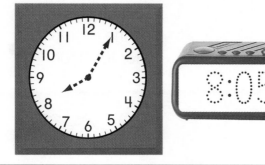

6. 40 minutes after 5

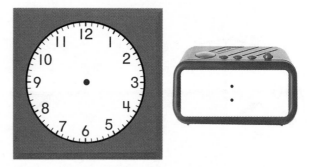

7. 25 minutes after 12

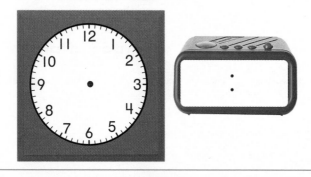

8. 20 minutes after 9

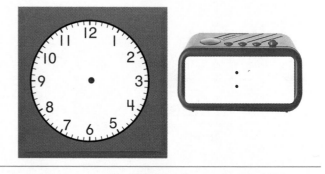

9. 55 minutes after 4

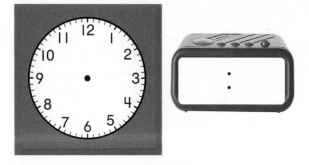

10. 35 minutes after 2

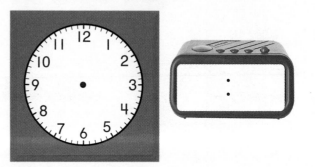

Problem Solving

Number Sense

About what time does each activity start?
Circle the better estimate. Use a clock if you like.

11. The relay race starts at 11:25.

about 11:00   about 11:30

12. The long jump starts at 1:55.

about 1:30   about 2:00

Home Activity Ask your child to tell time on different clocks around the house. Homework Workbook 5-3

Name_____ **Problem-Solving Strategy**

Use Logical Reasoning

Match the labels with the pictures.

Take a trip.   Get dressed.   Time at school each day.

| about 5 minutes | about 5 hours | about 5 days |

Understand

You need to decide about how long
each activity takes.

Plan

Decide which activity takes the most time
and which takes the least time.

Solve

Match each activity to the time it will take.

| about 5 minutes | about 5 hours | about 5 days |

Look Back

Are your answers reasonable?

 California Content Standards *Measurement and Geometry 1.4*
Tell time to the nearest quarter hour and know relationships of time.
Number Sense 6.1. Also Mathematical Reasoning 2.0.

How long does each activity take?
Match the label with the picture.

1. Brush your teeth.   Paint a fence.   Watch a movie.

•   •   •
•   •   •

| about 2 hours | about 2 minutes | about 2 days |

2. Visit the zoo.   Feed your fish.   Play soccer.

•   •   •
•   •   •

| about 1 minute | about 1 hour | about 1 day |

 Math Reasoning

Circle the activities that take about the same time. Explain.

3.

Rake leaves.   Blow up a balloon.   Open a gift.

Home Activity Discuss with your child activities that take about a day, an hour, or a minute. Homework Workbook 5-4

Name _____ **Telling Time**

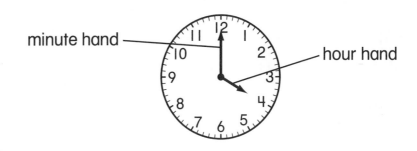

minute hand ——— hour hand

Record the matching time.

1.
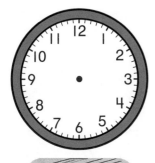
8:25

2.

:

3.

:

4.

:

5.

10:25

6.

1:45

7.

:

8.

11:50

9.

:

California Content Standards *Measurement and Geometry 1.4*
Tell time to the nearest quarter hour and know relationships of time.
Also Mathematical Reasoning 2.0.

Record the matching time.

10.

2:15

11.

:

12.

11:05

13.

:

14.

12:05

15.

:

Problem Solving

Draw the clock hands.
Write the time.

16. Dan starts to set the
    table at 5:00. It takes
    him 10 minutes.
    When does he finish?

:

17. Maria starts cleaning
    her room at 9:25.
    It takes her 1 hour.
    When does she finish?

:

Home Activity Ask your child to tell the time at breakfast,
dinner, or bedtime. Homework Workbook 5-5

Write the time.

1.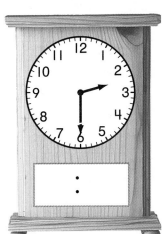

[:   ]

2.

[:   ]

3.

[:   ]

4. Write the time.

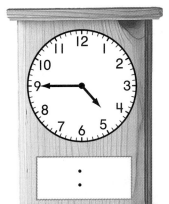
[:   ]

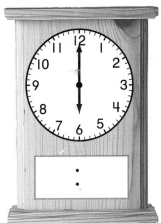
[:   ]

[:   ]

[:   ]

Draw the clock hands. Write the time.

5.    15 minutes after 8

[:   ]

6.    35 minutes after 12

[:   ]

7. Circle the activities that take about the same time.

Make a cake.

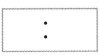

Comb your hair.

Play a game.

Name_____

1. $4 + 4 = \boxed{}$

| 12 | 9 | 8 | NH |
| ○ | ○ | ○ | ○ |

2. $15 - 7 = \boxed{}$

| 2 | 7 | 9 | 8 |
| ○ | ○ | ○ | ○ |

3. $\begin{array}{r} 56 \\ + 10 \\ \hline \end{array}$

| 45 | 66 | 67 | NH |
| ○ | ○ | ○ | ○ |

4. $\begin{array}{r} 20 \\ - 13 \\ \hline \end{array}$

| 7 | 3 | 6 | 13 |
| ○ | ○ | ○ | ○ |

5. $\begin{array}{r} 23¢ \\ + 54¢ \\ \hline \end{array}$

| 31¢ | 68¢ | 77¢ | NH |
| ○ | ○ | ○ | ○ |

6. $\begin{array}{r} 60¢ \\ - 42¢ \\ \hline \end{array}$

| 22¢ | 18¢ | 28¢ | NH |
| ○ | ○ | ○ | ○ |

7.

$3.15 $2.55 $1.48 $1.63

○   ○   ○   ○

Oral Directions *Mark the correct answer. NH means "Not here." Mark it whenever the answer is not given.*

#1–6. Add or subtract.
#7. Which toy could you buy for $1.50?

Name_____ **A.M. and P.M.**

The time from midnight until noon is A.M.
The time from noon until midnight is P.M.

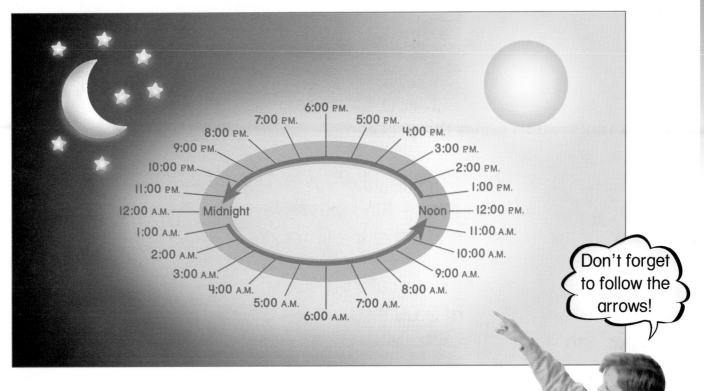

Use the diagram to solve the problems.

1. Benita went to bed at 9:00 P.M.
   She woke up at 6:00 A.M.
   How long did she sleep?   _9 hours_

2. In Springview, school begins at 9:00 A.M.
   Students are in school for 6 hours.
   At what time is school over?   _____

3. The pilot took off in her plane at 10:00 P.M.
   She landed at 1:00 A.M.
   How long was her flight?   _____

4. Grandpa began making cookies at 11:00 A.M.
   He finished washing the dishes 3 hours later.
   At what time did he finish?   _____

California Content Standards *Measurement and Geometry 1.5 Determine the duration of intervals of time in hours. Also Mathematical Reasoning 1.0.*

one hundred fifty-five **155**

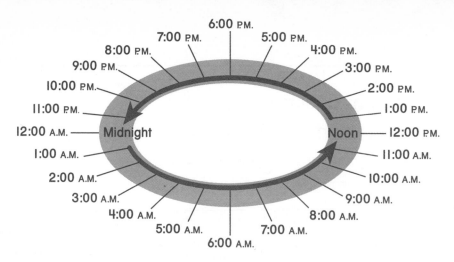

Use the diagram to solve the problems.

5. Anad has soccer practice at 11:00 A.M. It lasts 2 hours.
   Then he goes to the library for 1 hour.
   At what time does Anad leave the library? ⠂⠂⠂2:00 P.M.⠂⠂⠂

6. Leon went into the museum at 10:00 A.M.
   He left the museum at 2:00 P.M.
   How long was he there?

7. Lin eats lunch at 12:00 P.M. and dinner
   at 6:00 P.M. How long is it between his
   lunch and dinner?

8. Zoe does chores for 2 hours, starting
   at 12:00 P.M. After that, she plays
   outside for 3 hours. What time is it then?

9. Kate's family left for Grandma's house
   at 8:00 A.M. They traveled for 6 hours.
   What time did they arrive?

 **Problem Solving**

10. Write something you might do at each time.

    7:00 P.M.   7:00 A.M.

    _____   _____

🏠 **Home Activity** Ask your child to tell how many hours pass
between 12:00 A.M. and 12:00 P.M. Homework Workbook 5-6

Name_____ **Elapsed Time**

10:00   12:00   2 hours

The swim meet started at 10 o'clock. Now it is 12 o'clock. It took 2 hours.

Write the start and end times.
Write how many hours passed.

1.

Watch a baseball game.

Start   End

: ____   : ____

_____ hours

2.

Visit an amusement park.

Start   End

: ____   : ____

_____ hours

3.

Go to the circus.

Start   End

: ____   : ____

_____ hours

California Content Standards *Measurement and Geometry 1.5 Determine the duration of intervals of time in hours. Also Statistics, Data Analysis, and Probability 1.0 (🔑).*

Draw hands on each clock to show the later time.
Write the time. Use a clock if you like.

4.  8:00   I hour and
30 minutes later      9:30

5.  2:00   2 hours later      :

6.  5:00   3 hours later   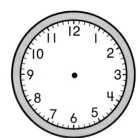   :

7.  10:00   I hour and
30 minutes later   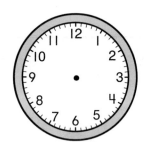   :

 **Problem Solving**

Solve. Use a clock if you like.

8. My school starts at 9:00.
It takes me a half hour to walk to school.
It takes me I hour to get ready for school.
What time should I get up?

_____ : _____

Home Activity Help your child practice elapsed time by
noting the time when he or she goes to bed and gets up.
Homework Workbook 5-7

Name_____ **Reading Schedules**

Hopscotch Around the World

Hopscotch has different names in different places.

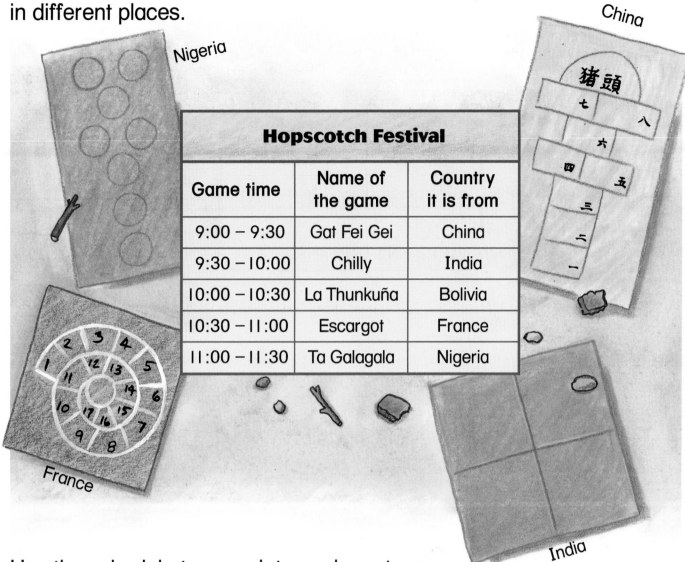

Nigeria

China

France

India

Hopscotch Festival

Game time	Name of the game	Country it is from
9:00 – 9:30	Gat Fei Gei	China
9:30 – 10:00	Chilly	India
10:00 – 10:30	La Thunkuña	Bolivia
10:30 – 11:00	Escargot	France
11:00 – 11:30	Ta Galagala	Nigeria

Use the schedule to complete each sentence.
Use a clock if you like.

1. Each game is _____ minutes long.

2. Hopscotch from China starts at _____.

3. Hopscotch from Nigeria ends at _____.

4. Hopscotch from India starts at _____.

5. From the start of the first game
   to the end of the second game is _____ hour.

6. The festival will last _____ hours and _____ minutes.

School Day Schedule	
Time	Activity
9:00 – 10:30	Reading
10:30 – 11:15	Language Arts
11:15 – 12:15	Math
12:15 – 1:00	Lunch
1:00 – 1:30	Music
1:30 – 2:15	Science
2:15 – 2:45	Art

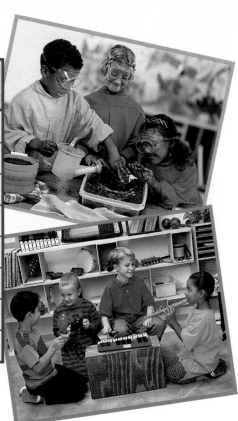

Use the schedule.

Write the time and draw the clock hands.

7. Reading starts at

9:00

8. Math starts at

:

9. Science starts at

:

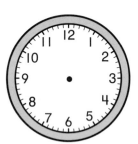

10. Art ends at

:

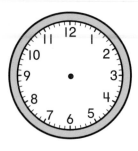

11. Lunch ends at

:

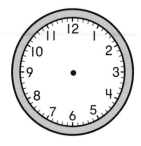

12. Math ends at

:

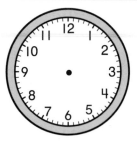

Home Activity Help your child choose a program from a TV schedule to watch together. Homework Workbook 5-8

Name_____ **Problem-Solving Application**

Using a Calendar

Complete the calendar for this month.

Month _____ Year _____

Word Bank

calendar

Sunday	Monday	Tuesday	Wednesday	Thursday	Friday	Saturday

Use the calendar to answer each question.

Think: What do you need to find out?

1. How many Sundays are in this month? _____

2. What is the date of the second Monday? _____

3. What day of the week is the 19th? _____

4. What is the date of the last Friday? _____

5. What day of the week is the 25th? _____

6. On what day of the week will the next month start? _____

7. On what day of the week did last month end? _____

California Content Standards *Measurement and Geometry 1.4 Know relationships of time. Also Statistics, Data Analysis, and Probability 1.0 (🔑), 1.1, 1.4.*

one hundred sixty-one **161**

One Year

			January							February								March							April			
S	M	T	W	T	F	S	S	M	T	W	T	F	S	S	M	T	W	T	F	S	S	M	T	W	T	F	S
				1	2	3	1	2	3	4	5	6	7	1	2	3	4	5	6	7					1	2	3	4
4	5	6	7	8	9	10	8	9	10	11	12	13	14	8	9	10	11	12	13	14	5	6	7	8	9	10	11
11	12	13	14	15	16	17	15	16	17	18	19	20	21	15	16	17	18	19	20	21	12	13	14	15	16	17	18
18	19	20	21	22	23	24	22	23	24	25	26	27	28	22	23	24	25	26	27	28	19	20	21	22	23	24	25
25	26	27	28	29	30	31								29	30	31					26	27	28	29	30		

			May							June							July							August			
S	M	T	W	T	F	S	S	M	T	W	T	F	S	S	M	T	W	T	F	S	S	M	T	W	T	F	S
					1	2		1	2	3	4	5	6				1	2	3	4							1
3	4	5	6	7	8	9	7	8	9	10	11	12	13	5	6	7	8	9	10	11	2	3	4	5	6	7	8
10	11	12	13	14	15	16	14	15	16	17	18	19	20	12	13	14	15	16	17	18	9	10	11	12	13	14	15
17	18	19	20	21	22	23	21	22	23	24	25	26	27	19	20	21	22	23	24	25	16	17	18	19	20	21	22
24/31	25	26	27	28	29	30	28	29	30					26	27	28	29	30	31		23/30	24/31	25	26	27	28	29

			September							October							November							December			
S	M	T	W	T	F	S	S	M	T	W	T	F	S	S	M	T	W	T	F	S	S	M	T	W	T	F	S
		1	2	3	4	5					1	2	3	1	2	3	4	5	6	7			1	2	3	4	5
6	7	8	9	10	11	12	4	5	6	7	8	9	10	8	9	10	11	12	13	14	6	7	8	9	10	11	12
13	14	15	16	17	18	19	11	12	13	14	15	16	17	15	16	17	18	19	20	21	13	14	15	16	17	18	19
20	21	22	23	24	25	26	18	19	20	21	22	23	24	22	23	24	25	26	27	28	20	21	22	23	24	25	26
27	28	29	30				25	26	27	28	29	30	31	29	30						27	28	29	30	31		

Use the calendar to complete each sentence.

8. The month just before June is _____ .

9. The month just after September is _____ .

10. Two months after July is _____ .

11. The fourth month of the year is _____ .

12. Two months before May is _____ .

 Math Reasoning

13. Larry's birthday is in February.

   Rita's birthday is 2 months before Larry's.

   Rita's birthday is in _____ .

Home Activity Ask your child to look at a calendar to tell you today's date, the date in three days, and any holidays or special occasions. Homework Workbook 5-9

Name_____ **Equivalent Times**

How many minutes are in one hour?

The minute hand moves from one number to the next number in 5 minutes.

Count by fives around the clock.

There are __60__ minutes in one hour.

Use the clock above to find each answer.

1. How many minutes are in
    a quarter hour?   _____ minutes

2. How many quarter hours
    are in one hour?   _____ quarter hours

3. How many minutes are in
    a half hour?   _____ minutes

4. How many half hours are
    in one hour?   _____ half hours

5. Tell how to count by tens on the clock.

    _____

    _____

California Content Standards *Measurement and Geometry 1.4*
Tell time to the nearest quarter hour and know relationships of time.
Also Statistics, Data Analysis, and Probability 1.0, 1.4 (⚷).

one hundred sixty-three **163**

Use the calendar to
answer the questions.

6. How many
   days are
   in a week? _____ days

7. How many
   months are
   in a year? _____ months

8. Which month has
   the fewest days?

   _____

9. Which months
   have 30 days?

   _____

   _____

   _____

10. How many days
    does October have?

    _____ days

One Year

January
S	M	T	W	T	F	S
				1	2	3
4	5	6	7	8	9	10
11	12	13	14	15	16	17
18	19	20	21	22	23	24
25	26	27	28	29	30	31

February
S	M	T	W	T	F	S
1	2	3	4	5	6	7
8	9	10	11	12	13	14
15	16	17	18	19	20	21
22	23	24	25	26	27	28

March
S	M	T	W	T	F	S
1	2	3	4	5	6	7
8	9	10	11	12	13	14
15	16	17	18	19	20	21
22	23	24	25	26	27	28
29	30	31				

April
S	M	T	W	T	F	S
			1	2	3	4
5	6	7	8	9	10	11
12	13	14	15	16	17	18
19	20	21	22	23	24	25
26	27	28	29	30		

May
S	M	T	W	T	F	S
					1	2
3	4	5	6	7	8	9
10	11	12	13	14	15	16
17	18	19	20	21	22	23
24/31	25	26	27	28	29	30

June
S	M	T	W	T	F	S
	1	2	3	4	5	6
7	8	9	10	11	12	13
14	15	16	17	18	19	20
21	22	23	24	25	26	27
28	29	30				

July
S	M	T	W	T	F	S
			1	2	3	4
5	6	7	8	9	10	11
12	13	14	15	16	17	18
19	20	21	22	23	24	25
26	27	28	29	30	31	

August
S	M	T	W	T	F	S
						1
2	3	4	5	6	7	8
9	10	11	12	13	14	15
16	17	18	19	20	21	22
23/30	24/31	25	26	27	28	29

September
S	M	T	W	T	F	S
		1	2	3	4	5
6	7	8	9	10	11	12
13	14	15	16	17	18	19
20	21	22	23	24	25	26
27	28	29	30			

October
S	M	T	W	T	F	S
				1	2	3
4	5	6	7	8	9	10
11	12	13	14	15	16	17
18	19	20	21	22	23	24
25	26	27	28	29	30	31

November
S	M	T	W	T	F	S
1	2	3	4	5	6	7
8	9	10	11	12	13	14
15	16	17	18	19	20	21
22	23	24	25	26	27	28
29	30					

December
S	M	T	W	T	F	S
	1	2	3	4	5	
6	7	8	9	10	11	12
13	14	15	16	17	18	19
20	21	22	23	24	25	26
27	28	29	30	31		

Problem Solving

11. Dolores is going on a trip for 18 days.
    Matt is going on a trip for 3 weeks.
    Who will be away longer?
    Explain.

    _____

164 one hundred sixty-four

 Home Activity Help your child use the calendar to find out
how many days are in a year. Homework Workbook 5-10

Solve.

1. Jill went to the beach at 11:00 A.M. She left at 2:00 P.M. How long was she there?

   _____

2. The puppet show began at 2:00 P.M. It lasted 2 hours. What time did it end?

   _____

Write the start and end times.
Write how many hours passed.

3. **Start**   **End**

    :   :

_____ hours

4. **Start**   **End**

    :   :

_____ hours

Use the schedule to solve. Write the time.

5. The Nature Walk starts at

       :

6. Story Time ends at

       :

Camp Schedule	
Time	**Activity**
9:15 – 10:45	Arts and Crafts
10:45 – 11:30	Nature Walk
11:30 – 12:00	Story Time

7. Ilia read for 1 hour.
   Nick read for 75 minutes.
   Who read for a longer time? _____

1.
| 5 | 7 | 15 | NH |
| ○ | ○ | ○ | ○ |

2.
| 2 hours | 3 hours | 5 hours | NH |
| ○ | ○ | ○ | ○ |

3.
| 4:30 P.M. | 5:30 P.M. | 7:00 P.M. | 8:30 P.M. |
| ○ | ○ | ○ | ○ |

4.
$$\begin{array}{r} 8 \\ 9 \\ + 7 \\ \hline \end{array}$$

| 25 | 24 | 29 | NH |
| ○ | ○ | ○ | ○ |

5. 8, 11, 14, 17, 20, 23

| Add 2 | Add 4 | Add 5 | NH |
| ○ | ○ | ○ | ○ |

6. 40, 35, 30, 25, 20

| Subtract 10 | Subtract 7 | Subtract 5 | Subtract 2 |
| ○ | ○ | ○ | ○ |

Oral Directions *Mark the correct answer. NH means "Not here." Mark it whenever the answer is not given.*

#1. Pete picked 11 apples. He gave 4 apples to Mark. How many apples does Pete have left?
#2. The class arrived at the zoo at 10:00 A.M. They left at 3:00 P.M. How long were they at the zoo?

#3. The movie began at 6:30 P.M. It lasted 2 hours. What time did the movie end?
#4. Add.
#5–6. Identify each pattern.

Name_____

Record the matching time.

1.
 12:15

2.

3. Draw hands on the clock to show the later time. Write the time.

 7:00   4 hours later

4. Draw the missing hands to complete the pattern. Write each time.

:_____ 8:30 :_____ :_____

Draw the clock hands. Write the time.

5. 10 minutes after 4

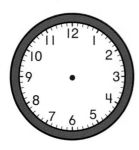

:_____

6. 35 minutes after 12

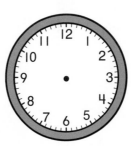

:_____

Can you do the activity in one minute?
Circle **yes** or **no**.

7. Wash your hands.

    yes   no

8. Rake leaves.

    yes   no

9. Write the start and end times.
   Write how many hours passed.

Start   End

_____ P.M.   _____ A.M.   _____ hours

Use the schedule to answer the questions.

Summer Festival	
Time	Event
9:00 – 10:30	Relay Race
10:30 – 11:00	Pie-eating Contest
11:00 – 12:00	Egg Toss
12:00 – 12:30	Pet Parade

10. What time does the
    Pet Parade start? _____

11. What event
    ends at 10:30? _____

12. What event takes place between

    11:00 and 12:00? _____

Use the calendar to answer the questions.

March						
S	M	T	W	T	F	S
			1	2	3	4
5	6	7	8	9	10	11
12	13	14	15	16	17	18
19	20	21	22	23	24	25
26	27	28	29	30	31	

13. How many days
    are there in a week? _____

14. What is the date of
    the 4th Thursday? _____

15. What day of the
    week is the 20th? _____

Name _____

1. eat a sandwich   color a picture   draw a star   take a walk
   ○   ○   ○   ○

2. write your name   dust a table   weed a garden   blink your eyes
   ○   ○   ○   ○

3.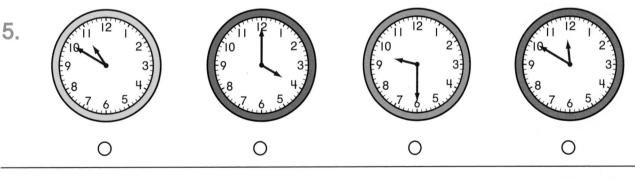
   ○   ○   ○   ○

4.
   ○   ○   ○   ○

5.
   ○   ○   ○   ○

6.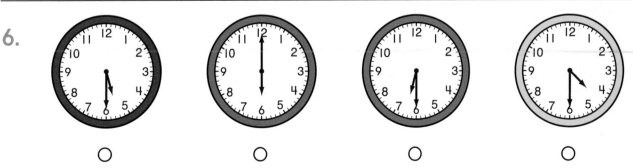
   ○   ○   ○   ○

Oral Directions *Mark the correct answer. NH means "Not here." Mark it whenever the answer is not given.*

#1. Mark the activity that takes about 1 minute.
#2. Mark the activity that takes about 1 hour.

#3. Mark the clock that shows 30 minutes after 3.
#4. Mark the clock that shows 10:45.
#5. Mark the clock that shows 50 minutes after 11.
#6. Mark the clock that shows five-thirty.

7.

    ◯   ◯   ◯   ◯

---

8.   5:00 P.M.   6:00 P.M.   3:00 A.M.   5:00 A.M.

        ◯   ◯   ◯   ◯

County Zoo Schedule	
Time	**Activity**
10:00	Zoo Opens
11:30 – 12:00	Lion Feeding
1:00 – 2:00	Seal Training
3:00 – 4:00	Dolphin Show
4:30	Zoo Closes

9.   10:00   3:00   4:00   4:30

       ◯   ◯   ◯   ◯

10.   10:00   11:00   1:30   NH

       ◯   ◯   ◯   ◯

July						
S	M	T	W	T	F	S
			1	2	3	4
5	6	7	8	9	10	11
12	13	14	15	16	17	18
19	20	21	22	23	24	25
26	27	28	29	30	31	

11.   July 17   July 24   July 30   NH

       ◯   ◯   ◯   ◯

12.   Monday   Tuesday   Sunday   Saturday

       ◯   ◯   ◯   ◯

---

13.   30 minutes   15 minutes   60 minutes   100 minutes

       ◯   ◯   ◯   ◯

Oral Directions *Mark the correct answer. NH means "Not here." Mark it whenever the answer is not given.*

#7. Band practice starts at 4:00. It lasts 45 minutes. Mark the clock that shows when band practice ends.
#8. Chad goes to the library at 1:00 P.M. and stays for one hour. Then he plays at a friend's house for three hours. What time is it when Chad leaves his friend's house?

#9. Mark the time the Dolphin Show begins.
#10. Mark the time the Lion Feeding ends.
#11. Jan's birthday is July 10. Kiko's birthday is two weeks later. When is Kiko's birthday?
#12. On what day of the week will the next month start?
#13. How many minutes are in one hour?

170 one hundred seventy

Diagnosing Readiness
for Chapter 6

1. Write how many.

 _____ stones

 _____ stones

2. Use <, >, or = to make the statement true.

22 ◯ 23

86 ◯ 68

51 ◯ 51

3. Write the missing numbers.

35, 36, _____, 38, _____, _____

56, _____, _____, 53, _____, 51

To the Family

Looking Back	Chapter 6	Looking Ahead
Previously in Grade 2 children learned about numbers to 100. They counted groups of objects in tens and ones and compared and ordered numbers by using symbols.	**Subtracting Two-Digit Numbers** Children count, read, and write numbers to 1,000 and identify the place value for each digit. Children will also use symbols to compare and order numbers.	Later in Grade 2 children will add and subtract three-digit numbers.

Page 171 Your child solved problems that review math skills from previous chapters and will help your child with the skills in Chapter 6.

Math at Home Look for three-digit numbers while you are shopping. Ask your child to tell you how many hundreds, tens, and ones are in each number. You can do the same with dollars and cents.

Math Literature To read more stories with your child about exploring numbers to 1,000, look for these books in your local library.
Millions of Cats by Wanda Gag (Paper Star, 1996)
Math Curse by John Scieszka and Lane Smith (Viking, 1995)

California Content Standards in Chapter 6 Lessons*

	Teach and Practice	Practice		Teach and Practice	Practice
Number Sense			**Statistics, Data Analysis, and Probability**		
1.0 Students understand the relationship between numbers, quantities, and place value in whole numbers up to 1,000.	10, 11		2.0 (🔑) Students demonstrate an understanding of patterns and how patterns grow and describe them in general ways.		7, 8, 12
1.1 (🔑) Count, read, and write whole numbers to 1,000 and identify the place value for each digit.	1–5	6, 8, 9	2.1 Recognize, describe, and extend patterns and determine a next term in linear patterns.	7, 12	2
1.2 Use words, models, and expanded forms to represent numbers to 1,000.	6	1–5	2.2 Solve problems involving simple number patterns.		12
1.3 (🔑) Order and compare whole numbers to 1,000 by using the symbols <, =, >.	8, 9		**Mathematical Reasoning**		
6.0 Use estimation strategies in computation and problem solving.		10	2.0 Students solve problems and justify their reasoning.		6, 8, 9
Algebra and Functions			2.1 Defend the reasoning used and justify the procedures selected.		3, 4
1.0 Students model, represent, and interpret number relationships to create and solve problems involving addition and subtraction.		12			

* The symbol (🔑) indicates a key standard as designated in the Mathematics Framework for California Public Schools.
Full statements of the California Content Standards are found at the beginning of this book following the Table of Contents.

Name_____ **Patterns with Hundreds**

Count by hundreds. Follow the pattern.

 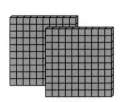 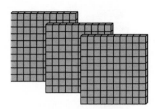

Word Bank
hundreds

I hundred 　　　2 hundreds 　　　3 hundreds
100 　　　　　　　200 　　　　　　　300

Count by hundreds. Write the numbers.
Use models if you like.

1.　　　　I hundred

Hundreds	Tens	Ones
1	0	0

100

2.　　　　2 hundreds

Hundreds	Tens	Ones

_____

3.　　　　3 hundreds

Hundreds	Tens	Ones

_____

4.　　　　4 hundreds

Hundreds	Tens	Ones

_____

5.　　　　5 hundreds

Hundreds	Tens	Ones

_____

6.　　　　6 hundreds

Hundreds	Tens	Ones

_____

7.　　　　7 hundreds

Hundreds	Tens	Ones

_____

8.　　　　8 hundreds

Hundreds	Tens	Ones

_____

9.　　　　9 hundreds

Hundreds	Tens	Ones

_____

10.　　　　10 hundreds

Hundreds	Tens	Ones

_____

California Content Standards *Number Sense 1.1 (🔑) Count, read, and write whole numbers to 1,000 and identify the place value for each digit. Also Number Sense 1.2.*

Count by hundreds. Write the numbers.

11.

Hundreds	Tens	Ones

12.

Hundreds	Tens	Ones

13.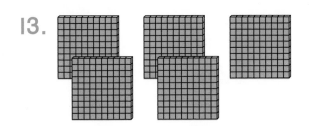

Hundreds	Tens	Ones

14.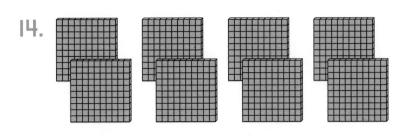

Hundreds	Tens	Ones

15.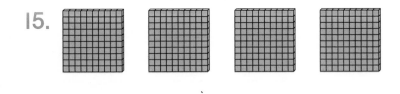

Hundreds	Tens	Ones

16.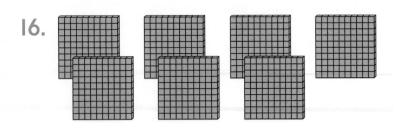

Hundreds	Tens	Ones

Home Activity Give your child some small objects such as dried beans to group and count by hundreds. Homework Workbook 6-1

Name_____

Understanding Hundreds, Tens, and Ones

What You Need

models

spinner

Workmat 4

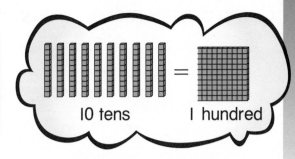

10 tens = 1 hundred

① Spin the spinner 2 times. Record each spin.

② Take that many tens. Regroup 10 tens as 1 hundred if you can.

③ Write how many hundreds, tens, and ones.

④ Write the number.

---

1. 1st spin _____ 2nd spin _____

Hundreds	Tens	Ones

2. 1st spin _____ 2nd spin _____

Hundreds	Tens	Ones

3. 1st spin _____ 2nd spin _____

Hundreds	Tens	Ones

4. 1st spin _____ 2nd spin _____

Hundreds	Tens	Ones

5. 1st spin _____ 2nd spin _____

Hundreds	Tens	Ones

6. 1st spin _____ 2nd spin _____

Hundreds	Tens	Ones

California Content Standards Number Sense 1.1 (🔑) Count, read, and write whole numbers to 1,000 and identify the place value for each digit. Also Number Sense 1.2, Statistics, Data Analysis, and Probability 2.1.

Use models to build each number.
Follow the rule. Regroup if you can.
Complete each chart. Read the numbers.

7. Add 1.

Hundreds	Tens	Ones
2	0	0
2	0	1

Hundreds	Tens	Ones
3	1	5

Hundreds	Tens	Ones
3	9	6

8. Add 10.

Hundreds	Tens	Ones
1	9	0
2	0	0

Hundreds	Tens	Ones
3	0	6

Hundreds	Tens	Ones
2	7	4

Home Activity Have your child tell you how he or she built the numbers on this page. Talk about the patterns that your child sees. Homework Workbook 6-2

Name_____ **Understanding Three-Digit Numbers**

I count hundreds, tens, and ones. Then I write the number.

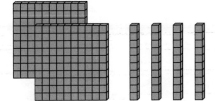

Hundreds	Tens	Ones
2	4	3

243

Write how many hundreds, tens, and ones.
Write the number. Read it.

1.

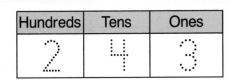

Hundreds	Tens	Ones

_____

2.

Hundreds	Tens	Ones

_____

3.

Hundreds	Tens	Ones

_____

4.

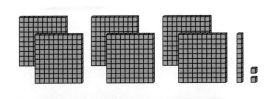

Hundreds	Tens	Ones

_____

5.

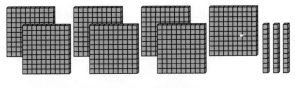

Hundreds	Tens	Ones

_____

6.

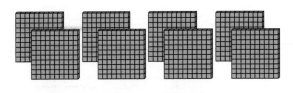

Hundreds	Tens	Ones

_____

California Content Standards *Number Sense 1.1 (🔑) Count, read, and write whole numbers to 1,000 and identify the place value for each digit. Also Number Sense 1.2, Mathematical Reasoning 2.1.*

Write how many hundreds, tens, and ones.
Write the number. Read it.

7.
___3___ hundreds ___7___ tens ___5___ ones   375

8.
_____ hundreds _____ ten _____ ones   _____

9.
_____ hundreds _____ tens _____ ones   _____

 **Problem Solving**

Solve each problem. Tell how you did it.

10. Nan has 6 bags with 100 beads in each bag. She also has 8 loose beads. How many beads does she have?

_____ beads

11. What if Nan also has 5 strings of beads? If each string has 10 beads, how many beads does she have in all?

_____ beads

Home Activity Say or write three-digit numbers like 425. Have your child read the number and tell how many hundreds, tens, and ones. Homework Workbook 6-3

Count by hundreds. Write the missing numbers.

1. 100, _____, 300, _____, _____, 600, 700, _____, _____,

Show each number in a different way.

2. 261 _____ hundreds _____ tens _____ one

3. 959 _____ hundreds _____ tens _____ ones

Write the numbers.

4.

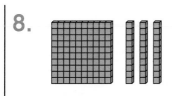 and

_____ and _____ is 1,000.

Write each number.

5. 6 hundreds 2 tens 8 ones | 6. seven hundred fourteen

_____ | _____

Write the numbers.

7.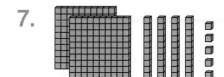

Hundreds	Tens	Ones

_____

8.

Hundreds	Tens	Ones

_____

9.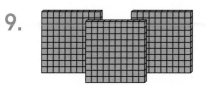

Hundreds	Tens	Ones

_____

Name_____

1. $9 + 6 = 15$ $6 + 9 = 15$ $15 - 9 = 6$

$9 + 5 = 14$ ○ $14 - 6 = 8$ ○ $15 - 6 = 9$ ○ $9 - 6 = 3$ ○

---

2.   52
   $+ 38$

| 90 | 14 | 26 | NH |
| ○ | ○ | ○ | ○ |

---

3.   61
   $- 29$

| 48 | 32 | 91 | NH |
| ○ | ○ | ○ | ○ |

---

4. $25 + 47 = 72,$

so $47 + 25 = \boxed{}$

| 22 | 52 | 71 | 72 |
| ○ | ○ | ○ | ○ |

5.

$1.82 ○ $1.77 ○ $1.88 ○   NH ○

---

6.   **Science Experiments Completed**

Name	Month 1	Month 2
Meg	9	8
Jill	7	7
Tim	6	9
Mike	5	9

| 29 | 27 | 33 | 24 |
| ○ | ○ | ○ | ○ |

Oral Directions *Mark the correct answer. NH means "Not here." Mark it whenever the answer is not given.*

#1. Mark the number sentence that completes the fact family.
#2. Add.
#3. Subtract.

#4. Use $25 + 47 = 72$ to solve $47 + 25$.
#5. Jane has 1 dollar, 2 quarters, 2 dimes, 1 nickel, and 2 pennies in her pocket. How much money does she have in all?
#6. How many science experiments did the students complete during month 2?

Name_____ **Understanding Place Value**

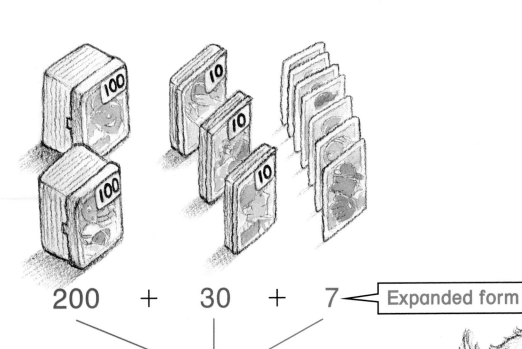

Each digit has a different value.

200 + 30 + 7 — Expanded form

237 — Standard form

Circle the matching number.

1.	300 + 60 + 1 (361) 316	2.	500 + 30 + 6 563 536
3.	700 + 20 + 9 729 792	4.	600 + 10 + 0 610 601
5.	100 + 70 + 3 173 371	6.	200 + 80 + 4 482 284
7.	400 + 40 + 3 434 443	8.	800 + 10 + 8 818 881

California Content Standards *Number Sense 1.2 Use words, models, and expanded form to represent numbers to 1,000. Also Number Sense 1.1 (🐾), Mathematical Reasoning 2.0.*

one hundred eighty-five **185**

Write the number in expanded form.

9. 824

_____ + _____ + _____

10. 259

_____ + _____ + _____

11. seven hundred forty-one

_____ + _____ + _____

12. six hundred thirteen

_____ + _____ + _____

Write the value of the red digit.

13.   370

_____

14.   947

_____

15.   583

_____

16.   416

_____

17.   672

_____

18.   805

_____

Problem Solving

Solve.

19. Tom has 345 marbles. How many sets of hundreds, tens, and ones does he have?

_____ hundreds   _____ tens   _____ ones

20. Nick has 6 more marbles than Tom. How many sets of hundreds, tens, and ones does Nick have?

_____ hundreds   _____ tens   _____ ones

Home Activity Name three-digit numbers, such as 579. Have your child tell you the value of each digit. Homework Workbook 6-6

Name_____ **Problem-Solving Strategy**

Find a Pattern

Look at the chart.
What numbers are missing in the first row?

301	302	303				307	308	309	310
311	312	313			316	317	318	319	320
321	322	323			326	327	328	329	330
331	332				336	337	338	339	340
341						347	348	349	350
351	352	353				357	358	359	360

Understand

You need to find the missing numbers
in the first row.

Plan

Find a number pattern.

Solve

Compare each number to the number
before it. Decide what number comes next.

The missing numbers in the first row are:

304, 305, 306

Each number
increases by 1.

Look Back

Do your answers make sense?
Use the pattern to complete the chart.

California Content Standards Statistics, Data Analysis, and Probability 2.1 Recognize, describe, and extend patterns and determine a next term in linear patterns. Also Statistics, Data Analysis, and Probability 2.0 (🔑).

1. Write the missing numbers.

901	902	903		905	906			909	910
911	912		914	915			918	919	920
921		923	924			927	928		
	932			935	936	937			
	942	943					948		
951			954						960
961	962				966	967			
	972	973					977		980
981				985	986			989	
991	992						998		1,000

Use the chart to continue each pattern.
Tell about the pattern you see.

2. 989, 988, 987, __986__, _____, _____, _____, _____

3. 922, 932, 942, _____, _____, _____, _____, _____

4. 909, 918, 927, _____, _____, _____, _____, _____

5. 993, 984, 975, _____, _____, _____, _____, _____

Use the chart to make your own pattern.

6. _____, _____, _____, _____, _____, _____, _____

Home Activity Ask your child to find patterns in the chart that go across, up and down, and diagonally. Homework Workbook 6-7

Name_____ **Comparing Numbers to 1,000**

First compare the hundreds. | If the hundreds are the same, compare the tens.

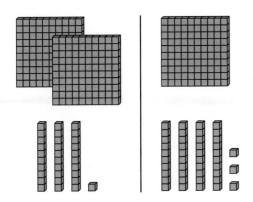

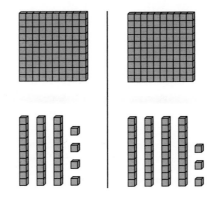

What do you do if the tens are the same? What if the ones are the same?

231 is **greater than** 143.

231 > 143

134 is **less than** 143.

134 < 143

Circle <, >, or =.

1. 325 ⬭>⬭ 251
   (< above, = below)

2. 425 > 446
   (< above, = below)

3. 237 > 437
   (< above, = below)

4. 156 > 156
   (< above, = below)

5. 583 > 581
   (< above, = below)

6. 698 > 700
   (< above, = below)

7. 802 > 802
   (< above, = below)

8. 920 > 92
   (< above, = below)

California Content Standards *Number Sense 1.3 (🔑) Order and compare whole numbers to 1,000 by using the symbols <, =, >. Also Number Sense 1.1 (🔑), Mathematical Reasoning 2.0.*

Compare. Write $<$, $>$, or $=$.

9. 267 $\bigcirc$ 276   829 $\bigcirc$ 819   300 $\bigcirc$ 299

10. 742 $\bigcirc$ 724   351 $\bigcirc$ 352   409 $\bigcirc$ 409

11. 698 $\bigcirc$ 800   572 $\bigcirc$ 527   200 $\bigcirc$ 201

12. 186 $\bigcirc$ 68   660 $\bigcirc$ 460   716 $\bigcirc$ 761

13. 950 $\bigcirc$ 950   437 $\bigcirc$ 347   513 $\bigcirc$ 517

14. 333 $\bigcirc$ 233   699 $\bigcirc$ 700   811 $\bigcirc$ 788

15. 472 $\bigcirc$ 473   150 $\bigcirc$ 150   602 $\bigcirc$ 502

16. 89 $\bigcirc$ 598   265 $\bigcirc$ 264   999 $\bigcirc$ 998

Math Reasoning

Use the clues to find each number.

17. It is greater than 498.
It is less than 507.
It has a 9 in the tens place.

The number is _____.

18. It is greater than 621.
It is less than 629.
It has a 6 in the ones place.

The number is _____.

Home Activity Show your child a three-digit number. Ask him or her to write one number that is greater than and another that is less than your number. Homework Workbook 6-8

Name_____ **Ordering Numbers to 1,000**

445   446   447   448   449   450   451   452   453   454   455

449 is just **after** 448.

450 is just **before** 451.

451 is **between** 450 and 452.

Write the number that comes just **after**.

1. 106, _107_   614, _____   548, _____

2. 329, _____   263, _____   409, _____

3. 777, _____   950, _____   899, _____

Write the number that comes just **before**.

4. _417_, 418   _____, 221   _____, 776

5. _____, 802   _____, 163   _____, 689

6. _____, 320   _____, 919   _____, 500

Write the number that comes **between**.

7. 333, _334_, 335   558, _____, 560

8. 205, _____, 207   997, _____, 999

9. 499, _____, 501   809, _____, 811

California Content Standards *Number Sense 1.3 (🔑) Order and compare whole numbers. Also Number Sense 1.1. Mathematical Reasoning 2.0.*

one hundred ninety-one   **191**

Write the missing numbers.

10. 316, 317, , _____, _____, _____, 322, _____

11. 431, 432, _____, _____, 435, _____, _____, 438

12. _____, 568, _____, _____, _____, 572, _____, _____

13. 650, _____, _____, _____, 654, _____, _____, _____

14. _____, 729, _____, _____, _____, _____, _____, 735

15. 897, _____, _____, _____, _____, 902, _____, _____

16. _____, 995, _____, _____, _____, 999, 1,000

Math Reasoning

Logical Thinking

Match the marbles to the correct person.

17. Pete has more marbles than Bea.
Bob has fewer marbles than Pete.
Bea has more marbles than Bob.

Bob	252 marbles
Bea	136 marbles
Pete	140 marbles

192 one hundred ninety-two

Home Activity Name a three-digit number. Have your child identify the numbers that come before and after your number.
Homework Workbook 6-9

Name_____ **Rounding to the Nearest Hundred**

418 is between 400 and 500.
418 is closer to 400.

485 is between 400 and 500.
485 is closer to 500.

Use the number line.
Look for the closer hundred. Complete.

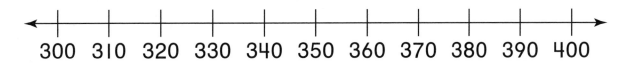

300 310 320 330 340 350 360 370 380 390 400

1. 391 is between __300__ and __400__.

   391 is closer to _____.

2. 335 is between _____ and _____.

   335 is closer to _____.

3. 379 is closer to _____.   319 is closer to _____.

California Content Standards *Number Sense 1.0 Students understand the relationship between numbers, quantities, and place value in whole numbers up to 1,000. Also Number Sense 6.0.*

Use the number line.
Look for the closer hundred. Complete.

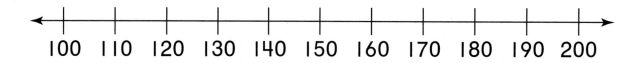

100 110 120 130 140 150 160 170 180 190 200

4. 177 is closer to _200_.   119 is closer to _____.

5. 132 is closer to _____.   156 is closer to _____.

6. 145 is closer to _____.   163 is closer to _____.

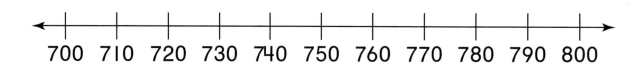

700 710 720 730 740 750 760 770 780 790 800

7. 709 is closer to _____.   790 is closer to _____.

8. 771 is closer to _____.   752 is closer to _____.

9. 736 is closer to _____.   733 is closer to _____.

 Math Reasoning

Number Sense
Use the number line.

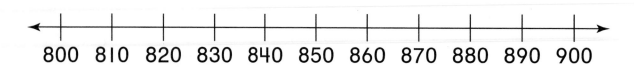

800 810 820 830 840 850 860 870 880 890 900

10. What number is halfway between 800 and 900? _____

Home Activity Ask your child to explain how he or she found the closest hundred in each problem. Homework Workbook 6-10

Name_____ **Ordinal Numbers**

1st first	2nd second	3rd third	4th fourth	5th fifth	6th sixth	7th seventh	8th eighth	9th ninth	10th tenth

Write the word to show the order of each item.

1.

third

2.

_____

3.

_____

4.

_____

5.

_____

6.

_____

7.

_____

8.

_____

9.

_____

California Content Standards *Number Sense 1.0 Students understand the relationship between numbers, quantities, and place value in whole numbers up to 1,000.*

one hundred ninety-five **195**

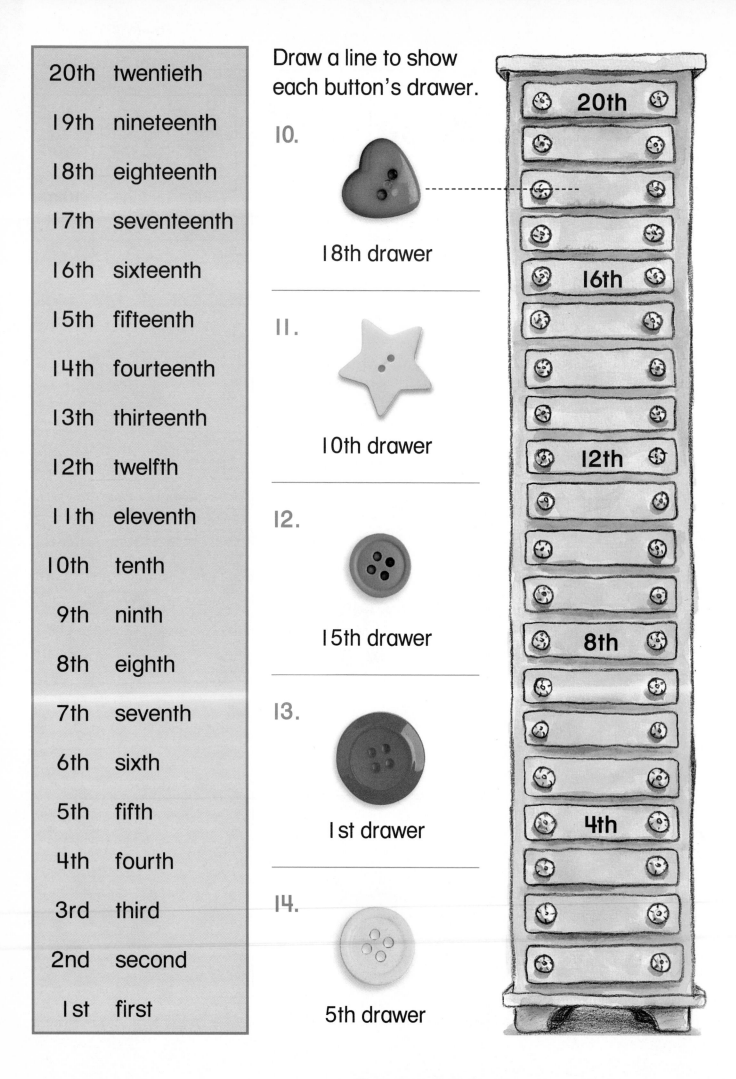

20th	twentieth
19th	nineteenth
18th	eighteenth
17th	seventeenth
16th	sixteenth
15th	fifteenth
14th	fourteenth
13th	thirteenth
12th	twelfth
11th	eleventh
10th	tenth
9th	ninth
8th	eighth
7th	seventh
6th	sixth
5th	fifth
4th	fourth
3rd	third
2nd	second
1st	first

Draw a line to show each button's drawer.

10.

18th drawer

11.

10th drawer

12.

15th drawer

13.

1st drawer

14.

5th drawer

196 one hundred ninety-six

Name_____

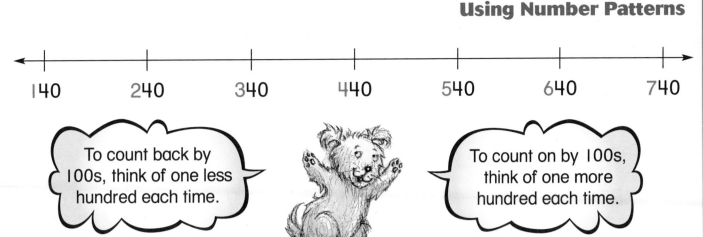

←———|———————|———————|———————|———————|———————|———————|———→
  140   240   340   440   540   640   740

Count on and back by 100s or 10s.

Think: Look for patterns.

Tell about the patterns you find.

1.   125,   225,   _325_,   425,   525,   _625_, _725_

2.   530,   540,   _____,   560,   _____, _____, _____

3.   322,   332,   _____,   352,   _____, _____, _____

4.   _____, _____,   407,   507,   607,   _____, _____

5.   _____,   644,   654,   664,   _____, _____,   694

6.   110,   _____,   130,   140,   150,   _____, _____

7.   _____,   499,   599,   699,   _____, _____, _____

8.   10,   110,   _____,   310,   _____,   510,   _____

9.   902,   _____, _____,   932,   _____, _____, _____

10. _____,   560,   _____,   580,   _____,   600,   _____

California Content Standards *Statistics, Data Analysis, and Probability 2.1 Determine a next term in linear patterns. Also Statistics, Data Analysis, and Probability 2.0 (🔑), 2.2, Algebra and Functions 1.0.*

one hundred ninety-seven **197**

Write the number that is 2 **hundreds more**.

11.   367   441   230   673

     567   _____   _____   _____

Write the number that is 2 **hundreds less**.

12.   781   513   949   803

     _____   _____   _____   _____

Write the number that is 2 **tens more**.

13.   415   720   945   570

     _____   _____   _____   _____

Write the number that is 2 **tens less**.

14.   330   225   714   501

     _____   _____   _____   _____

 Math Reasoning

Number Sense

15. If $25 + 10 = 35$, then $250 + 100 =$ _____.

16. If $48 + 10 = 58$, then $480 + 100 =$ _____.

17. If $63 + 10 = 73$, then $630 + 100 =$ _____.

Home Activity To practice using number patterns, ask your child to count on or back by 100s or 10s from different numbers. Homework Workbook 6-12

Name_____ **Diagnostic Checkpoint**

Write the missing numbers.

1. _____, 414, _____, 416, 417, _____, 419, _____

2. 329, _____, _____, 332, _____, _____, 335, _____

Complete each pattern.

3. 199, 299, _____, 499, _____, _____, 799

4. 740, _____, 760, 770, 780, _____, _____

5. 32, _____, _____, _____, 432, 532, _____

Write the number in expanded form.

6. 723

_____ + _____ + _____

7. five hundred forty-one

_____ + _____ + _____

Write the value of the red digit.

8. 382

_____

9. 917

_____

10. 456

_____

Compare. Write <, >, or =.

11. 510 ◯ 486

12. 749 ◯ 794

13. 610 ◯ 610

14. 156 ◯ 165

15. 911 ◯ 910

16. 399 ◯ 400

| 1. | 3 weeks is ____ days | 3 ○ | 30 ○ | 21 ○ | NH ○ |

| 2. | 120 minutes is ____ hours | 1 ○ | 2 ○ | 3 ○ | 45 ○ |

| 3. | $\begin{array}{r} 76 \\ -\ 29 \\ \hline \end{array}$ | 95 ○ | 53 ○ | 47 ○ | 43 ○ |

| 4. | $\begin{array}{r} 37 \\ +\ 55 \\ \hline \end{array}$ | 92 ○ | 82 ○ | 91 ○ | 22 ○ |

5. $\begin{array}{r} 63 \\ -\ 24 \\ \hline 39 \end{array}$

| $\begin{array}{r} 39 \\ +\ 63 \\ \hline \end{array}$ ○ | $\begin{array}{r} 63 \\ +\ 39 \\ \hline \end{array}$ ○ | $\begin{array}{r} 63 \\ +\ 24 \\ \hline \end{array}$ ○ | $\begin{array}{r} 39 \\ +\ 24 \\ \hline \end{array}$ ○ |

6.

Students with Collections

Room A	Room B	Room C	Room D
19	12	23	15

○ 23 students

○ 7 students

○ 8 students

○ 38 students

Oral Directions *Mark the correct answer. NH means "Not here." Mark it whenever the answer is not given.*

#1–2. Mark the missing number.
#3. Subtract.

#4. Add.
#5. Which addition sentence would help you check
63 − 24 = 39?
#6. How many more students in Room C have collections than in Room D?

1. **4 hundreds 7 tens 9 ones**

478 497 479 749
○   ○   ○   ○

2. **six hundred seventeen**

670 617 770 607
○   ○   ○   ○

3. **665, 765, 865, ____**

866 965 875 975
○   ○   ○   ○

4. **520, 510, 500, ____**

501 499 400 490
○   ○   ○   ○

5. **346**

400 40 4 NH
○   ○   ○   ○

6. **291 ◯ 292**

<   >   =   NH
○   ○   ○   ○

Oral Directions *Mark the correct answer. NH means "Not here." Mark it whenever the answer is not given.*

#1–2. Mark the matching number.
#3–4. Count on or back by 100s or 10s.
#5. Mark the number that tells the value of the red digit.
#6. Mark the symbol that makes the statement true.

7.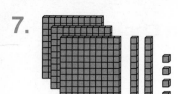

   ○ 3 hundreds 4 tens 2 ones

   ○ 3 hundreds 3 tens 4 ones

   ○ 2 hundreds 2 tens 4 ones

   ○ 3 hundreds 2 tens 4 ones

8.

   ○ 567

   ○ 576

   ○ 570

   ○ 756

9.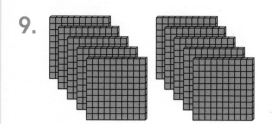

   ○ 10

   ○ 100

   ○ 1,000

   ○ NH

---

10. 399, ____	500 ○	400 ○	398 ○	499 ○
11. ____, 650	651 ○	640 ○	649 ○	648 ○
12. 552, ____, 554	551 ○	555 ○	550 ○	553 ○
13. 999, ____	100 ○	1,000 ○	998 ○	899 ○

Oral Directions *Mark the correct answer. NH means "Not here." Mark it whenever the answer is not given.*

#7–9. Which tells how many?

#10. Mark the number that comes after 399.
#11. Mark the number that comes just before 650.
#12. Mark the number that comes between 552 and 554.
#13. Mark the number that comes just after 999.

Diagnosing Readiness

for Chapter 7

START BICYCLE RACE

1. 48
  + 15

2. What number comes next?

    378, 379, 380, _____

3. 67
  − 29

4. Cross out the money
    amounts written incorrectly.

    $1.25   1.25$ 38¢   ¢38

5. Mike rode his bike 22 miles.
    Kim rode her bike 38 miles.
    How many more miles
    did Kim ride than Mike?
    Write the number sentence.

    _____

FINISH

To the Family

Looking Back	Chapter 7	Looking Ahead
In Chapters 2 and 3, children added and subtracted two-digit numbers with and without regrouping.	**Adding and Subtracting Three-Digit Numbers** Children add and subtract three-digit numbers and add and subtract money. Children check subtraction using addition.	Children will add and subtract numbers up to 10,000 in Grade 3.

Page 205 Your child solved problems that review math skills from previous chapters and will help your child with the skills in Chapter 7.

Math at Home The chapter theme is travel. Use maps to find distances between cities. Work with your child to make up and solve problems where you add and subtract miles between cities.

Math Literature Read math or theme-related stories with your child. Look for the following books in your local library.
Rush Hour by Christine Loomis (Houghton Mifflin, 1996)
A Million Fish . . . More or Less by Patricia C. McKissack (Econo-Clad Books, 1999)

California Content Standards in Chapter 7 Lessons*

	Teach and Practice	Practice		Teach and Practice	Practice
Number Sense			**1.3** Solve addition and subtraction problems by using data from simple charts, picture graphs, and number sentences.		7
2.0 Students estimate, calculate, and solve problems involving addition and subtraction of two- and three-digit numbers.	8		**Statistics, Data Analysis, and Probability**		
2.2 (🔑) Find the sum or difference of two whole numbers up to three digits long.	2–7, 11	8, 12	**1.4** Ask and answer simple questions related to data representations.		7
2.3 Use mental arithmetic to find the sum or difference of two two-digit numbers.	1, 11		**2.0** (🔑) Students demonstrate an understanding of patterns and how patterns grow and describe them in general ways.		1
5.0 Students model and solve problems by representing, adding, and subtracting amounts of money.		9			
5.1 (🔑) Solve problems using combinations of coins and bills.	9, 10		**2.2** Solve problems involving simple number patterns.		1
5.2 (🔑) Know and use the decimal notation and the dollar and cent symbols for money.		9, 10	**Mathematical Reasoning**		
			1.1 Determine the approach, materials, and strategies to be used.	12	
6.0 Students use estimation strategies in computation and problem solving.	8		**1.2** Use tools, such as manipulatives or sketches, to model problems.	9	2, 3, 5, 6
Algebra and Functions			**2.0** Students solve problems and justify their reasoning.		5, 6, 10–12
1.1 (🔑) Use the commutative and associative rules to simplify mental calculations and to check results.		4	**2.1** Defend the reasoning used and justify the procedures selected.		12
1.2 Relate problem situations to number sentences involving addition and subtraction.		2, 3, 10–12			

* The symbol (🔑) indicates a key standard as designated in the Mathematics Framework for California Public Schools.
Full statements of the California Content Standards are found at the beginning of this book following the Table of Contents.

Name_____ **Adding and Subtracting Mentally**

You can use basic facts and patterns
to add and subtract using mental math.

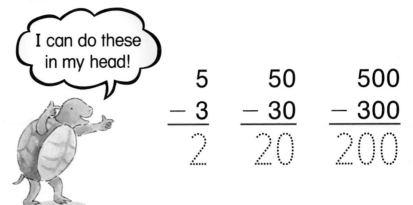

I can do these in my head!

2	20	200	5	50	500
+ 6	+ 60	+ 600	− 3	− 30	− 300
8	80	800	2	20	200

Add or subtract. Use mental math.

1.
4	40	400
+ 3	+ 30	+ 300

2.
5	50	500
− 4	− 40	− 400

3.
1	10	100
+ 3	+ 30	+ 300

4.
6	60	600
− 1	− 10	− 100

5.
4	40	400
+ 1	+ 10	+ 100

6.
8	80	800
− 5	− 50	− 500

7.
3	30	300
+ 5	+ 50	+ 500

8.
7	70	700
− 4	− 40	− 400

California Content Standards *Number Sense 2.3 Use mental arithmetic to find the sum or difference of two two-digit numbers. Also Statistics, Data Analysis, and Probability 2.0 (◆), 2.2.*

two hundred seven **207**

Add or subtract. Use mental math.

9.
40	200	300	50	400
+ 20	+ 100	+ 200	+ 30	+ 500
60				

10.
60	900	700	40	20
− 20	− 300	− 500	− 10	− 10

11.
800	90	200	800	70
+ 100	− 70	+ 500	− 100	+ 10

12.
700	500	60	600	90
− 100	+ 300	+ 10	− 200	− 30

 ## Math Reasoning

Use mental math!

Number Sense

Add or subtract. What patterns do you see?

13.
3	33	333
+ 4	+ 44	+ 444

14.
4	44	444
+ 1	+ 11	+ 111

15.
9	99	999
− 2	− 22	− 222

16.
8	88	888
− 5	− 55	− 555

Home Activity Give your child two numbers to add or subtract, such as 400 + 300. Talk about how knowing 4 + 3 can help. Homework Workbook 7-1

Name_____ **Adding Three-Digit Numbers**

Sunshine Grove has 162 orange trees and 253 grapefruit trees. How many trees are there in all?

① Add the ones. Regroup if you need to.

H	T	O
		2
1	6	2
+ 2	5	3
		5

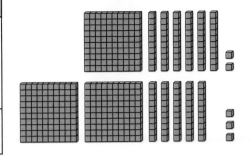

② Add the tens. Regroup if you need to.

H	T	O
1		
1	6	2
+ 2	5	3
	1	5

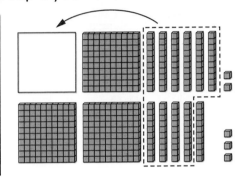

③ Add the hundreds.

H	T	O
1		
1	6	2
+ 2	5	3
4	1	5

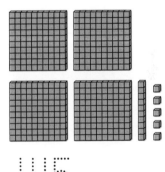

415 trees

Use models and Workmat 4. Add.

1.
H	T	O
4	8	6
+ 2	0	7

2.
H	T	O
1	4	4
+ 2	7	3

3.
H	T	O
3	5	2
+ 1	9	6

California Content Standards Number Sense 2.2 (🔑) Find the sum of two whole numbers. Also Algebra and Functions 1.2, Mathematical Reasoning 1.2.

two hundred nine **209**

Use models and Workmat 4.
Find each sum.

4.

H	T	O
☐	☐	
3	6	4
+ 2	8	1
6	4	5

H	T	O
☐	☐	
6	3	8
+ 1	4	0

H	T	O
☐	☐	
5	4	8
+	2	6

5.

H	T	O
☐	☐	
7	8	0
+ 1	3	6

H	T	O
☐	☐	
2	0	9
+ 2	2	7

H	T	O
☐	☐	
1	8	3
+ 6	5	5

6.

H	T	O
☐	☐	
2	5	7
+ 4	9	1

H	T	O
☐	☐	
3	0	0
+ 3	5	9

H	T	O
☐	☐	
6	7	4
+ 2	5	1

Problem Solving

Use models to solve. Write a number sentence.

7. One morning, 248 people rode the boat
for a close look at the falls. Later, 190 people
rode the boat. How many people rode in all?

_____

▲ Niagara Falls

Home Activity Ask your child to explain what regrouping is
and how it works. Homework Workbook 7-2

Name_____ **Three-Digit Addition**

How far is it from San Francisco to Los Angeles on Highway 101?

① Add the ones. Regroup if you need to.

H	T	O
1	9	6
+ 2	2	7
		3

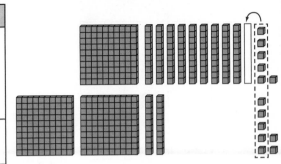

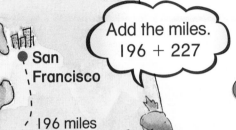

Add the miles. 196 + 227

② Add the tens. Regroup if you need to.

H	T	O
	1	
1	9	6
+ 2	2	7
	2	3

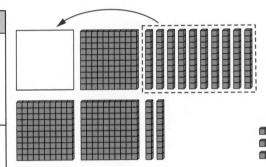

San Francisco

196 miles

San Miguel

227 miles

Los Angeles

③ Add the hundreds.

H	T	O
1	1	
1	9	6
+ 2	2	7
4	2	3

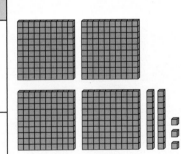

423 miles

Use models and Workmat 4. Add.

1.

H	T	O
3	8	6
+ 2	3	5

2.

H	T	O
1	7	0
+ 1	6	8

3.

H	T	O
3	2	2
+ 1	9	9

California Content Standards *Number Sense 2.2 (⟶) Find the sum of two whole numbers. Also Algebra and Functions 1.2, Mathematical Reasoning 1.2.*

Use models and Workmat 4.
Find each sum.

4.

H	T	O
☐	☐	
2	7	4
+	8	9
3	6	3

H	T	O
☐	☐	
7	1	0
+ 2	6	0

H	T	O
☐	☐	
4	3	4
+	2	6

5.

H	T	O
☐	☐	
5	9	3
+ 1	3	6

H	T	O
☐	☐	
3	0	9
+ 2	4	6

H	T	O
☐	☐	
1	6	8
+ 3	5	5

6.

H	T	O
☐	☐	
1	0	0
+ 4	3	5

H	T	O
☐	☐	
2	7	1
+ 1	7	9

H	T	O
☐	☐	
6	3	2
+	6	8

Problem Solving

Algebra

Use models to solve. Write a number sentence.

7. Sal drove 342 miles from San Diego to
Fresno. He then drove 174 miles from Fresno
to Sacramento. How many miles did he drive
from San Diego to Sacramento?

212 two hundred twelve

Home Activity Ask your child to explain what he or she did
in each problem. Homework Workbook 7-3

Name_____ **Practicing Addition**

Lone Star
Texas Ranch
236 Herefords
318 Angus

How can you find out
how many cattle there
are altogether?

① Add the ones.
Regroup if you need to.

H	T	O
□	⋮	
2	3	6
+ 3	1	8
		4

② Add the tens.
Regroup if you need to.

H	T	O
□	1	
2	3	6
+ 3	1	8
	5	4

③ Add the hundreds.

H	T	O
□	1	
2	3	6
+ 3	1	8
5	5	4

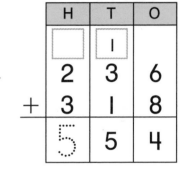

554 cattle

Add. Use models if you like.

1.
$$\begin{array}{r} 274 \\ + 183 \\ \hline 457 \end{array}$$
$$\begin{array}{r} 623 \\ + 105 \\ \hline \end{array}$$
$$\begin{array}{r} 539 \\ + 84 \\ \hline \end{array}$$
$$\begin{array}{r} 417 \\ + 268 \\ \hline \end{array}$$
$$\begin{array}{r} 285 \\ + 629 \\ \hline \end{array}$$

2.
$$\begin{array}{r} 720 \\ + 196 \\ \hline \end{array}$$
$$\begin{array}{r} 865 \\ + 9 \\ \hline \end{array}$$
$$\begin{array}{r} 155 \\ + 385 \\ \hline \end{array}$$
$$\begin{array}{r} 247 \\ + 391 \\ \hline \end{array}$$
$$\begin{array}{r} 582 \\ + 68 \\ \hline \end{array}$$

3.
$$\begin{array}{r} 604 \\ + 137 \\ \hline \end{array}$$
$$\begin{array}{r} 271 \\ + 319 \\ \hline \end{array}$$
$$\begin{array}{r} 596 \\ + 235 \\ \hline \end{array}$$
$$\begin{array}{r} 442 \\ + 46 \\ \hline \end{array}$$
$$\begin{array}{r} 353 \\ + 150 \\ \hline \end{array}$$

California Content Standards Number Sense 2.2 (🔑) Find the sum of two whole numbers up to three digits long. Also Algebra and Functions 1.1 (🔑).

Write in vertical form. Then add.

4. 581 + 173   229 + 430   675 + 98   386 + 8

$$\begin{array}{r} {}^{1}581 \\ + 173 \\ \hline 754 \end{array}$$

5. 129 + 183   454 + 172   407 + 3   572 + 300

Math Reasoning   Algebra

Number Sense

6. If you know 581 + 173 = 754,
    how much is 173 + 581?   173
                                        + 581

Explain.

_____

_____

_____

Home Activity Ask your child to identify problems on this page that required regrouping. Homework Workbook 7-4

Name_____

Add or subtract. Use mental math.

1.
$$\begin{array}{r} 1 \\ +\ 4 \\ \hline \end{array} \qquad \begin{array}{r} 10 \\ +\ 40 \\ \hline \end{array} \qquad \begin{array}{r} 100 \\ +\ 400 \\ \hline \end{array} \qquad \begin{array}{r} 7 \\ -\ 3 \\ \hline \end{array} \qquad \begin{array}{r} 70 \\ -\ 30 \\ \hline \end{array} \qquad \begin{array}{r} 700 \\ -\ 300 \\ \hline \end{array}$$

Find each sum.

2.

H	T	O
☐	☐	
3	4	5
+ 2	9	3

H	T	O
☐	☐	
4	0	6
+ 1	3	7

H	T	O
☐	☐	
6	5	2
+ 2	7	4

3.
$$\begin{array}{r} 428 \\ +\ 233 \\ \hline \end{array} \qquad \begin{array}{r} 90 \\ +\ 438 \\ \hline \end{array} \qquad \begin{array}{r} 572 \\ +\ 245 \\ \hline \end{array} \qquad \begin{array}{r} 300 \\ +\ 400 \\ \hline \end{array} \qquad \begin{array}{r} 285 \\ +\ 350 \\ \hline \end{array}$$

4.
$$\begin{array}{r} 167 \\ +\ 56 \\ \hline \end{array} \qquad \begin{array}{r} 105 \\ +\ 281 \\ \hline \end{array} \qquad \begin{array}{r} 318 \\ +\ 511 \\ \hline \end{array} \qquad \begin{array}{r} 20 \\ +\ 698 \\ \hline \end{array} \qquad \begin{array}{r} 376 \\ +\ 114 \\ \hline \end{array}$$

Use models to solve. Write a number sentence.

5. On Friday, 341 people ate lunch at the Cave Cafe. On Saturday, 264 people ate lunch at Cave Cafe. How many people ate lunch on those two days?

....

1. **four hundred twenty**

42	402	420	40020
○	○	○	○

2. | 361 | 352 | 351 | NH |
   |-----|-----|-----|----|
   | ○ | ○ | ○ | ○ |

3.

Oak Street School	
School Begins	8:00 A.M.
School Ends	3:00 P.M.

   ○ 5 hours
   ○ 7 hours
   ○ 11 hours
   ○ NH

4. **135**   **67**

202 marbles	192 marbles	72 marbles	68 marbles
○	○	○	○

5.

$2.60	$2.41	$1.49	$1.41
○	○	○	○

Oral Directions *Mark the correct answer. NH means "Not here." Mark it whenever the answer is not given.*

#1. Which number stands for the same value as the number in words?
#2. I am a number between 350 and 370. I have 2 ones. What number am I?

#3. How long does school last at Oak Street School?
#4. James collected 135 marbles. Rosa collected 67 marbles. How many marbles did they collect in all?
#5. Ray had these bills and coins in his pocket. He then bought a toy truck for $1.19. How much money does he have left?

Name_____ **Subtracting Three-Digit Numbers**

123 people hiked into
the Grand Canyon.
315 people rode mules.
How many fewer people
hiked than rode mules?

① Subtract the ones. Regroup if you need to.

H	T	O
3	1	5
− 1	2	3
		2

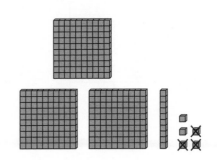

② Subtract the tens. Regroup if you need to.

H	T	O
2	11	
3	1	5
− 1	2	3
	9	2

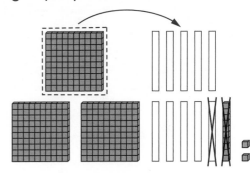

③ Subtract the hundreds.

H	T	O
2	11	
3	1	5
− 1	2	3
1	9	2

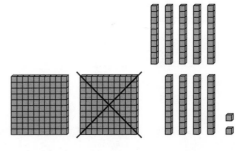

__192__ fewer people

Use models and Workmat 4. Subtract.

1.

H	T	O
4	5	3
− 2	1	7

2.

H	T	O
3	2	7
− 1	5	4

3.

H	T	O
5	7	6
− 3	4	2

Use models and Workmat 4. Subtract.

4.

H	T	O
	2	14
2	3̶	4̶
− 1	2	6
1	0	8

H	T	O
6	2	1
− 3	0	8

H	T	O
4	6	7
− 1	8	4

5.

H	T	O
2	8	5
− 1	4	2

H	T	O
3	4	5
− 1	8	2

H	T	O
7	3	6
− 4	4	2

6.

H	T	O
5	7	3
− 2	4	8

H	T	O
8	2	1
− 5	0	0

H	T	O
6	8	5
− 2	9	4

Math Reasoning

Which two numbers will make each sum or difference?
Write the numbers.

7. Difference of 125 _____ and _____

8. Difference of 342 _____ and _____

9. Sum of 537 _____ and _____

391

516

174

363

Home Activity Ask your child to explain how he or she knows when it is necessary to regroup in subtraction.
Homework Workbook 7-5

Name_____ **Subtracting with Zeros**

The Hermosa Bike Club planned a 250-mile bike trip. After the first week, they had ridden 122 miles. How many miles do they have left to bike?

① Subtract the ones. Regroup if you need to.

H	T	O
	4	10
2	5̷	0̷
− 1	2	2
		8

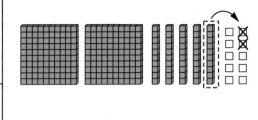

There are not enough ones in 250. You need to regroup.

② Subtract the tens. Regroup if you need to.

H	T	O
	4	10
2	5̷	0̷
− 1	2	2
	2	8

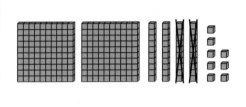

③ Subtract the hundreds.

H	T	O
	4	10
2	5̷	0̷
− 1	2	2
1	2	8

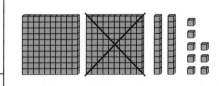

128 miles

Use models and Workmat 4. Subtract.

1.

H	T	O
3	5	3
− 1	0	6

2.

H	T	O
4	0	8
− 2	5	1

3.

H	T	O
6	0	6
− 1	2	2

California Content Standards *Number Sense 2.2 (⬤⬤) Find the difference of two whole numbers up to three digits long. Also Mathematical Reasoning 1.2, 2.0.*

two hundred nineteen **219**

Use models and Workmat 4. Subtract.

4.

H	T	O
	3	11
4	4̶	1̶
− 2	3	4
2	0	7

H	T	O
4	1	0
− 2	0	7

H	T	O
5	1	2
− 1	0	0

5.

H	T	O
2	7	2
− 1	1	0

H	T	O
4	2	3
− 2	3	2

H	T	O
1	5	2
−	2	3

6.

H	T	O
7	0	3
− 1	5	2

H	T	O
9	5	0
−	2	0

H	T	O
5	6	2
− 1	9	2

Math Reasoning

Number Sense

7. Maria started the problem 105 − 9 by regrouping 1 hundred into 10 tens. Use models and Workmat 4 to complete the problem.

H	T	O
0	10	
1̶	0̶	5
−		9

Home Activity Ask your child to explain how he or she completed each of the exercises on this page. Homework Workbook 7-6

Name_____ **Practicing Subtraction**

346 adults and 182 children visited the Gateway Arch in St. Louis, Missouri. How many more adults visited the arch?

Gateway Arch ▶

① Subtract the ones. Regroup if you need to.

H	T	O
3	4	6
− 1	8	2
		4

② Subtract the tens. Regroup if you need to.

H	T	O
2	14	
3	4	6
− 1	8	2
	6	4

③ Subtract the hundreds.

H	T	O
2	14	
3	4	6
− 1	8	2
1	6	4

164 more adults

Subtract. Use models if you like.

1.
```
   536        952        470        715        429
 − 270      − 618      −   9      − 225      − 374
```

2.
```
   391        865        529        463        308
 − 166      − 634      − 273      − 436      − 126
```

3.
```
   783        672        819        568        608
 − 577      − 345      − 596      −  50      −  45
```

California Content Standards *Number Sense 2.2 (🔑) Find the difference of two whole numbers. Also Algebra and Functions 1.3, Statistics, Data Analysis, and Probability 1.4.*

two hundred twenty-one **221**

Write in vertical form. Subtract.

4. 426 − 118   923 − 561   861 − 307   409 − 45

$$\begin{array}{r} \overset{1\;16}{4\cancel{2}\cancel{6}} \\ -\;118 \\ \hline 308 \end{array}$$

5. 438 − 215   647 − 9   533 − 218   464 − 146

Problem Solving

Use the table to solve.
Write the number sentence.

Park Visitors		
	adults	children
Oak Park	328	452
Sand Park	436	331
Stone Park	218	422

6. How many more children than adults visited Stone Park?

_____

7. How many adults and children visited Oak Park in all?

_____

Home Activity Ask your child to show you exercises on this page that require regrouping 1 ten as 10 ones and exercises that require regrouping 1 hundred as 10 tens. Homework Workbook 7-7

Name_____ **Estimating to Check Answers**

① Solve the problem.

524 people visited the park.
340 other people visited the
zoo. How many more people
visited the park?

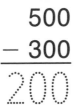

4 12
5̶2̶4
− 340
184

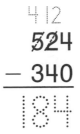

You can estimate
to see if your answer
is reasonable.

② Estimate to check your answer.

524 is closer to 500.
340 is closer to 300.

500
− 300
200

184 is close
to 200.

③ Write your answer.

184 more people

Solve the problem.
Estimate to check your answer.
Write the answer.

Solve   **Check**

1. Jill drove 322 miles.
   Sam drove 485 miles.
   How many miles did
   they drive altogether?

   _____ miles

   + _____   + _____

2. Mary read 687 pages.
   Phil read 413 pages.
   How many more pages
   did Mary read?

   _____ pages

   − _____   − _____

California Content Standards *Number Sense 6.0 Students use estimation strategies in computation and problem solving. Number Sense 2.0. Also Number Sense 2.2.*

Solve the problem.
Estimate to check your answer.
Write the answer.

Solve   **Check**

3. Steve collected 182 rocks.
   Luisa collected 312 rocks.
   How many rocks did
   they collect altogether?

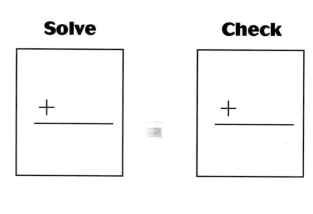

_____ rocks

4. 862 people ran in the race.
   271 people watched the race.
   How many more people
   ran than watched the race?

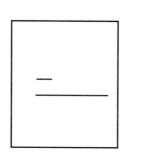

_____ people

5. Rosa saved 212 pennies.
   Dave saved 128 pennies.
   How many pennies did
   they save altogether?

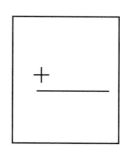
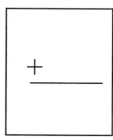

_____ pennies

Math Reasoning

Number Sense

Estimate   **Add**

6. Ron said 284 − 116 = 168.
   Use both estimation and
   addition to check his answer.

Home Activity Ask your child to explain how he or she
solved each problem on this page. Homework Workbook 7-8

Name_____ **Problem-Solving Strategy**

Act It Out

Lea had $4.00 when she went to the store.
She had 28¢ when she left the store.
What toy did she buy?

Understand

You need to find which toy Lea bought.

Plan

Use coins and bills to act out the problem.

Trade bills
for coins.

Solve

• Show the $4.00 Lea
  had to start.

• Take away the 28¢
  Lea had left.

• Count the money left. It is what the toy cost.

$3.72

Since the airplane cost $3.72, Lea bought the airplane.

Look Back

Is your answer reasonable?

 California Content Standards *Number Sense 5.1 (☞) Solve problems using combinations of coins and bills. Mathematiacal Reasoning 1.2. Also Number Sense 5.0, 5.2 (☞).*

two hundred twenty-five **225**

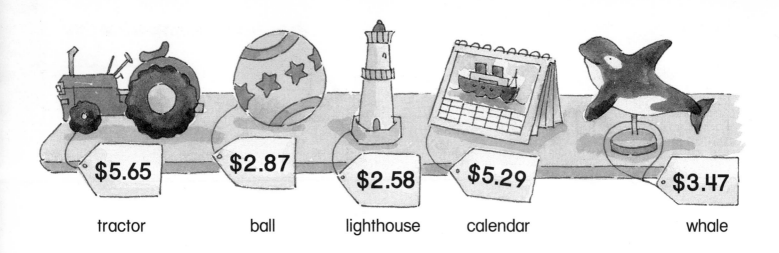

$5.65 — tractor
$2.87 — ball
$2.58 — lighthouse
$5.29 — calendar
$3.47 — whale

What did each person buy?
Use coins to act it out.

1. Andy had $6.00 when he went to the
store. When he left the store, he had 35¢.
How much money did he spend?

_____

Which toy did Andy buy?

_____

2. Becky had $3.00 when she went to the
store. She had 42¢ when she left the store.
How much did she spend?

_____

Which toy did Becky buy?

_____

3. Masa had $5.00 when he went to the
store. When he left, he had $1.53.
How much money did he spend?

_____

Which toy did Masa buy?

_____

Home Activity Play "store" with your child to have him or
her practice making purchases. Homework Workbook 7-9

Name_____ **Adding and Subtracting Money**

I had $6.00. I bought a puzzle for $2.67 and postcards for $1.23.

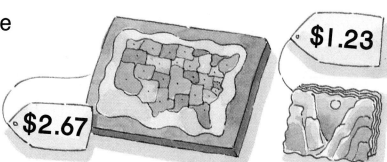

$2.67

$1.23

How much did I spend?
Add.

1

$2.67
+ 1.23
‾‾‾‾‾
$ 3.90

How much do I have left?
Subtract.

5 10

$6.00
− 3.90
‾‾‾‾‾
$2.10

Add or subtract.

1. $3.48 $2.05 $6.00 $7.50 $9.41
   + 2.45   − 0.15   + 2.35   − 2.25   − 6.26

2. $5.94 $4.65 $9.25 $5.26 $3.42
   + 0.75   + 2.19   − 7.80   − 2.08   + 1.08

3. $8.14 $7.04 $4.25 $6.56 $8.78
   − 5.62   + 0.89   − 1.08   + 1.93   − 5.83

4. $6.23 $8.28 $2.52 $4.44 $6.45
   − 1.61   − 3.25   + 4.18   + 1.82   − 3.63

California Content Standards Number Sense 5.1 (🔑) Solve problems using combinations of coins and bills. Also Number Sense 5.2 (🔑), Mathematical Reasoning 2.0.

two hundred twenty-seven **227**

Add or subtract.

5.
$$\begin{array}{r} 318 \\ \$7.\cancel{48} \\ -\ 1.19 \\ \hline \$6.29 \end{array}$$
$$\begin{array}{r} \$1.26 \\ +\ 2.66 \\ \hline \end{array}$$
$$\begin{array}{r} \$3.56 \\ -\ 1.81 \\ \hline \end{array}$$
$$\begin{array}{r} \$4.54 \\ +\ 1.28 \\ \hline \end{array}$$
$$\begin{array}{r} \$5.23 \\ -\ 2.61 \\ \hline \end{array}$$

6.
$$\begin{array}{r} \$3.29 \\ +\ 4.64 \\ \hline \end{array}$$
$$\begin{array}{r} \$2.48 \\ +\ 6.03 \\ \hline \end{array}$$
$$\begin{array}{r} \$8.17 \\ -\ 3.42 \\ \hline \end{array}$$
$$\begin{array}{r} \$7.73 \\ -\ 2.56 \\ \hline \end{array}$$
$$\begin{array}{r} \$0.83 \\ +\ 3.45 \\ \hline \end{array}$$

7.
$$\begin{array}{r} \$8.47 \\ -\ 5.93 \\ \hline \end{array}$$
$$\begin{array}{r} \$6.08 \\ -\ 3.64 \\ \hline \end{array}$$
$$\begin{array}{r} \$2.71 \\ +\ 0.78 \\ \hline \end{array}$$
$$\begin{array}{r} \$1.57 \\ +\ 4.83 \\ \hline \end{array}$$
$$\begin{array}{r} \$6.00 \\ -\ 4.30 \\ \hline \end{array}$$

Problem Solving

Solve. Show your work.

8. Pam buys stickers for $3.22 and a poster for $2.48. She gives the clerk $6.00. How much change does she get?

_____ change

9. Ken buys a ball for $1.56 and a cap for $5.34. He gives the clerk $7.00. How much change does he get?

_____ change

Home Activity Help your child practice adding and subtracting money. Homework Workbook 7-10

Name_____ **Choosing a Computation Method**

What are some ways to add
or subtract three-digit numbers?

Mental Math	Models	Paper and Pencil

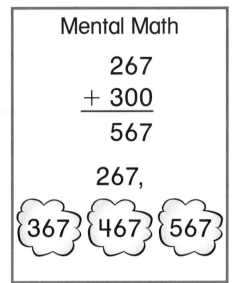

267
+ 300
————
567

267,

367 467 567

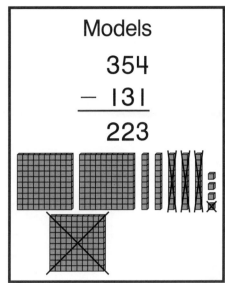

354
– 131
————
223

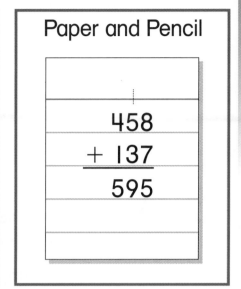

458
+ 137
————
595

Add or subtract.
Choose your own method. Tell why.

1.   473   525   673   136   394
    + 282   – 361   + 251   + 218   – 237
    ————
     755

2.   607   284   413   726   845
    – 362   + 509   + 165   – 432   – 630

3.   289   574   850   443   939
    + 603   – 436   + 65   – 281   – 644

4. 100 + 400 = _____   327 + 10 = _____

5. 600 – 200 = _____   457 – 100 = _____

California Content Standards *Number Sense 2.2* ( ) *Find
the sum or difference of two whole numbers up to three digits long.
Number Sense 2.3. Also Mathematical Reasoning 2.0.*

Choose a way to solve each problem.
Circle your choice. Then solve.

Sometimes one way is easier than another.

6.   428   **a.** models
    + 236   **b.** paper and pencil
            c. mental math

7.   649   **a.** models
    − 100   **b.** paper and pencil
            c. mental math

8.   168   **a.** models
    + 280   **b.** paper and pencil
            c. mental math

9.   591   **a.** models
    − 258   **b.** paper and pencil
            c. mental math

10.   354   **a.** models
    + 200   **b.** paper and pencil
            c. mental math

11.   706   **a.** models
    − 544   **b.** paper and pencil
            c. mental math

 Problem Solving

Solve.

12. 289 people came to the bicycle race in the morning and 318 more came in the afternoon. How many came in all?

_____ people

13. What if 195 people left the bicycle race in the afternoon? How many people were still at the race at the end of the day?

_____ people

Home Activity Ask your child to explain the different ways to add or subtract three-digit numbers like 371 + 220.
Homework Workbook 7-11

Name_____

Problem-Solving Application

Too Much Information

Cross out the information you do not need. Then solve.

Empire State Building ▽

Think: What do you need to find out?

1. The Empire State Building is 381 m tall. ~~It has 102 floors.~~ The World Trade Center is 417 m tall. Which building is taller? How much taller?

▲ World Trade Center

The World Trade Center is 36 m taller.

2. The General Sherman Tree is 275 ft tall. Its lowest branch is 130 ft above the ground. The tree is 103 ft around. How many feet is it from the lowest branch to the top of the tree?

_____ ft

▲ General Sherman Tree

3. The Space Needle is 607 ft tall. 273 people visited the building in the morning. 346 people visited in the afternoon. How many people visited in all?

_____ people

▲ Space Needle

California Content Standards *Mathematical Reasoning 1.1 Determine the approach, materials, and strategies to be used. Also Number Sense 2.2 (⚭), Mathematical Reasoning 2.0, 2.1.*

two hundred thirty-one **231**

Cross out the information you do not need. Solve.

4. At the fair, 207 adults and 463 children rode the Ferris wheel. 350 children rode the merry-go-round. How many people rode the ferris wheel?

_____ people

▲ Western Idaho Fair

5. The Astrodome is 208 ft high. At an Astros ballgame, 693 people ate hot dogs. 426 of those people were adults. How many children ate hot dogs?

_____ children

▲ The Houston Astrodome

 Math Reasoning

Number Sense

What information do you need to solve the problem?

Sometimes you do not have enough information to solve a problem.

6. The Clark family drove to the Smoky Mountains in 2 days. They drove 200 miles on Day 1. How many miles did they drive on Day 2?

_____

_____

Home Activity Ask your child what he or she wanted to find out in each problem and why some facts were eliminated.
Homework Workbook 7-12

Name_____ **Diagnostic Checkpoint**

Find each difference.

1.

H	T	O
☐	☐	☐
3	5	2
− 1	9	1

H	T	O
☐	☐	☐
4	7	5
− 2	6	3

H	T	O
☐	☐	☐
6	4	2
− 3	2	7

2.
```
   600        763        435        546        874
 − 400      − 327      − 253      − 190      −  32
```

Add or subtract.

3.
```
  $3.25      $5.63      $6.80      $7.52      $2.45
 + 2.17     + 3.74     − 3.23     − 0.60     + 1.32
```

4.
```
   300        293        582        706        454
 +   7      − 124      − 166      − 253      + 271
```

What did you buy?
Use coins and bills to act it out.

button
$0.59
$0.78
$0.25
pen   post card

5. You have $1.00 to spend.
When you leave the store,
you have 41¢. How much
did you spend? $____.____

What did you buy? _____

Name _____

1.

Favorite Ice Cream	
Vanilla	24
Chocolate	35
Strawberry	17

- ○ 18 more votes
- ○ 11 more votes
- ○ 9 more votes
- ○ NH

2.

$1.32   47¢   1.45$ $0.05
○   ○   ○   ○

3. ____ > 675

657   674   99   680
○   ○   ○   ○

4.

1:45   2:09   2:45   NH
○   ○   ○   ○

5. 325, 335, 345, 355, ____, ____, ____

356, 357, 358	365, 375, 385	355, 365, 375	NH
○	○	○	○

6.

$1.47 $1.40   47¢   7¢
○   ○   ○   ○

Oral Directions *Mark the correct answer. NH means "Not here." Mark it whenever the answer is not given.*

#1. A second-grade class voted for their favorite flavor of ice cream. How many more votes did chocolate get than vanilla?

#2. Which money amount is NOT written correctly?
#3. Find the number that is greater than 675.
#4. What time is it?
#5. Which numbers come next?
#6. Which amount shows one dollar and forty-seven cents?

Name_____

Add.

1.
```
   400        370       $2.56      529        643
 + 300       + 47      + 3.36     +   7      + 232
```

2.
```
 $4.08        791        359       272        586
 + 2.63      + 144      + 135     + 460      + 333
```

Subtract.

3.
```
   800       $5.73       906       647        758
 - 500       - 4.65     - 551     -  86      - 224
```

4.
```
   348        480       $6.34      228        554
 - 262       - 163      - 3.52    -   9      - 462
```

Cross out the information you do not need. Solve.

5. The Jackson family has to drive 650 miles to visit Mount Rushmore. The faces of 4 presidents are carved in the mountains. The Jacksons have gone 335 miles. How many more miles do they have to go?

▲ Mount Rushmore

_____ miles

Write in vertical form. Add or subtract.

6.   348 − 109   457 + 350   189 + 331   781 − 345

Subtract. Check by adding.

7.   440   645
      − 27   +   − 362   +   _____

What did each person buy?
Use coins to act it out.

kite  $3.71 ball  $3.49 car  $3.59 yo yo  $3.61

8. Jill had $5.00 when she went
   to the store. When she left the
   store, he had $1.51. How
   much money did he spend? _____

   Which toy did Jill buy? _____

9. Jose had $6.00 when he went
   to the store. When he left the
   store, he had $2.29. How
   much money did he spend? _____

   Which toy did Jose buy? _____

Name_____

1.	336 + 255	581 ○	591 ○	681 ○	691 ○
2.	745 − 217	528 ○	532 ○	962 ○	NH ○
3.	407 − 172	375 ○	275 ○	239 ○	235 ○
4.	185 + 249	424 ○	434 ○	435 ○	NH ○

5. Irma collected 125 shells on the beach. She gave 42 of the shells to a friend. Her friend sorted the shells into 6 boxes. How many shells did Irma have left?

○ Irma collected 125 shells on the beach.

○ She gave 42 of the shells to a friend.

○ Her friend sorted the shells into 6 boxes.

○ How many shells did Irma have left?

Oral Directions *Mark the correct answer. NH means "Not here." Mark it whenever the answer is not given.*

#1–4. Add or subtract.
#5. Which sentence is NOT needed to solve the problem? Irma collected 125 shells on the beach. She gave 42 of the shells to a friend. Her friend sorted the shells into 6 boxes. How many shells did Irma have left?

6. $1.35
+ 1.84

| $3.19 ○ | $2.59 ○ | $2.19 ○ | NH ○ |

7. $4.21
− 2.14

| $2.35 ○ | $2.15 ○ | $2.07 ○ | $1.07 ○ |

8.   279
− 123

| 123 + 279 ○ | 156 + 123 ○ | 146 + 123 ○ | NH ○ |

9.

| $3.79 ○ | $3.21 ○ | $2.21 ○ | $2.11 ○ |

10.

NH

○   ○   ○   ○

Oral Directions *Mark the correct answer. NH means "Not here." Mark it whenever the answer is not given.*

#6–7. Add or subtract.
#8. Which addition problem could be used to check the subtraction sentence 279 − 123?

#9. Jen had $4.00. She spent $1.79 on a toy dog. How much money does she have left? Use bills and coins to act out the problem.
#10. Ted had $3.00. When he left the store, he had $1.31. Which toy did he buy? Use bills and coins to act out the problem.

Diagnosing Readiness
for Chapter 8

1. Circle the shorter crayon.

2. Circle the longer pencil.

3. Which is heavier?

4. Circle the container that holds the most. Put an X on the one that holds the least.

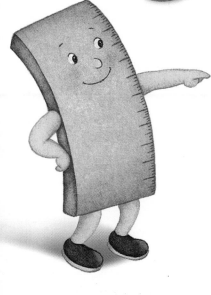

5. Circle the picture that shows how to measure using cubes.

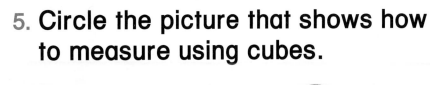

To the Family

Looking Back	Chapter 8	Looking Ahead
In Grade 1 children compared the length, weight, and volume of objects and measured using nonstandard units.	In this chapter children measure length, weight, and volume using nonstandard and standard units. Children will measure the length of objects to the nearest inch and/or centimeter.	In Grade 3 children will work with determining area, volume, and perimeter and choose appropriate tools and units of measure.

Page 239 Your child solved problems that review math skills from previous chapters and will help your child with the skills in Chapter 8.

Math at Home Measure the length of the room using a heel-to-toe process. Ask your child to do the same and talk about why the measurements are different.

Math Literature To read more about measurement, look for these books in your library.
Length by Henry Pluckrose (Children's Press, 1995)
How Big Is a Foot? by Rolf Myller (Young Yearling, 1991)

California Content Standards in Chapter 8 Lessons*

	Teach and Practice	Practice		Teach and Practice	Practice
Number Sense			1.3 (🔑) Measure the length of an object to the nearest inch and/or centimeter.	2, 3, 5	
6.1 Recognize when an estimate is reasonable in measurements.	2, 4–11	3			
Measurement and Geometry			**Mathematical Reasoning**		
1.0 Students understand that measurement is accomplished by identifying a unit of measure, iterating (repeating) that unit, and comparing it to the item to be measured.	4, 6-13		1.0 Students make decisions about how to set up a problem.		11
			1.1 Determine the approach, materials, and strategies to be used.	13	
1.1 Measure the length of objects by iterating (repeating) a nonstandard or standard unit.	1–3		1.2 Use tools, such as manipulatives or sketches, to model problems.		9, 10
			2.0 Students solve problems and justify their reasoning.	12	4, 7, 8, 12
1.2 Use different units to measure the same object and predict whether the measure will be greater or smaller when a different unit is used.	1, 5		2.1 Defend the reasoning used and justify the procedures selected.		

* The symbol (🔑) indicates a key standard as designated in the Mathematics Framework for California Public Schools.
  Full statements of the California Content Standards are found at the beginning of this book following the Table of Contents.

Name_____ **Understanding Length and Height**

This book is about 12 cubes long.

This book is about 3 crayons long.

Word Bank

length
height

Choose an object in your classroom to measure.

| desk | pencil | book | door | table |

Choose a unit of measure.

| clip | cube | crayon | eraser | block |

Measure the object. Choose a different unit
and measure again. Complete the chart.

What I Measured	Unit of Measure	Measurement
1. _____	_____	about _____
	_____	about _____
2. _____	_____	about _____
	_____	about _____

California Content Standards *Measurement and Geometry
1.2 Use different units to measure the same object and predict
whether the measure will be greater or smaller when a different unit
is used. Measurement and Geometry 1.1.*

Write the name of an object and two different units of measure.
Predict which measure will be greater. Circle that unit.
Then measure and complete the chart.

Objects:

| chair | teacher's desk | chalkboard | shelves | scissors |

Units of Measure:

| clip | cube | crayon | eraser | block |

What I Measured	Unit of Measure	Measurement
3. _____	_____ _____	about _____ about _____
4. _____	_____ _____	about _____ about _____
5. _____	_____ _____	about _____ about _____
6. _____	_____ _____	about _____ about _____

Home Activity Ask your child to use different units, such as paper clips or blocks, to measure the same object around your home. Have your child predict which measure will be greater or smaller when a different unit is used. Homework Workbook 8-1

Name_____ **Inches and Feet**

This paper clip is about 1 inch long.

There are 12 inches in 1 foot.

Find objects like the ones shown.
Work with a partner. Estimate.
Then use a ruler to measure.

Word Bank

inch (in.)
foot (ft)

	Estimate	**Measure**
1. crayon	about _____ inches	about _____ inches
2. eraser	about _____ inches	about _____ inches
3. marker	about _____ inches	about _____ inches
4. sneaker	about _____ inches	about _____ inches

California Content Standards *Measurement and Geometry 1.3 (🔑) Measure the length of an object to the nearest inch. Measurement and Geometry 1.1. Number Sense 6.1.*

two hundred forty-three **243**

About how many inches or feet
would the real thing be?
Circle the better estimate.

5.

2 feet tall

(6 feet tall)

man

6.

11 inches long

1 inch long

hammer

7.

2 inches long

12 inches long

nail

8.

50 feet long

5 feet long

workbench

9.

2 feet long

20 feet long

toolbox

10.

1 inch long

10 inches long

screwdriver

Problem Solving

Solve.

11. Patti had a stick one foot long.
She cut off a piece five inches
long for her birdhouse.
How long is the stick now?

_____ inches

 Home Activity Help your child use a ruler to measure household items in inches. Homework Workbook 8-2

Name_____

Understand

You need to measure a path that is not a straight line.

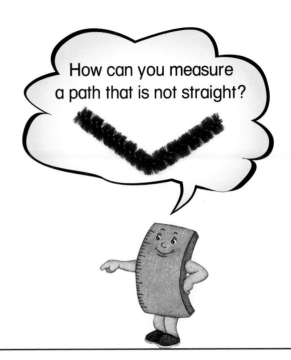

How can you measure a path that is not straight?

Plan

Measure each part and add or measure with a string.

Solve

Measure the path.

Measure each part.   or   Measure with string.

I inch   I inch

Then add the parts.

Then measure the string with a ruler.

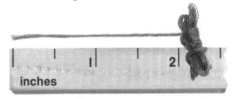

inches

I inch + I inch = 2 inches

Look Back

Does your answer make sense?

Measure.

I.

about _____ inches

California Content Standards *Measurement and Geometry 1.3 (🔑) Measure the length of an object to the nearest inch. Measurement and Geometry 1.1. Also Number Sense 6.1.*

two hundred forty-five **245**

Measure.

2.

about _____ inches

3.

about _____ inches

4.

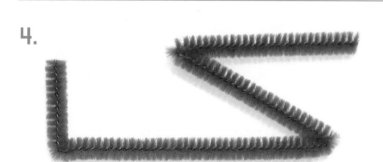

about _____ inches

Math Reasoning

Visual Thinking

Which path is longer?

5. Estimate. Write **A** or **B**.

_____

6. Measure to check.

A _____ inches **B** _____ inches

A

B

Home Activity Create a path at home that is not straight.
Have your child measure its length. Homework Workbook 8-3

Name_____ **Inches, Feet, and Yards**

The door is 3 feet wide. 3 feet is the same as 1 yard.

Word Bank

yard (yd)

Would you measure the real thing in inches, feet, or yards? Circle the best unit.

1.

length of tube

(inches)

feet

yards

2.

height of a girl

inches

feet

yards

3.

length of a paint box

inches

feet

yards

4.

height of an easel

inches

feet

yards

5.

length of a brush

inches

feet

yards

6.

length of a room

inches

feet

yards

California Content Standards *Number Sense 6.1 Recognize when an estimate is reasonable in measurements. Measurement and Geometry 1.0. Also Mathematical Reasoning 2.0.*

two hundred forty-seven **247**

About how long or tall would the real object be?
Circle the best estimate.

7.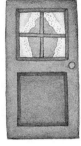

7 inches

(7 feet)

7 yards

height of door

8.

5 inches

5 feet

5 yards

length of a marker

9.

1 inch

1 foot

1 yard

length of a table

10.

6 inches

6 feet

6 yards

height of a bookcase

11.

2 inches

2 feet

2 yards

length of a large clip

12.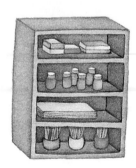

13 inches

13 feet

13 yards

length of a bus

Math Reasoning

Number Sense

13. Cindy and Mike each measured the bookcase.
Cindy's measure was 2 yards.
Mike's measure was 6 feet.
Could they **both** be correct?
Tell why or why not.

 Home Activity Point out things at home. Ask your child if it is easier to measure these things in inches, feet, or yards.
Homework Workbook 8-4

Name_____ **Centimeters and Meters**

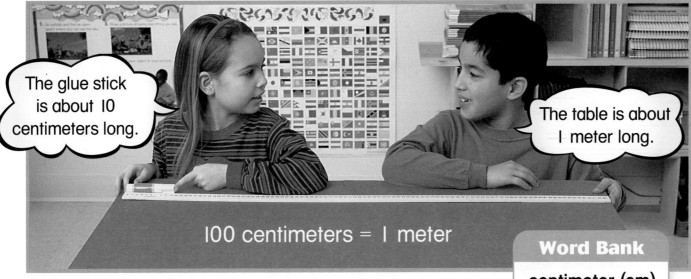

The glue stick is about 10 centimeters long.

The table is about 1 meter long.

100 centimeters = 1 meter

Find objects like the ones shown. Estimate.
Then use a ruler to measure.

Word Bank

centimeter (cm)
meter (m)

	Estimate	Measure
1. eraser	about _____ cm	about _____ cm
2. marker	about _____ cm	about _____ cm
3. chalk	about _____ cm	about _____ cm
4. chalkboard	about _____ m	about _____ m

California Content Standards *Measurement and Geometry*
1.3 (⚷) Measure the length of an object to the nearest centimeter.
Measurement and Geometry 1.2, Number Sense 6.1.

About how long or tall would the real object be?
Circle the better estimate.

5.

(15 cm)

15 m

height of a birdhouse

6.

2 cm

2 m

length of a picnic table

7.

1 cm

1 m

height of a doghouse

8.

40 cm

40 m

length of a swing seat

9.

50 cm

50 m

length of a flower box

10.

3 cm

3 m

length of a fence

Math Reasoning

Estimation

11. Find objects that you think are about 10 centimeters long
or tall. Use a ruler to check. Tell about what you find.

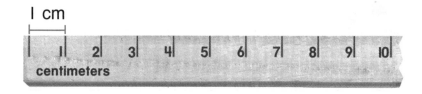

1 cm

1 2 3 4 5 6 7 8 9 10
centimeters

Home Activity Ask your child to find things in your home
that are about one centimeter long and about one meter long.
Homework Workbook 8-5

Name_____

Circle the answer.

1. Will it take more cubes or crayons to measure the book?

   cubes   crayons

Use an inch ruler to measure.

2.

   screwdriver

   about _____ inches

Measure the length of the path.

3.

   about _____ inches

Use a centimeter ruler to measure.

4.

   chalk

   about _____ centimeters

Would you measure the real thing in inches, feet, or yards?

5.

   4 inches

   4 feet

   4 yards

6.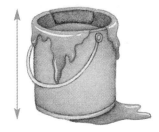

   10 inches

   10 feet

   10 yards

Name_____

1. **3 hundreds   8 tens   4 ones**

285   348   384   NH

○   ○   ○   ○

2. **six hundred fifty-nine**

609   659   759   NH

○   ○   ○   ○

3.

○   1 cm

○   2 cm

○   5 cm

○   10 cm

4.

○   52 beads

○   100 beads

○   104 beads

○   156 beads

5.

20	20	20	20
+10	+20	+30	+☐
30	40	50	60

○   20
○   40
○   60
○   80

6.

○   3:15
○   4:00
○   4:15
○   5:15

Oral Directions *Mark the correct answer. NH means "Not Here." Mark it whenever the answer is not given.*

#1–2. Mark the number.
#3. About how long is the screw? Measure it using a centimeter ruler.

#4. There are 52 beads in each container. How many beads are there in all?
#5. Find the pattern. Mark the number that solves the problem.
#6. What time does the clock show?

Name_____ **Understanding Weight**

The marker weighs less than 10 cubes.

Word Bank

weight

Find objects like the ones shown.
Does each object weigh **more** or **less** than 10 cubes?
Circle your estimate. Then use a scale to measure.

	Estimate	Measure
1. book	more less	more less
2. eraser	more less	more less
3. ruler	more less	more less
4. box of crayons	more less	more less

California Content Standards *Number Sense 6.1 Recognize when an estimate is reasonable in measurements. Measurement and Geometry 1.0.*

two hundred fifty-three **253**

Which object could you put on the right side
of the scale to make the scale look like this?
Circle the best choice.

5.

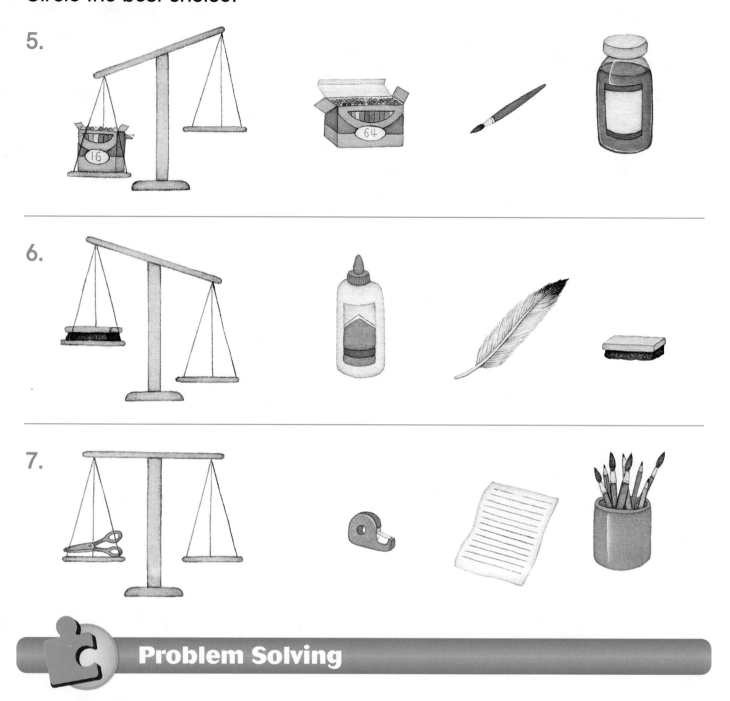

6.

7.

Problem Solving

8. What is wrong with this picture?
Draw or write to show how the scale should look.

Home Activity Hand your child an object and then challenge
him or her to find other things that are heavier, lighter, and
about the same weight. Homework Workbook 8-6

Name_____ **Pounds**

less than 1 pound

about 1 pound

more than 1 pound

Does it weigh more or less than 1 pound?
Write **more** or **less**.

Word Bank

pound (lb)

1.

less

2.

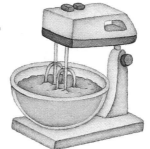

_____

3.

_____

4.

_____

5.

_____

6.

_____

California Content Standards Number Sense 6.1 Recognize
when an estimate is reasonable in measurements. Measurement
and Geometry 1.0. Also Mathematical Reasoning 2.0.

Read each scale to find the weight.
Write the weight to the nearest pound.

7.

2 pounds

8.

_____ pound

9.

_____ pounds

10.

_____ pounds

11.

_____ pounds

12.

_____ pounds

13. Circle the item that weighs about 1 pound.

Math Reasoning

Visual Thinking

14. Suzi says that the small basket weighs more than the big basket. Do you think she is right? Explain your answer.

Home Activity Help your child identify items in the kitchen that are more than, less than, or about 1 pound. Homework Workbook 8-7

Name_____ **Cups, Pints, and Quarts**

2 cups fill 1 pint.   4 cups or 2 pints fill 1 quart.

Circle the containers you can fill.

Word Bank

cup (c)
pint (pt)
quart (qt)

1.

1 pint

2.

1 quart

3.

1 quart

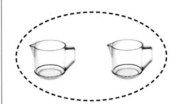

4.

2 quarts

California Content Standards *Number Sense 6.1 Recognize when an estimate is reasonable in measurements. Measurement and Geometry 1.0. Also Mathematical Reasoning 1.2.*

Complete the chart.
Write how many cups, pints, or quarts.

	Cups	Pints	Quarts
5.	4	2	1
6.			2
7.	12		
8.		8	
9.			5

10. What patterns do you see?

Problem Solving

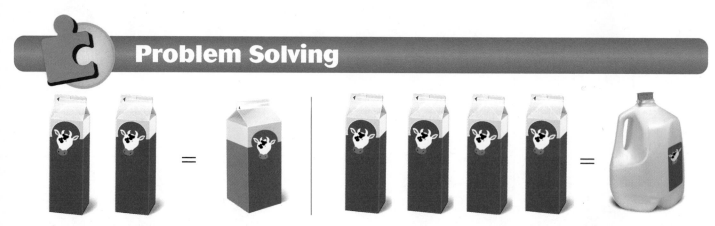

2 quarts fill a half gallon.   4 quarts fill a gallon.

Use the pictures to solve. Write **more** or **less**.

11. 5 quarts is _____ than 1 gallon.

12. 3 quarts is _____ than 1 gallon.

13. 3 quarts is _____ than a half gallon.

Home Activity Ask your child to compare cup, pint, and quart containers in your home or at the grocery store.
Homework Workbook 8-10

Name_____ **Liters**

less than 1 liter   about 1 liter   more than 1 liter

Word Bank

liter (L)

Does it hold more or less than 1 liter?
Write **more** or **less**.

1.

less

2.

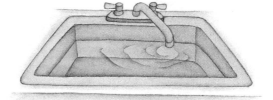

_____

3.

_____

4.

_____

5.

_____

6.

_____

California Content Standards *Number Sense 6.1 Recognize when an estimate is reasonable in measurements. Measurement and Geometry 1.0. Also Mathematical Reasoning 1.0.*

two hundred sixty-three **263**

About how many liters does it hold?
Circle the better estimate.

7.

30 liters

(3 liters)

8.

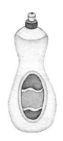

1 liter

60 liters

9.

1 liter

10 liters

10.

5 liters

50 liters

11.

1 liter

40 liters

12.

1 liter

20 liters

Problem Solving

Solve.

13. Ken's family drinks 2 liters of juice each week. How many liters does his family drink in 10 weeks?

_____ liters

14. It takes 5 liters of water to fill Jen's bucket. Jen used 15 liters of water. How many buckets did she fill?

_____ buckets

Home Activity Ask your child to find containers that hold more than, less than, or about 1 liter. Homework Workbook 8-11

Name_____ **Temperature**

Temperatures Around the World

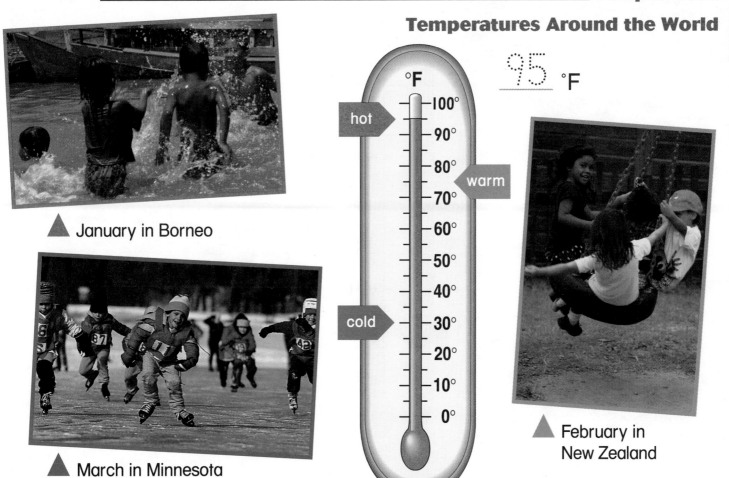

_95_ °F

January in Borneo

March in Minnesota

cold

warm

hot

February in
New Zealand

Write each temperature.
Circle the hottest temperature in red.
Circle the coldest temperature in blue. Tell how you know.

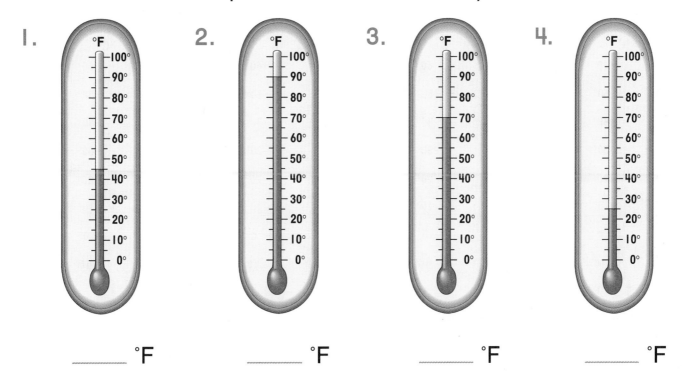

1. _____ °F

2. _____ °F

3. _____ °F

4. _____ °F

California Content Standards *Measurement and Geometry*
1.0 Students understand that measurement is accomplished by
identifying a unit of measure. Also Mathematical Reasoning 2.0.

two hundred sixty-five **265**

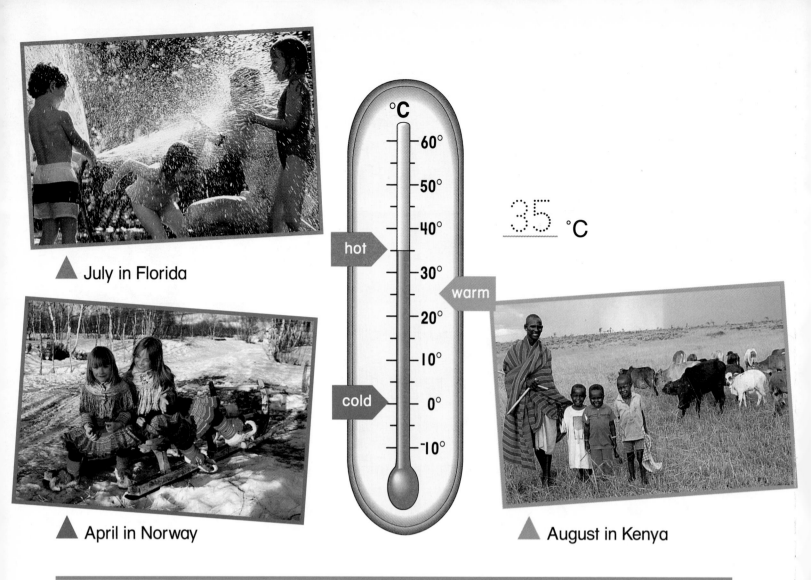

July in Florida

April in Norway

35 °C

hot

warm

cold

August in Kenya

Write each temperature.
Circle the hottest temperature in red.
Circle the coldest temperature in blue. Tell how you know.

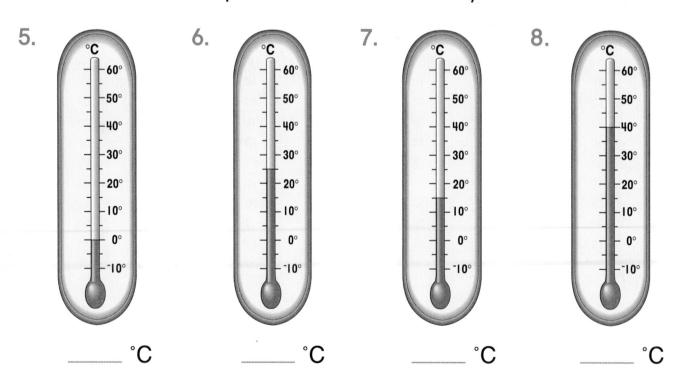

5. _____ °C

6. _____ °C

7. _____ °C

8. _____ °C

Home Activity Talk about the temperature each day and what kind of clothing is appropriate. Homework Workbook 8-12

Name_____ **Problem-Solving Application**

Choosing Reasonable Answers

Circle the tool you would use to answer each question.

Think: What do you need to find out?

1. How long is it?

2. How much does it hold?

3. Which object is heavier?

4. How cold is it?

California Content Standards *Mathematical Reasoning 1.1 Determine the approach, materials, and strategies to be used. Measurement and Geometry 1.0.*

two hundred sixty-seven **267**

Circle the correct unit of measure
to answer each question.

5. How heavy is it?

inches   (pounds)

cups   °F

---

6. How long is it?

inches   pounds

pints   °F

---

7. How tall is it?

feet   pounds

quarts   °F

---

8. How much does it hold?

centimeter   grams

liter   °C

---

9. How hot is it?

centimeters   kilograms

liters   °C

 Home Activity Have your child identify things at home that
can be measured with a ruler, scale, measuring cup, or ther-
mometer. Homework Workbook 8-13

About how much does it weigh?
Circle the better estimate.

1.

I pound

10 pounds

Would you measure the apple
in grams or kilograms?
Circle your choice.

2.

grams

kilograms

Circle the two that hold about the same.

3.

4.

5.

Write each temperature.

6.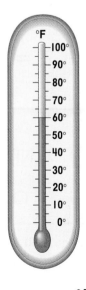

_____ °F   _____ °C

Circle the correct unit of
measure to answer
the question.

7. How much
does it hold?

centimeter   gram

liter   °F

1. **283**   **280**

   $<$ $=$ $>$ NH
   ○   ○   ○   ○

2. **399**   **400**

   $<$ $=$ $>$ NH
   ○   ○   ○   ○

3. **454, _____, 514**

   426   445   501   541
   ○   ○   ○   ○

4. **619, _____, 650**

   618   642   651   660
   ○   ○   ○   ○

5. **529**
   + 370

   ○ 899
   ○ 999
   ○ 259
   ○ NH

6. **843**
   − 692

   ○ 255
   ○ 251
   ○ 151
   ○ NH

7. **491**
   − 82

   ○ 411
   ○ 409
   ○ 579
   ○ NH

8. **185**
   + 228

   ○ 163
   ○ 403
   ○ 413
   ○ NH

9. **$2.85**   **$1.60**

   $1.25 $0.25 $1.05   NH
   ○   ○   ○   ○

10. + + (?) + (?) = 46¢

      NH

   ○   ○   ○   ○

Oral Directions *Mark the correct answer. NH means "Not here." Mark it whenever the answer is not given.*

#1–2. Compare. Mark the symbol that makes the statement true.
#3. Mark the number that is between 454 and 514.

#4. Mark the number that is between 619 and 650.
#5–8. Add or subtract.
#9. Lora had $2.85. She bought a necklace for $1.60. How much change did she get?
#10. Tyler had 4 coins in his pocket worth 46 cents. He had one quarter and one dime. What are the other two coins in his pocket?

270   two hundred seventy

Name_____

Circle the answer.

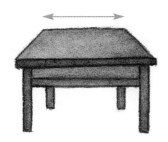

1. Will it take more cubes or
    straws to measure the desk?

    straws   cubes

Use an inch ruler to measure.

2.

about _____ inches

3.

about _____ inches

4.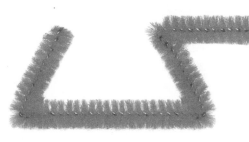

about _____ inches

Circle the tool you would use to answer each question.

5. How long is it?

6. Which object is heavier?

7. How much does it hold?

About how much does it weigh? Circle the better estimate.

8.

I pound

10 pounds

Would you measure it in grams or Kilograms? Circle your choice.

9.

grams

kilograms

About how much would the real object hold?

10.

more than
I cup

less than
I cup

11.

more than
I liter

less than
I liter

About how long is the real object?

12.

13 inches

13 feet

13 yards

13.

9 inches

9 feet

9 yards

Circle the hotter temperature.

14.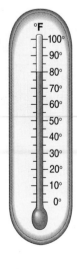

°F
—100°
—90°
—80°
—70°
—60°
—50°
—40°
—30°
—20°
—10°
—0°

°F
—100°
—90°
—80°
—70°
—60°
—50°
—40°
—30°
—20°
—10°
—0°

Measure using a centimeter ruler.

15.

about _____ centimeters

1.

- ○ 1 inch
- ○ 2 inches
- ○ 6 inches
- ○ 12 inches

2.

- ○ 1 foot
- ○ 2 feet
- ○ 4 feet
- ○ 40 feet

3.

- ○ 1 cm
- ○ 3 cm
- ○ 10 cm
- ○ 20 cm

4.

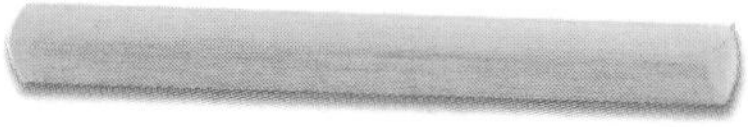

- ○ inches
- ○ feet
- ○ yards
- ○ NH

5.

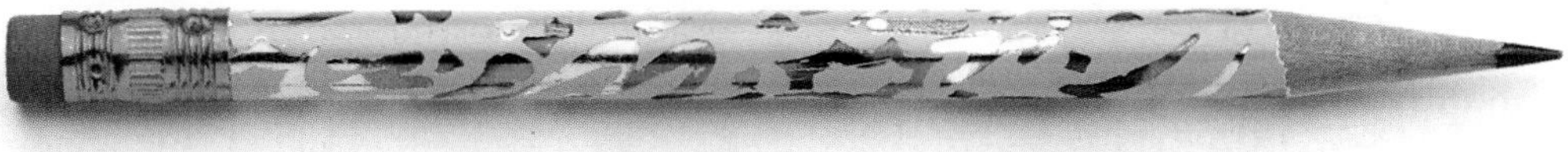

○   ○   ○   ○

Oral Directions *Mark the correct answer. NH means "Not here." Mark it whenever the answer is not given.*

#1. About how long is the sewing needle?
#2. About how tall is the girl?

#3. About how long is the nail?
#4. Mark the best unit to measure the piece of chalk.
#5. Will it take more cubes, clips, pennies, or beans to measure the pencil?

6.

- ○ I cup
- ○ I pint
- ○ I quart
- ○ I liter

7.

- ○ 50 liters
- ○ 10 liters
- ○ 5 liters
- ○ I liter

8.

- ○ yards
- ○ pounds
- ○ centimeters
- ○ °C

9.

- ○ kilograms
- ○ cups
- ○ inches
- ○ pounds

10.

○   ○   ○   ○

11.

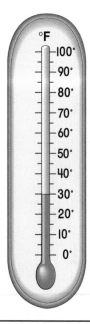

- ○ 20°F
- ○ 30°F
- ○ 40°F
- ○ NH

12.

- ○ I pound
- ○ 15 pounds
- ○ 150 pounds
- ○ NH

Oral Directions *Mark the correct answer. NH means "Not here." Mark it whenever the answer is not given.*

#6–7. Mark the unit that tells about how much each container will hold.
#8. Which unit of measure could you use to tell how heavy an object is?

#9. Which unit of measure could you use to tell how wide an object is?
#10. Which item is heavier than a kilogram?
#11. Mark the correct temperature.
#12. About how much would a real dog weigh?

Diagnosing Readiness

for Chapter 9

1. **How long is the pencil?**  _____ inches

2. **Circle the objects with the same kind of shape.**

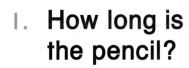

Does the shape have corners, faces, and edges? Write yes or no in each box.

	Corners	Faces	Edges
3. sphere			
4.  cube			

5. **I have 6 faces.**
   All 6 faces are the same.
   What shape am I?

Circle the correct shape.

To the Family

Looking Back	Chapter 9	Looking Ahead
In Grade 1 children identified and classified common geometric shapes and solids. In Chapter 8 children measured objects using rulers.	**Geometry** Children describe and classify geometric shapes and solids by common attributes, put together and take apart shapes to form other shapes, and measure to find the perimeter of shapes.	In Grade 3 children will classify shapes by their angles, measure the area of shapes, and find the volume of solids.

Page 275 Your child solved problems that review math skills from previous chapters and will help your child with the skills in Chapter 9.

Math at Home The chapter theme is shapes around us. With your child look for different shapes and solids in buildings and objects around you. For example, work with your child to identify objects that look like squares, triangles, cubes, cylinders, and cones.

Math Literature Read math or theme-related stories with your child. Look for the following books in your local library.
The Greedy Triangle by Marilyn Burns (Scholastic, 1995)
Round Trip by Ann Jonas (Mulberry Books, 1990)

California Content Standards in Chapter 9 Lessons*

	Teach and Practice	Practice		Teach and Practice	Practice
Algebra and Functions			**Mathematical Reasoning**		
1.3 Solve addition and subtraction problems by using data from simple charts, picture graphs, and number sentences.	9, 11		1.0 Students make decisions about how to set up a problem.		1, 2
Measurement and Geometry			1.1 Determine the approach, materials, and strategies to be used.		4
1.2 (🔑), Grade 3, Determine the area of solid figures by covering them with squares.		8	1.2 Use tools, such as manipulatives or sketches, to model problems.		3, 5, 10
1.3 (🔑), Grade 3, Find the perimeter of a polygon.	8		2.0 Students solve problems and justify their reasoning.		6
2.0 (🔑) Identify and describe the attributes of common figures in the plane.	5, 10		2.1 Defend the reasoning used and justify the procedures selected.		6
2.1 (🔑) Describe and classify plane and solid geometric shapes.	1–4		2.2 Make precise calculations and check the validity of the results in the context of the problem.		7
2.2 (🔑) Put shapes together and take them apart to form other shapes.	7	9	3.0 Students note connections between one problem and another.		4, 11
3.3, Grade 4, Identify congruent figures.	6				
Statistics, Data Analysis, and Probability					
1.4 Ask and answer simple questions related to data representations.	9, 11				

* The symbol (🔑) indicates a key standard as designated in the Mathematics Framework for California Public Schools.
  Full statements of the California Content Standards are found at the beginning of this book following the Table of Contents.

Name_____**Faces, Vertices, and Edges**

This crayon box is a rectangular prism.
It has 6 **faces**, 8 **vertices**,
and 12 **edges**.

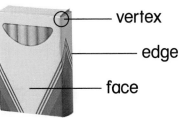

vertex

edge

face

Word Bank

face
vertex
edge

Find how many faces, vertices, and edges. Use solids if you like.

	solid	name	faces	vertices	edges
1.		cube	6	8	12
2.					
3.					
4.					
5.					
6.					

California Content Standards Measurement and Geometry
2.1 (🔑) Describe and classify solid geometric shapes. Also
Mathematical Reasoning 1.0.

two hundred seventy-nine **279**

Sort the solids.
Write the names in the boxes.

7.
Solids That Roll
_____
_____
_____

8.
Solids with Vertices
_____
_____
_____

9.
Solids with Flat Faces
_____ _____
_____ _____
_____ _____

Problem Solving

Solve each riddle.

10. What solid am I?
I can roll.
I don't have any faces
or edges.

_____

11. What solid am I?
I have 8 vertices.
All my faces
are squares.

_____

Home Activity Ask your child to take different shapes from home and show you the faces, edges, and vertices. Homework Workbook 9-2

Name_____ **Solid Shapes and Plane Shapes**

You can use a solid shape to draw
a plane shape.

If I draw around the
face of a cone, what
shape will I make?

Circle the solid shape you could use
to draw each shape at the left.

1. circle

2. square

3. rectangle

4. triangle

5. circle

California Content Standards *Measurement and Geometry 2.1*
(🔑) *Describe and classify plane and solid geometric shapes. Also*
Mathematical Reasoning 1.2.

two hundred eighty-one **281**

What if you drew around the face of each object?
Circle the shape you would make.

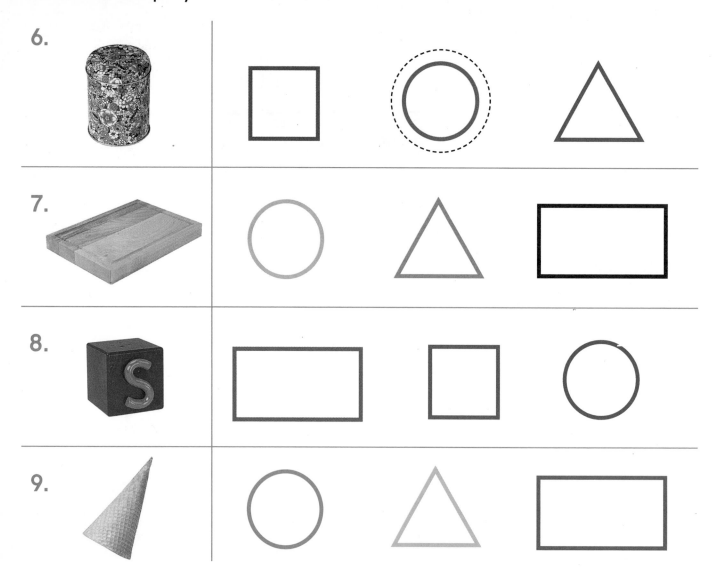

6.

7.

8.

9.

Math Reasoning

Visual Thinking

10. Draw a picture of the shapes you would
make if you traced each object.

 Home Activity Ask your child to place the faces of objects
on a sheet of paper and to trace the shape. Homework
Workbook 9-3

Name_____ **Slides, Flips, and Turns**

You can **slide**, **flip**, and **turn** shapes.

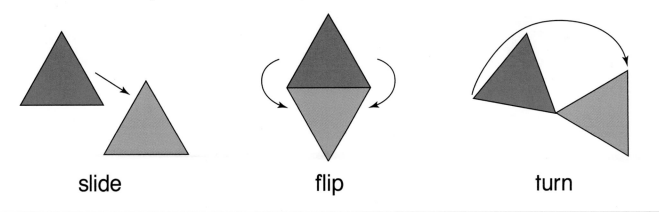

slide   flip   turn

Is it a **slide**, **flip**, or **turn**? Use pattern blocks to check.
Circle the answer.

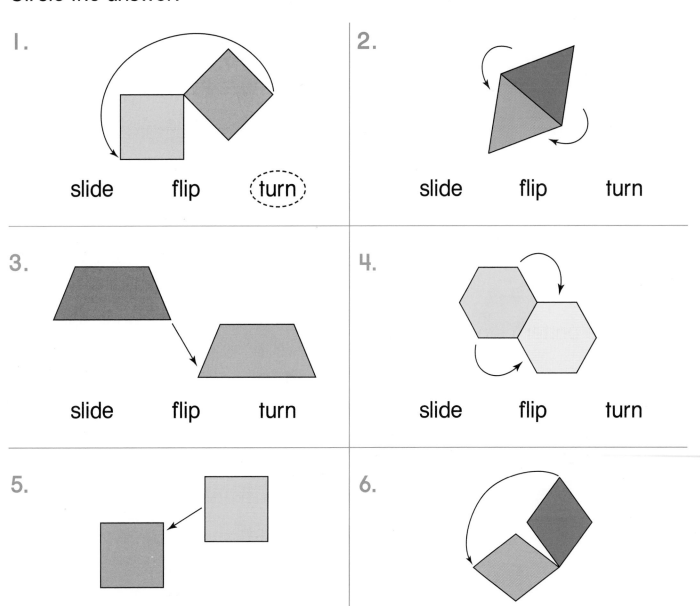

1.

slide   flip   (turn)

2.

slide   flip   turn

3.

slide   flip   turn

4.

slide   flip   turn

5.

slide   flip   turn

6.

slide   flip   turn

California Content Standards *Measurement and Geometry 2.0 (🔑) Identify and describe the attributes of common figures in the plane. Also Mathematical Reasoning 1.2.*

Write **slide**, **flip**, or **turn**. Use pattern blocks to check.

7.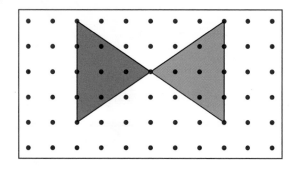

_____

8.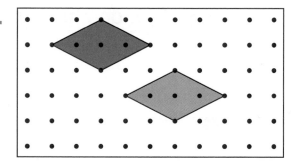

_____

9.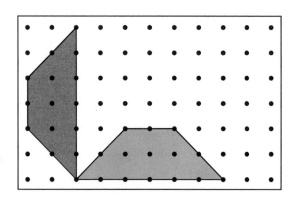

_____

10.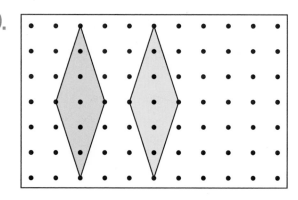

_____

Problem Solving

Solve. Use pattern blocks to help.

11. How many of each shape do you need to make a hexagon?

_____

_____

Hexagon

Home Activity Give your child an index card or a piece of paper. Ask him or her to show you how to slide, flip, and turn it. Homework Workbook 9-5

Name_____

1. Circle the objects that have the same kind of shape.

 |

2. Write the number of faces, vertices, and edges.

 _____ faces

_____ vertices

_____ edges

 _____ faces

_____ vertices

_____ edges

3. Circle the solid you would use to draw a triangle.

triangle

4. Write the number of vertices and sides.

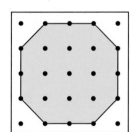 _____ vertices

_____ sides

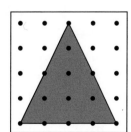 _____ vertices

_____ sides

5. Circle **slide, flip,** or **turn.**

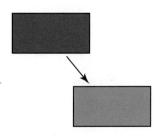

slide

flip

turn

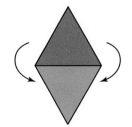

slide

flip

turn

Name_____

1.

153   100 + 50 + 3   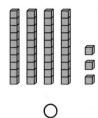   one hundred
                                                                        fifty-three

○   ○   ○   ○

---

2. 16 − 9 = ——

16 + 9 = 25   9 + 7 = 16   6 + 9 = 15   NH

○   ○   ○   ○

3.

○   ○   ○   ○

---

4. 1.45$ $1.45¢   1.45 $1.45

○   ○   ○   ○

5.

Event	Start	End
Relay Races	9:00	10:00
Games	10:00	12:00
Awards	1:00	2:00

10:00   11:00   12:00   NH

○   ○   ○   ○

Oral Directions *Mark the correct answer. NH means "Not here." Mark it whenever the answer is not given.*

#1: Which is NOT a way to show one hundred fifty-three?
#2: Which addition fact will help you subtract 16 − 9?

#3: Solve the riddle. Which solid am I? I have six faces. I have 12 edges.
#4: Which is the correct way to write one-dollar and forty-five cents?
#5: The table shows the times that different events take place at the school picnic. Damir's class eats lunch 2 hours after the relay races end. What time do they eat lunch?

Name_____ **Perimeter**

What is the distance around the rectangle?
Measure the number of inches around to find out.

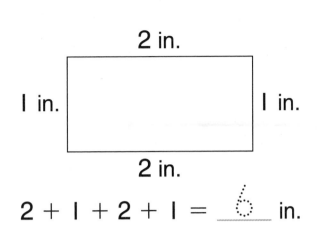

2 in.

I in.   I in.

2 in.

$2 + 1 + 2 + 1 =$ _6_ in.

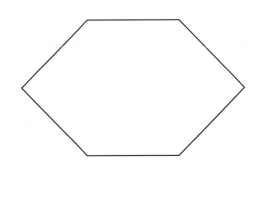

The distance around is called the **perimeter**. The perimeter is 6 inches.

Word Bank

perimeter

Find the perimeter of each shape.
Measure the number of inches around.

I.

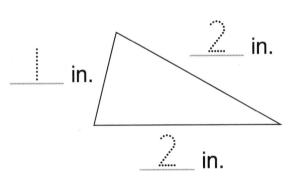

_1_ in.   _2_ in.

_2_ in.

_____ in.

2.

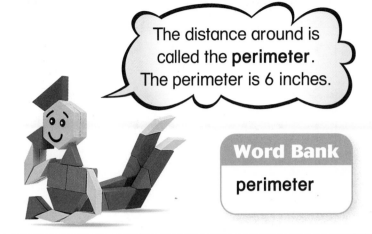

_____ in.

3.

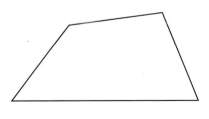

_____ in.

4.

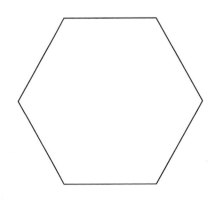

_____ in.

California Content Standards *Measurement and Geometry 1.3 ( ), Grade 3, Find the perimeter of a polygon. Also Measurement and Geometry 1.2 ( ), Grade 3.*

two hundred ninety-three **293**

5. Use the grid to draw a square and a rectangle that is not a square.
Make each side of the shapes 2, 3, or 4 centimeters long.
Write the perimeter of each shape.

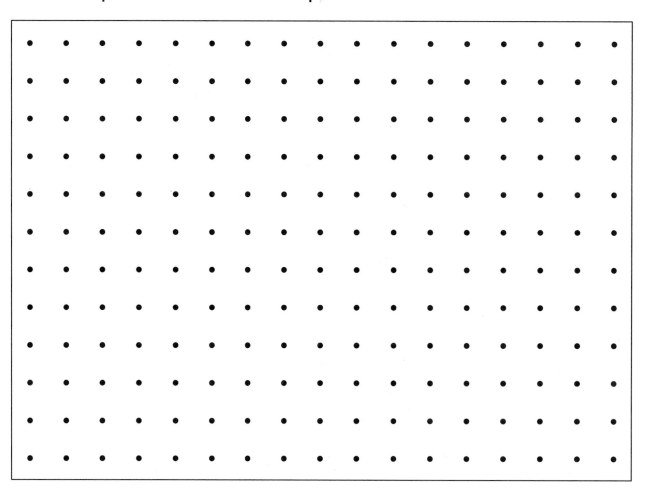

perimeter of square _____ cm   perimeter of rectangle _____ cm

Problem Solving

The number of square units equals the **area** of each shape. Find the area of each shape.

 = I square unit

6.

_____ square units   _____ square units   _____ square units

Home Activity Draw a triangle, square, or rectangle with sides that are 1, 2, or 3 inches in length. Ask your child to find the perimeter. Homework Workbook 9-8

Name_____

Look at the quilt below.

How many more 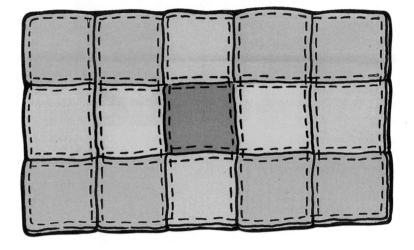 are there than
◻ , ◼ ,and ◻ together?

Algebra

Quilt Squares

Understand

You need to find how many
squares of each color there are.

Plan

You can make a graph.

Solve

Color a box for each
quilt square you see.

Then use the graph
to answer the question.

1. How many more ◻ are there
than ◻ , ◼ and ◻ together?   _____ more pink

Look Back

Does your answer make sense?

California Content Standards _Statistics, Data Analysis,
and Probability 1.4 Ask and answer questions related to data
representations. Algebra and Functions 1.3. Also Measurement
and Geometry 2.2 (🔑)._

two hundred ninety-five **295**

Make a bar graph.
Color 1 box for each quilt square.

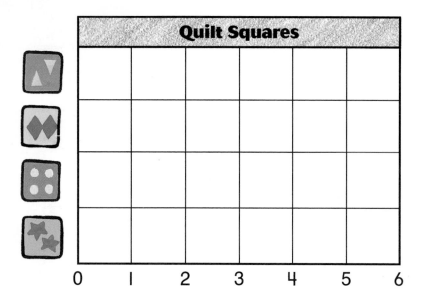

Quilt Squares

0 1 2 3 4 5 6

2. Circle the quilt squares that are used an equal number of times.

3. How many more are there than ? _____

4. How many and are there in all? _____

Math Reasoning

Visual Thinking

5. Pat made this quilt square out of small pieces of cloth.
   Put an X on the numbered piece that does not belong.

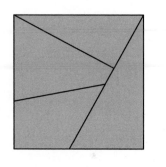 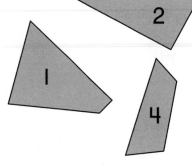 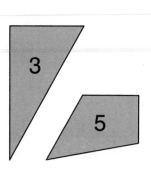

Home Activity Ask your child to explain the graph on this page. Homework Workbook 9-9

Name_____ **Symmetry**

Objects with a line of symmetry
have matching parts.

line of symmetry

matching parts

line of symmetry

matching parts

not a line of symmetry

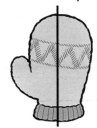

no matching parts

Does each picture have a line of symmetry?
Circle **yes** or **no**. If **yes**, draw a line of symmetry.

1.

(yes)

no

2.

yes

no

3.

yes

no

4.

yes

no

5.

yes

no

6.

yes

no

California Content Standards Measurement and Geometry
2.0 (🔑) Identify and describe the attributes of common figures
in the plane. Also Mathematical Reasoning 1.2.

Make the shapes show symmetry.
Draw to show the matching part.

7.
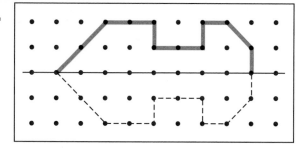

8.
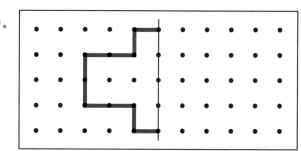

9.
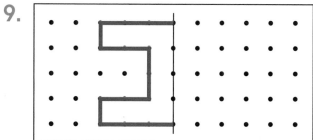

10.
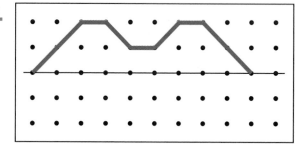

11.
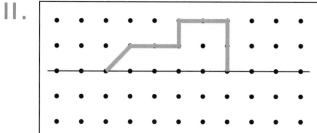

12.
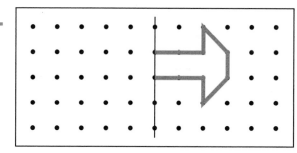

 Math Reasoning

Visual Thinking

Draw as many lines of symmetry as you can.

13.

14.
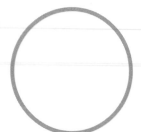

15.
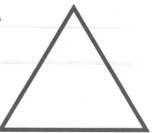

Home Activity Ask your child to find 2 or 3 household objects that have a line of symmetry. Homework Workbook 9-10

Name_____ **Problem-Solving Application**

Using Pictographs

Ms. Brown asked the children in her class to pick their favorite shape. The pictograph shows how many children picked each shape.

Favorite Shapes	= 2 children
Square	👤 👤 👤 👤 👤
Circle	👤 👤 👤
Rectangle	👤 👤 👤 👤
Triangle	👤

Use the graph to answer each question.

Think: Each child in the graph equals 2 children.

1. How many children picked each shape?

   _____ square   _____ rectangle   _____ circle   _____ triangle

2. How many more children picked the square than the rectangle?   _____ children

3. How many children picked the circle and the triangle?   _____ children

4. How many children are in Ms. Brown's class?   _____ children

California Content Standards *Statistics, Data, and Probability 1.4 Ask and answer questions related to data representations. Algebra and Functions 1.3. Also Mathematical Reasoning 3.0.*

Jason's class made shape patterns. The chart shows the number of children who used each shape.

Children Using a Shape			
Square	Circle	Rectangle	Triangle
4	8	6	10

5. Use the chart to make a pictograph.

Draw a ☺ to show 2 children.

Children Using a Shape ☺ = 2 children	
Square	
Circle	
Rectangle	
Triangle	

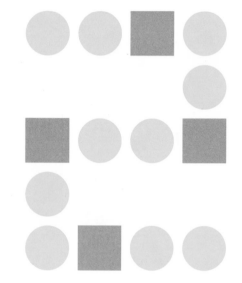

Use the pictograph to answer each question.

6. How many more children used circles than used squares? _____ children

7. Suppose 12 children used rectangles. How many ☺ would you draw in all? _____

Math Reasoning

Number Sense

Use the graph you made above.

8. What if each ☺ = 3 children?
   How many children used squares? _____ children

Home Activity Have your child explain the graph on this page. Homework Workbook 9-11

1. Cross out the shapes that are NOT congruent to the others.

2. Measure each shape. Write the perimeter.

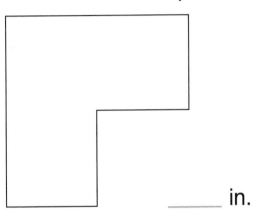   _____ in.

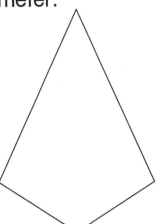   _____ in.

3. Does each picture have a line of symmetry?
   Circle **yes** or **no**. If **yes**, draw a line of symmetry.

   yes

no

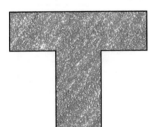   yes

no

Use the picture to make a graph.
Color a box for each shape.

Shapes				
Circle				
Square				
Triangle				
Rectangle (not square)				

0   1   2   3   4

4. Which shape was
   used most often? _____

Name_____

1. ○

   ○

   ○

   ○

---

2. $18 + 16 = 16 + \square$

34	18	2	NH
○	○	○	○

---

3. |

   ○   ○   ○   ○

4.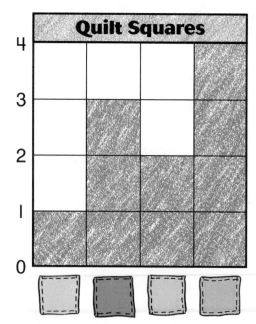

   ○ blue

   ○ orange

   ○ pink

   ○ NH

Oral Directions *Mark the correct answer. NH means "Not here." Mark it whenever the answer is not given.*

#1. Use your centimeter ruler to solve the problem. Anna cut a ribbon that was 7 centimeters long. Which of these shows the ribbon she cut?

#2. What number goes in the box to make the number sentence true?
#3. Which object has the same shape?
#4. Sue and Jow made a quilt using blue, orange, yellow, and pink squares. The graph shows how many of each color squares they used. Which color was used the most?

Name_____ **Chapter 9 Test**

1. Circle the shape you could make
   if you put the two rectangles together.

___

2. Draw a line of symmetry if you can.

 B **M** 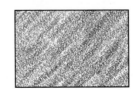 **L** **I**

___

3. Circle the figure that has the same size and shape.

___

4. Write **slide**, **flip**, or **turn**.

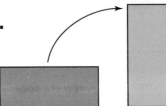

___

5. Look at the chart. Make a bar graph.
   Color one box for each time a sport was chosen.

Favorite Sports	
Sport	**Tally**
Baseball	ⲐⲎⲦ
Tennis	I
Soccer	I I I I
Swimming	I I I

Favorite Sports				
Baseball				
Tennis				
Soccer				
Swimming				

0   1   2   3   4   5

6. Write the number of faces, vertices, and edges.

 _____ faces

_____ vertices

_____ edges

 _____ faces

_____ vertices

_____ edges

7. Measure each shape. Write the perimeter.

 _____ cm

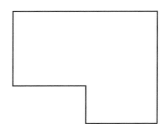 _____ cm

8. Write the number of vertices and sides.

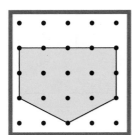 _____ vertices

_____ sides

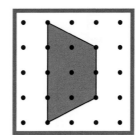 _____ vertices

_____ sides

Use the graph to answer each question.

9. How many children picked each color?

_____ red   _____ blue

_____ green   _____ yellow

10. How many more children picked blue than yellow?

_____ children

Favorite Color	🙂 = 2 children			
Red	🙂	🙂	🙂	
Blue	🙂	🙂	🙂	🙂
Green	🙂	🙂		
Yellow	🙂			

1.

○   ○   ○   ○

2.

   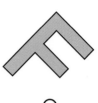

     ○   ○   ○   ○

3.

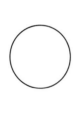 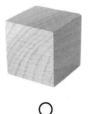  

NH

     ○   ○   ○   ○

4.

     ○   ○   ○   ○

5.

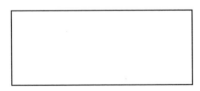

○ 16 centimeters around

○ 14 centimeters around

○ 12 centimeters around

○ 10 centimeters around

Oral Directions *Mark the correct answer. NH means "Not here." Mark it whenever the answer is not given.*

#1. Which shape is NOT the same size and shape as the others?

#2. Which shows the shape in the box after a flip?

#3. Which solid could you use to trace the circle?

#4. Solve the riddle: What shape am I? I have more than 3 vertices. I have fewer than 6 sides.

#5. Use your centimeter ruler to measure the sides of the rectangle. Find its perimeter.

6.

 ○ ○ ○ NH ○

7.

G ○   J ○   L ○   M ○

8.

   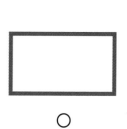

○   ○   ○   ○

9.

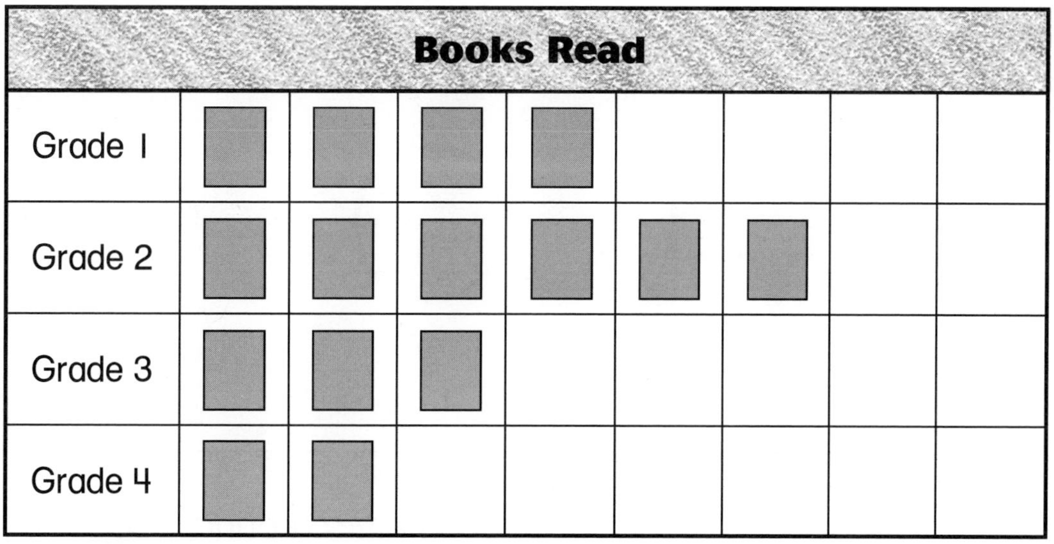

Books Read							
Grade 1	�damaged						

Books Read							
Grade 1	▪	▪	▪	▪			
Grade 2	▪	▪	▪	▪	▪	▪	
Grade 3	▪	▪	▪				
Grade 4	▪	▪					

Each ▪ stands for 2 books.

2 ○   4 ○   12 ○   NH ○

Oral Directions *Mark the correct answer. NH means "Not here." Mark it whenever the answer is not given.*

#6. Solve the riddle. Who am I? I can roll. I have two faces.
#7. Which letter has a line of symmetry?

#8. Which shape could you make if you put the two triangles together?
#9. The pictograph shows how many books were read in one day in a school book-reading contest. How many more books did the second grade read than the first grade?

306 three hundred six

Fractions and Probability

Diagnosing Readiness
for Chapter 10

1. How many equal parts does the spinner have? ____

2. What fraction of the spinner is green? ____

3. Which fraction is the least?

$\frac{1}{2}$ $\frac{1}{3}$ $\frac{1}{4}$

4. $\frac{1}{3}$ of the counters are red. How many are red? ____

5. If you put all the counters in one bag, which color counter would you be more likely to pick if you didn't look in the bag: yellow or red? _____

To the Family

Looking Back

In Grade 1 children were introduced to fractions up to $\frac{1}{4}$. Children also used patterns to predict what comes next in a series of numbers.

Chapter 10

Fractions and Probability

Children will work with equal parts, compare unit fractions, and find fractions of a group. They will also conduct simple probability experiments to determine possible outcomes.

Looking Ahead

Children will return to Fractions and Probability in Grade 3. They will learn to add and subtract fractions, and convert fractions to decimal equivalents. They will also conduct simple probability experiments to determine possible outcomes.

Page 307 Your child solved problems that review math skills from previous chapters and will help your child with the skills in Chapter 10.

Math at Home In the course of daily routines, help your child practice fractions and probability by asking him or her to predict outcomes, compare shapes, and tell you how to find a fraction of a set of objects.

Math Literature Read stories and do activities with your child. Look for the following books in your local library.
Eating Fractions by Bruce McMillan (Scholastic, 1991)
Fraction Fun by David A. Adler (Holiday House, 1997)

California Content Standards in Chapter 10 Lessons*

	Teach and Practice	Practice		Teach and Practice	Practice
Number Sense			1.2 Represent the same data set in more than one way (e.g., bar graphs and charts with tallies.)	11	
4.1 (🔑) Recognize, name, and compare unit fractions from 1/12 to 1/2.	1–5, 8	9, 10	1.4 Ask and answer simple questions related to data representations.		11
4.2 (🔑) Recognize fractions of a whole and parts of a group (e.g., one-fourth of a pie, two-thirds of 15 balls).	1–6, 9, 10		**Mathematical Reasoning**		
4.3 (🔑) Know that when all fractional parts are included, such as four-fourths, the result is equal to the whole and to one.	5, 7	10	2.0 Students solve problems and justify their reasoning.	12	13
Statistics, Data Analysis, and Probability			2.1 Defend the reasoning used and justify the procedures selected.		13
1.0 (🔑) Students collect numerical data and record, organize, display, and interpret the data on bar graphs and other representations.		11–13	2.2 Make precise calculations and check validity of the results in the context of the problem.	10	
1.1 Record numerical data in systematic ways, keeping track of what has been counted.	11–13				

* The symbol (🔑) indicates a key standard as designated in the Mathematics Framework for California Public Schools.
Full statements of the California Content Standards are found at the beginning of this book following the Table of Contents.

Name_____ **Equal Parts**

Each shape shows equal parts.

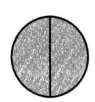 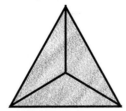 

halves   thirds   fourths
2 equal parts   3 equal parts   4 equal parts

Write the number of parts.
Circle **equal** or **not equal**.

1. 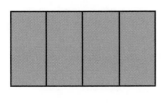 ⟨equal⟩ not equal _2_ parts	2. equal not equal _____ parts
3. 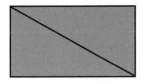 equal not equal _____ parts	4. equal not equal _____ parts
5. 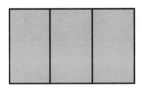 equal not equal _____ parts	6. 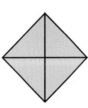 equal not equal _____ parts
7. 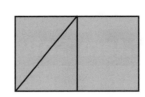 equal not equal _____ parts	8. 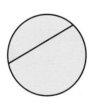 equal not equal _____ parts

California Content Standards Number Sense 4.2
Recognize fractions of a whole and parts of a group. Number Sense 4.1.

three hundred nine   **309**

Draw lines to show equal parts.

9. halves
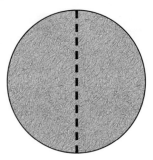

10. fourths

11. fourths

12. halves

13. thirds

14. fourths

 **Problem Solving**

Solve.

15. Sam and Lydia want to fold a piece of paper into fourths. Draw lines to show 2 different ways they could fold the paper. Describe another way.

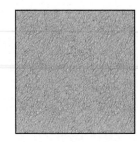

 **Home Activity** Have your child make equal parts by folding a sheet of paper into 2, 4, and 8 equal parts. Homework Workbook 10-1

Name_____ **Understanding Fractions to Fourths**

A fraction can name one equal part of a whole shape.

I of 2 equal parts	I of 3 equal parts	I of 4 equal parts
$\frac{1}{2}$ 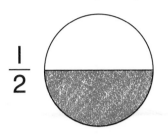	$\frac{1}{3}$ 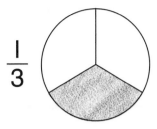	$\frac{1}{4}$ 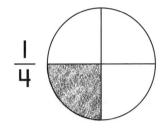
one half	one third	one fourth

Write the fraction of the shaded part.

I.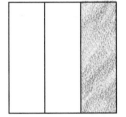
_____

2.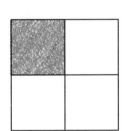
_____

3.
_____

4.
_____

5.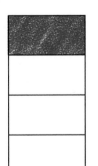
_____

6.
_____

7.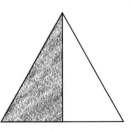
_____

8.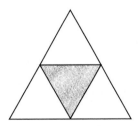
_____

9.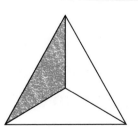
_____

California Content Standards *Number Sense 4.1 Recognize, name, and compare unit fractions from $\frac{1}{12}$ to $\frac{1}{2}$. Number Sense 4.2.*

Color to show the fraction.

10. $\frac{1}{2}$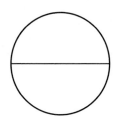

11. $\frac{1}{3}$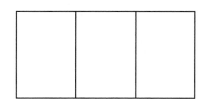

12. $\frac{1}{3}$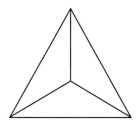

13. $\frac{1}{3}$

14. $\frac{1}{2}$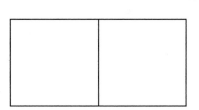

15. $\frac{1}{4}$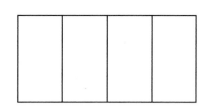

16. $\frac{1}{4}$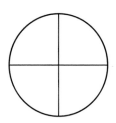

17. $\frac{1}{2}$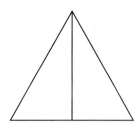

Problem Solving

18. Ronald wants to eat $\frac{1}{2}$ of a pizza. Color the $\frac{1}{2}$ that Ronald wants to eat. Susan wants to eat $\frac{1}{3}$ of a pizza. Color the $\frac{1}{3}$ piece that Susan will eat. Who is eating more pizza? _____

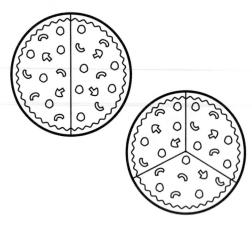

Home Activity Ask your child to make pictures showing $\frac{1}{2}$, $\frac{1}{3}$, and $\frac{1}{4}$. Homework Workbook 10-2

Name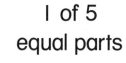_____ **Fractions to Eighths**

I of 5 equal parts	I of 6 equal parts	I of 7 equal parts	I of 8 equal parts
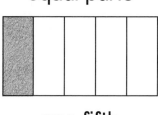	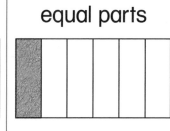	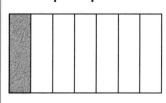	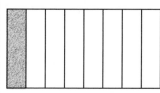
one fifth	one sixth	one seventh	one eighth
$\dfrac{1}{5}$	$\dfrac{1}{6}$	$\dfrac{1}{7}$	$\dfrac{1}{8}$

1. Color $\dfrac{1}{5}$ of each shape.

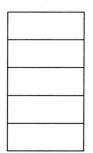
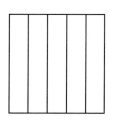

2. Color $\dfrac{1}{6}$ of each shape.

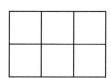
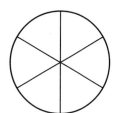
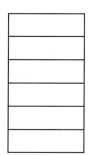

3. Color $\dfrac{1}{8}$ of each shape.

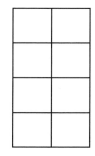
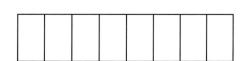
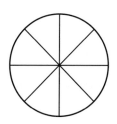

California Content Standards *Number Sense 4.1 Recognize, name, and compare unit fractions from $\frac{1}{12}$ to $\frac{1}{2}$. Number Sense 4.2.*

4. Circle the shape that shows $\frac{1}{7}$.

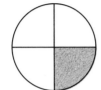 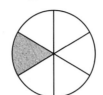 

5. Circle the shape that shows $\frac{1}{5}$.

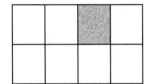 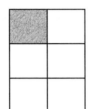 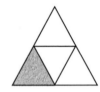

6. Circle the shape that shows $\frac{1}{8}$.

7. Circle the shape that shows $\frac{1}{6}$.

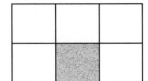 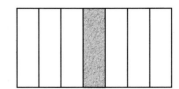

Problem Solving

8. A game spinner has 8 equal parts.
   Color each part a different color.

   What fraction is each part? _____

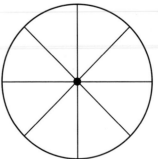

Home Activity Ask your child to draw pictures of objects divided into $\frac{1}{5}$, $\frac{1}{6}$, $\frac{1}{7}$, and $\frac{1}{8}$. Homework Workbook 10-3

Name_____ **Fractions to Twelfths**

1 of 9 equal parts	1 of 10 equal parts	1 of 11 equal parts	1 of 12 equal parts
	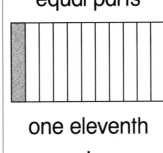		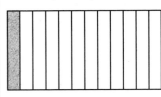
one ninth	one tenth	one eleventh	one twelfth
$\dfrac{1}{9}$	$\dfrac{1}{10}$	$\dfrac{1}{11}$	$\dfrac{1}{12}$

How many equal parts are in each shape?

1.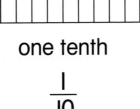

_____ equal parts

2.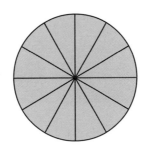

_____ equal parts

3.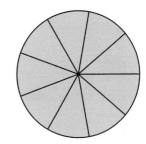

_____ equal parts

4.

_____ equal parts

5.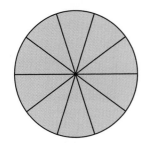

_____ equal parts

6.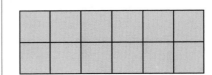

_____ equal parts

7.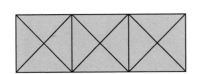

_____ equal parts

8.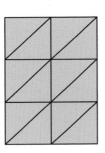

_____ equal parts

9.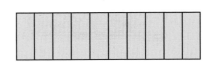

_____ equal parts

California Content Standards *Number Sense 4.1 Recognize, name, and compare unit fractions from $\frac{1}{12}$ to $\frac{1}{2}$. Number Sense 4.2.*

Jill had to fix one broken pane
in each window.
Write an X to show the broken pane.
Then write the fraction.

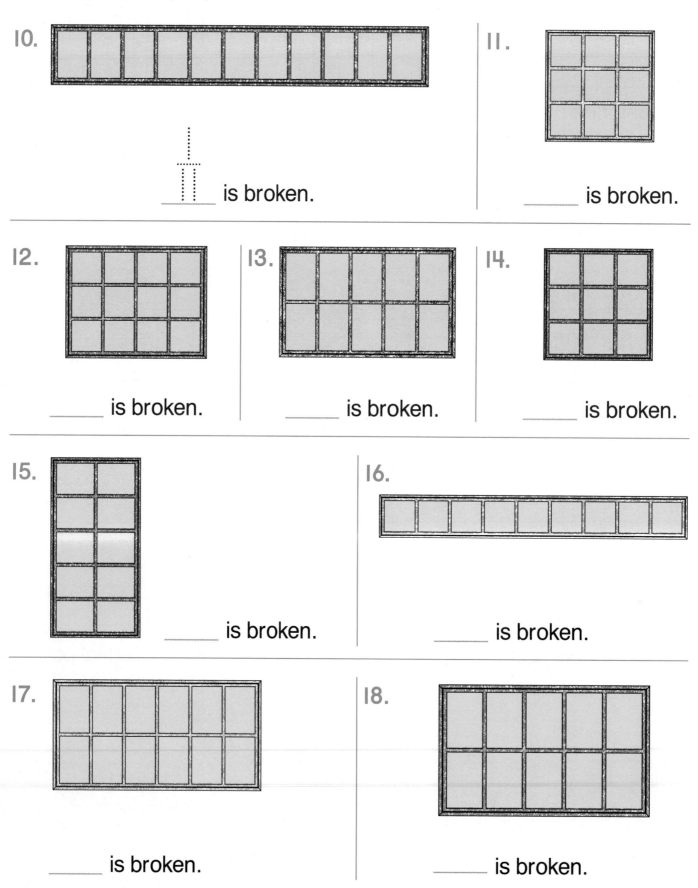

10. _____ is broken.

11. _____ is broken.

12. _____ is broken.

13. _____ is broken.

14. _____ is broken.

15. _____ is broken.

16. _____ is broken.

17. _____ is broken.

18. _____ is broken.

Home Activity Ask your child to draw rectangles with 9, 10, 11, and 12 equal sections. Have him or her represent the fraction by coloring one section of each rectangle. Homework Workbook 10-4

Name_____ **Comparing Unit Fractions**

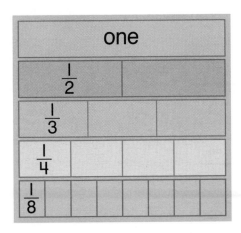

Use your fraction strips. Complete the chart to compare
fractions to the fraction in the middle.

	Fractions That Are Less		Fractions That Are Greater
1.	$\frac{1}{8}$	$\frac{1}{2}$	
2.		$\frac{1}{3}$	
3.		$\frac{1}{4}$	
4.		$\frac{1}{8}$	

> means is greater than
< means is less than

$\frac{1}{8} < \frac{1}{2}$ $\frac{1}{4} > \frac{1}{8}$

Write > or <. Use the chart to help you.

5. $\frac{1}{8}$ ◯ $\frac{1}{3}$ 6. $\frac{1}{2}$ ◯ $\frac{1}{4}$ 7. one ◯ $\frac{1}{8}$

8. $\frac{1}{2}$ ◯ one   9. $\frac{1}{3}$ ◯ $\frac{1}{4}$ 10. $\frac{1}{8}$ ◯ $\frac{1}{2}$

California Content Standards *Number Sense 4.1 Recognize,
name, and compare unit fractions from $\frac{1}{12}$ to $\frac{1}{2}$. Number Sense
4.2, 4.3.*

Write the fraction that tells how much is shaded.
For each pair, circle the fraction that is greater.

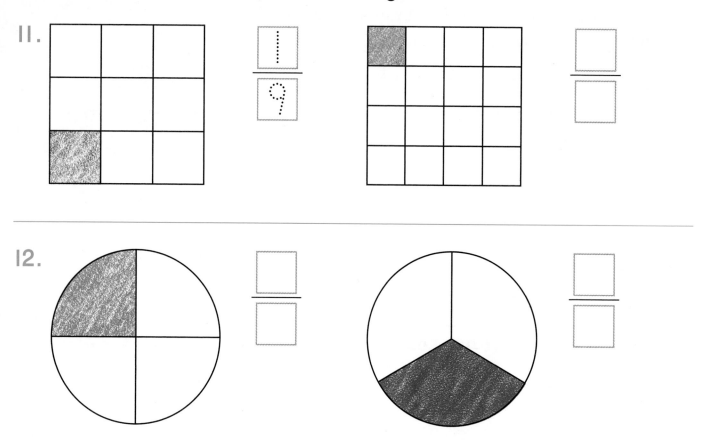

11.

$\frac{1}{9}$

12.

Write the fraction that tells how much is shaded.
For each pair, circle the fraction that is less.

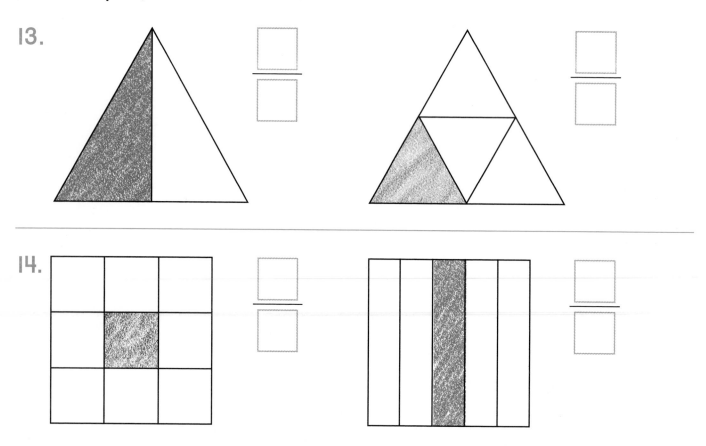

13.

14.

Home Activity Ask your child to tell you whether $\frac{1}{4}$ or $\frac{1}{2}$ is
the greater number. Have him or her explain why. Homework
Workbook 10-5

Name_____ **Working with Fractions**

A fraction can name more than one equal part of a whole shape.

The fractions name the number of equal parts that are shaded.

2 of 5 equal parts

$\frac{2}{5}$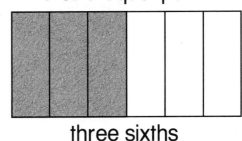

two fifths

3 of 6 equal parts

$\frac{3}{6}$

three sixths

Circle the fraction that names the shaded part.

1.

$\frac{2}{5}$ $\left(\frac{3}{5}\right)$ $\frac{4}{6}$

2.

$\frac{2}{6}$ $\frac{2}{8}$ $\frac{3}{6}$

3.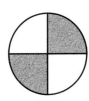

$\frac{2}{3}$ $\frac{1}{4}$ $\frac{2}{4}$

4.

$\frac{4}{7}$ $\frac{3}{6}$ $\frac{3}{7}$

5.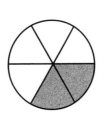

$\frac{2}{5}$ $\frac{4}{5}$ $\frac{2}{6}$

6.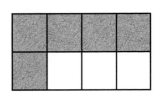

$\frac{5}{6}$ $\frac{5}{8}$ $\frac{6}{8}$

7.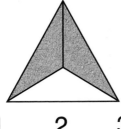

$\frac{1}{2}$ $\frac{2}{3}$ $\frac{3}{3}$

8.

$\frac{3}{4}$ $\frac{3}{5}$ $\frac{4}{4}$

9.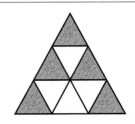

$\frac{5}{8}$ $\frac{5}{9}$ $\frac{7}{10}$

Color to show the number of shaded parts.
Write the fraction that names the shaded parts.

10.   2 shaded parts

$\frac{2}{8}$

11.   4 shaded parts

_____

12.   2 shaded parts

_____

13.   3 shaded parts

_____

14.   2 shaded parts

_____

15.   5 shaded parts

_____

16.   2 shaded parts

_____

17.   3 shaded parts

_____

Math Reasoning

Visual Thinking

18. Color each square to show the fraction. Circle the fractions that show the same amount of colored space.

$\frac{1}{2}$ $\frac{1}{3}$ $\frac{2}{4}$

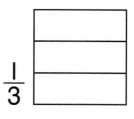

Home Activity Draw a simple shape, divide it into thirds or fourths, and shade more than one part. Ask your child to identify the fraction that names the shaded parts. Homework Workbook 10-6

Name_____ **Diagnostic Checkpoint**

Write the number of parts.

1.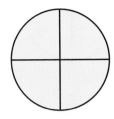

_____ parts

2.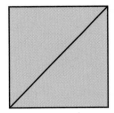

_____ parts

3.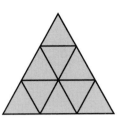

_____ parts

Color $\frac{1}{6}$ of each shape.

4.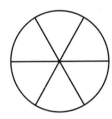

5.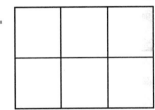

6.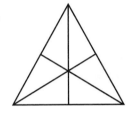

Write >, <, or =.

7. $\frac{1}{3}$ $\frac{1}{2}$

8. $\frac{1}{2}$ $\frac{1}{8}$

9. $\frac{1}{4}$ $\frac{1}{2}$

Write the fraction that tells how much is shaded.

10.

☐
—
☐

11.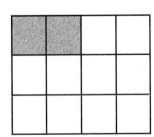

☐
—
☐

12.

☐
—
☐

Name_____

1.

○   ○   ○   ○

2.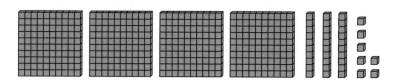

734   400   437   430

○   ○   ○   ○

3.

○   ○   ○   ○

4.

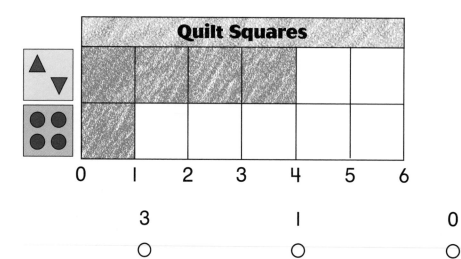

4   3   1   0

○   ○   ○   ○

Oral Directions *Mark the correct answer. NH means "Not here." Mark it whenever the answer is not given.*

#1. Mark under the clock that reads 11:45.
#2. Mark under the answer that tells how many hundreds, tens, and ones there are in the picture.
#3. Mark under the shape that shows $\frac{1}{5}$.
#4. How many more triangle quilt squares are there than circle squares?

Name_____ **Fractions Equal to One**

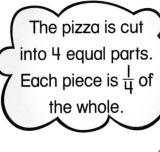

The pizza is cut into 4 equal parts. Each piece is $\frac{1}{4}$ of the whole.

If we eat all 4 pieces, we will have eaten $\frac{4}{4}$ of the pizza.

$\frac{4}{4} =$ I whole.

What other fractions equal I whole?

Color to show I whole.
Write the fraction that equals I whole.

1.  $\dfrac{3}{3} = $ I

2. 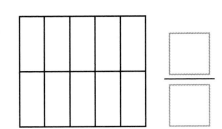 $\dfrac{\square}{\square} = $ I

3. 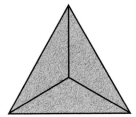 $\dfrac{\square}{\square} = $ I

4. 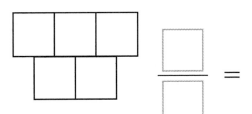 $\dfrac{\square}{\square} = $ I

5. 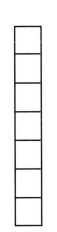 $\dfrac{\square}{\square} = $ I

6. 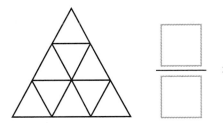 $\dfrac{\square}{\square} = $ I

California Content Standards *Number Sense 4.3 Know that when all fractional parts are included, such as four-fourths, the result is equal to the whole and to one.*

Color to show 1 whole.

Write the fraction that equals 1 whole.

7. 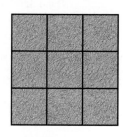 $\frac{9}{9} = 1$

8. 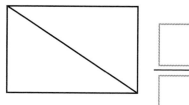 $\frac{\Box}{\Box} = 1$

9. 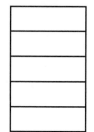 $\frac{\Box}{\Box} = 1$

10. 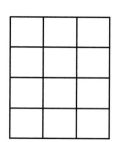 $\frac{\Box}{\Box} = 1$

11. 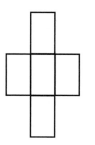 $\frac{\Box}{\Box} = 1$

12. 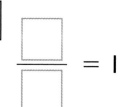 $\frac{\Box}{\Box} = 1$

13.  $\frac{\Box}{\Box} = 1$

14. $\frac{\Box}{\Box} = 1$

 Math Reasoning

15. If a rectangle were cut into 100 equal parts, what fraction of the rectangle would equal one whole? Explain.

_____

_____

Home Activity Ask your child to tell you how many fifths would equal one whole (5). Homework Workbook 10-7

Name_____ **Equal Fractions**

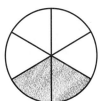

I can see that two sixths is the same size as one third. That means $\frac{2}{6} = \frac{1}{3}$.

$$\frac{2}{6} = \frac{1}{3}$$

Write the fractions that make each statement true.

1.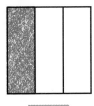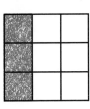

$$\frac{1}{3} = \frac{3}{9}$$

2.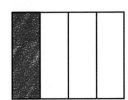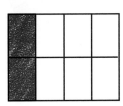

$$\frac{\square}{\square} = \frac{\square}{\square}$$

3.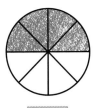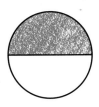

$$\frac{\square}{\square} = \frac{\square}{\square}$$

4.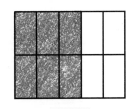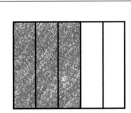

$$\frac{\square}{\square} = \frac{\square}{\square}$$

5.

$$\frac{\square}{\square} = \frac{\square}{\square}$$

6.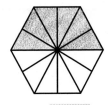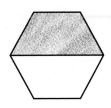

$$\frac{\square}{\square} = \frac{\square}{\square}$$

California Content Standards *Number Sense 4.1*
Recognize, name, and compare unit fractions from $\frac{1}{12}$ to $\frac{1}{2}$.

Write fractions that make each statement true.

7.

$$\frac{\boxed{}}{\boxed{}} = \frac{\boxed{}}{\boxed{}}$$

8.

$$\frac{\boxed{}}{\boxed{}} = \frac{\boxed{}}{\boxed{}}$$

9.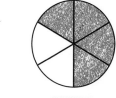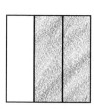

$$\frac{\boxed{}}{\boxed{}} = \frac{\boxed{}}{\boxed{}}$$

10.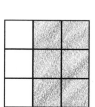

$$\frac{\boxed{}}{\boxed{}} = \frac{\boxed{}}{\boxed{}}$$

11.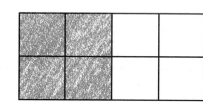

$$\frac{\boxed{}}{\boxed{}} = \frac{\boxed{}}{\boxed{}} = \frac{\boxed{}}{\boxed{}}$$

Math Reasoning

12. $\dfrac{1}{2} = \dfrac{2}{\boxed{}} = \dfrac{3}{\boxed{}} = \dfrac{4}{\boxed{}} = \dfrac{5}{\boxed{}} = \dfrac{6}{\boxed{}}$

Home Activity Draw two squares that are the same size. Have your child color one square to show halves and the other square to show fourths. Then ask your child to name different fractions that are equal. For example, $\frac{1}{2} = \frac{3}{6}$ or $\frac{1}{3} = \frac{2}{6}$.

Homework Workbook 10-8

326 three hundred twenty-six

Name_____ **Fractions of a Group**

What You Need

12 red and yellow
two-sided counters

cup

1. Put counters in the cup and shake.

2. Spill them out. Color to show how the counters landed.

3. Write the fractions.

---

1. Use 4 counters.

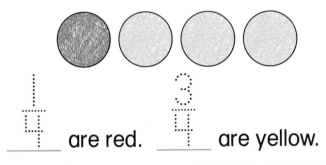

$\frac{1}{4}$ _____ are red. $\frac{3}{4}$ _____ are yellow.

2. Use 5 counters.

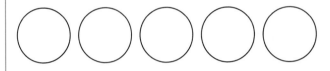

_____ are red. _____ are yellow.

---

3. Use 6 counters.

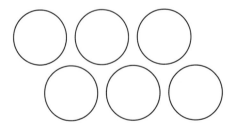

_____ are red. _____ are yellow.

4. Use 8 counters.

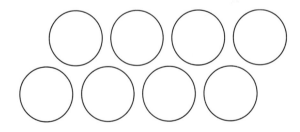

_____ are red. _____ are yellow.

---

5. Use 12 counters.

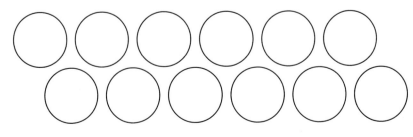

_____ are red. _____ are yellow.

California Content Standards *Number Sense 4.2 Recognize fractions of a whole and parts of a group. Also Number Sense 4.1.*

three hundred twenty-seven **327**

Find $\frac{2}{3}$ of 12 counters.

Show 12 counters.

Make 3 groups.

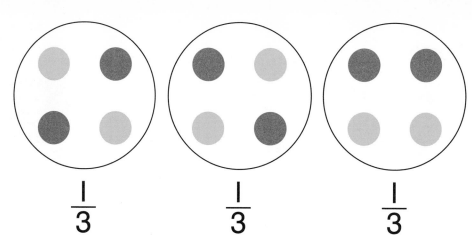

$\frac{1}{3}$ $\frac{1}{3}$ $\frac{1}{3}$

$\frac{1}{3}$ of 12 is 4.

It is the number of counters in one group.

$\frac{2}{3}$ of 12 is 8.

It is the number of counters in two groups.

Circle part of each group to show the fraction.

6. $\frac{2}{5}$

7. $\frac{5}{6}$

8. $\frac{3}{5}$

9. $\frac{3}{4}$

10. $\frac{2}{3}$

Home Activity Show your child 6 pennies, some placed heads up and other tails up. Ask your child what fraction names the pennies that are heads up. Homework Workbook 10-9

Name_____

Coach Green made 15 hamburgers for the members of her T-Ball team.

If she puts $\frac{1}{3}$ of the hamburgers on each plate, how many burgers are on each plate?

This means that $\frac{1}{3}$ of 15 is 5.

I put the hamburgers into 3 equal groups. Each group has 5 burgers.

Solve each problem.
Use counters to help you.

1. Katrina has 12 pieces of fruit. If $\frac{2}{4}$ are mangos, how many are mangos?

   $\frac{2}{4}$ of 12 = 6

2. Lenny's Skate Shop has 10 pairs of Zippy skates. Lenny sold $\frac{2}{5}$ of the Zippy skates. How many did he sell?

   $\frac{2}{5}$ of 10 = _____

3. Frisky the cat has 6 kittens. If $\frac{2}{3}$ of the kittens have white paws, how many have white paws?

   $\frac{2}{3}$ of 6 = _____

4. Randy read 8 books. $\frac{1}{4}$ of the books were about animals. How many books were about animals?

   $\frac{1}{4}$ of 8 = _____

California Content Standards *Number Sense 4.2 Recognize fractions of a whole and parts of a group. Mathematical Reasoning 2.2. Also Number Sense 4.1, 4.3.*

Solve each problem.
Use counters to help you.

5. There are 10 muffins. $\frac{2}{5}$ of the muffins are cherry. How many muffins are cherry?

$\frac{2}{5}$ of 10 = **4**

6. Mom buys 8 apples. $\frac{3}{4}$ of the apples are yellow. How many apples are yellow?

$\frac{3}{4}$ of 8 = _____

7. Sue has 8 pennies. $\frac{2}{4}$ of the pennies were minted in 2000. How many pennies were minted in 2000?

$\frac{2}{4}$ of 8 = _____

8. Dad made 16 sandwiches. $\frac{1}{2}$ of the sandwiches have cheese. How many sandwiches are made with cheese?

$\frac{1}{2}$ of 16 = _____

9. Keiko has 12 stamps. $\frac{6}{6}$ of the stamps are square. How many of the stamps are square?

$\frac{6}{6}$ of 12 = _____

10. Jim sees 16 parked cars. $\frac{5}{8}$ of the cars are big. How many cars are big?

$\frac{5}{8}$ of 16 = _____

Math Reasoning

Solve. Explain how to find the answer.

11. A calendar has 12 months. $\frac{2}{3}$ of the names of the months have an *R* in them. How many months do **not** have an *R* in them? _____

Home Activity Show your child 12 objects, such as beans. Ask him or her to tell you how to find $\frac{3}{4}$ of 12. (9) Homework Workbook 10-10

Name_____ **Recording Data from a Survey**

Take a survey. Ask 10 classmates to choose the indoor activity they like best. Make a tally mark for each answer. Then write the total.

Favorite Indoor Activities		
Activity	Tally	Total
Playing board games		
Doing arts and crafts		
Reading stories		
Playing computer games		

Use the chart to answer each question.

1. Which activity was chosen the most?

   _____

2. Which activity was chosen the least?

   _____

3. Suppose you asked all your classmates. Which activity do you think would be chosen the most? Why?

   _____

   _____

4. Which activity do you like best?

   _____

California Content Standards *Statistics, Data Analysis, and Probability 1.1 Record numerical data in systematic ways, keeping track of what has been counted. Statistics, Data Analysis, and Probability 1.2. Also Statistics, Data Analysis, and Probablity 1.0, 1.4.*

Terry took a survey. He asked children in his neighborhood to choose the activity they liked best.

5. Complete the chart to show what Terry found out.

Favorite Outdoor Activities		
Activity	Tally	Total
Bike riding	⊥⊥⊥⊤ ⅠⅠ	7
Jumping rope	ⅠⅠ	
In-line skating	ⅠⅠⅠⅠ	
Playing hide-and-seek	⊥⊥⊥⊤	

6. Make a bar graph. Color one box for each time an activity was chosen.

Favorite Outdoor Activities

Bike riding

Jumping rope

In-line skating

Playing hide-and-seek

0   1   2   3   4   5   6   7   8

Use the graph to answer each question.

7. Which activity was chosen the most? _____

8. Which activity was chosen the least? _____

9. How many more children liked bike riding better

than in-line skating? _____

10. How many children did Terry survey?

_____

Home Activity Ask your child to explain how he or she collected information and what he or she learned. Homework Workbook 10-11

Name_____ **Problem-Solving Strategy**

Make a Table

A bag has 5 blue cubes and 5 red cubes in it. How many times can you pick a blue cube from the bag in 20 tries?

Understand

You need to do the experiment.
You need a way to record your results.

Plan

You can make a table to record your results.

Solve

Do the experiment.
Replace the cube after each pick.
Make a tally mark by the color for each cube you draw.
After 20 tries, write the totals.

Color	Tally	Total
blue		
red		

Look Back

Do you have 20 tally marks in all?
Answer the question.
How many times out of 20 tries did you pick a blue cube?

_____ times

 California Content Standards *Statistics, Data Analysis, and Probability 1.1 Record numerical data in systematic ways, keeping track of what has been counted. Mathematical Reasoning 2.0. Also Statistics, Data Analysis, and Probability 1.0.*

With a classmate, find the total of the two numbers after you roll two number cubes with numbers 1–6. Roll the cubes at least 20 times.

If you roll a 1 and a 2, record a tally mark in the 3 row.

1. Record your data in a table.

Roll	Tallies	Total
1		
2		
3		
4		
5		
6		
7		
8		
9		
10		
11		
12		

2. Which number came up the most often? _____

3. How does a table help you? _____

_____

Home Activity With your child, look for tables in newspapers, magazines, encyclopedias, or other sources and talk about what they show. Homework Workbook 10-12

Name_____ **Probability**

Put red and blue cubes in a bag. What color are you more likely to pick?

Think: How many of each color cube are in the bag?

Pick 1 cube without looking. Color a box to show your pick. Put the cube back. Repeat 9 more times.

1. Put 5 red and 5 blue cubes in the bag.
   What color are you more likely to pick?   red   blue

Pick	1	2	3	4	5	6	7	8	9	10
Color										

2. Put 2 red and 8 blue cubes in the bag.
   What color are you more likely to pick?   red   blue

Pick	1	2	3	4	5	6	7	8	9	10
Color										

3. Put 1 red and 9 blue cubes in the bag.
   What color are you more likely to pick?   red   blue

Pick	1	2	3	4	5	6	7	8	9	10
Color										

California Content Standards *Statistics, Data Analysis, and Probability 1.1 Record numerical data in systematic ways, keeping track of what has been counted. Also Statistics, Data Analysis, and Probability 1.0, Mathematical Reasoning 2.0, 2.1.*

three hundred thirty-five **335**

Which color are you more likely to pick? Circle the answer.

4.

red   (blue)

5.
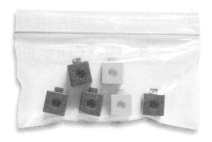

red   yellow

6.

orange   green

7.

purple   yellow

8.

blue   green

9.
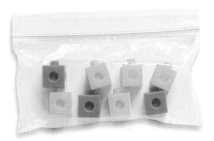

yellow   green

 Math Reasoning

10. Suppose you put 5 red cubes, 5 yellow cubes, and 5 blue cubes in a bag. You pick one cube, record the color, and put the cube back. You do this 20 times. Which color do you think you would pick the most? Explain.

Home Activity Ask your child to put 3 red crayons and 1 blue crayon in a bag. Have your child tell which color is more likely to be picked. Homework Workbook 10-13

1. Write the fractions to make the statement true.

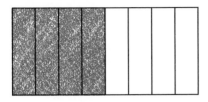

$$\frac{\square}{\square} = \frac{\square}{\square}$$

Write the fraction for each color.

2.

_____ are red. _____ are yellow.

3.

_____ are red. _____ are yellow.

4. Which colors are you more likely to pick? Circle the answer.

yellow   green

blue   red

Favorite Fruit Survey		
Grapes	ЖНГ ІІІ	8
Apples	ІІІІ	4
Cherries	ЖНГ ІІІІ	9
Guavas	І	1

5. How many more people chose cherries than guavas? _____

6. Which fruit was chosen the most? _____

Name_____

1.	415	615	425	215	435
		○	○	○	○

2.	$48 - 30 = \square$	38	18	20	8
		○	○	○	○

3.	$80 + 20 = \square$	90	60	100	10
		○	○	○	○

4.

$3.81	$1.54	$3.00	$3.76
○	○	○	○

5.

51    18

$51 - 18 = 33$	$33 + 18 = 51$	$51 + 18 = 69$	$18 + 18 = 36$
○	○	○	○

6.	$30 > 20$	$50 > 49$	$38 < 36$	$11 > 10$
	○	○	○	○

Oral Directions *Mark the correct answer. NH means "Not here." Mark it whenever the answer is not given.*

#1. What number is 2 hundreds less than 415?
#2. Subtract. Count back by tens.

#3. Add. Use mental math.
#4. What is the total amount?
#5. Brad has 51 pennies. Ryan gives him 18 more. Choose the number sentence to tell how many pennies Brad has now.
#6. Mark the statement that is NOT true.

Name_____

Write the fraction of the shaded part.

1.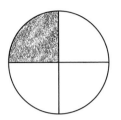

_____

2.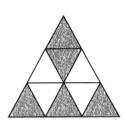

_____

Circle part of each group to show the fraction.

3. $\frac{2}{5}$

4. $\frac{1}{3}$

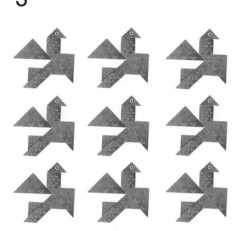

Draw lines to show equal parts.

5. fourths

6. halves

Use fraction strips. Write $>$, $<$, or $=$.

7. $\frac{1}{3}$ ◯ $\frac{1}{9}$

8. 1 ◯ $\frac{4}{5}$

9. $\frac{2}{10}$ ◯ $\frac{1}{5}$

Which color are you more likely to pick?
Circle the answer.

10.

red   blue

11.

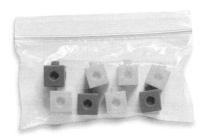

yellow   green

Solve.

12. Humble the dog has 6 puppies. If $\frac{2}{3}$ of the puppies are sleeping, how many are sleeping?

$\frac{2}{3}$ of 6 = _____ puppies

13. Emily and her Dad cooked 8 hot dogs. They ate $\frac{1}{4}$ of the hot dogs. How many hot dogs did they eat?

$\frac{1}{4}$ of 8 = _____ hot dogs

Cubes were picked from a bag.
The results are written in the table.

Color	Tally	Total
red	I I I	
blue	H H H	
yellow	H H H I I	
green	I I	
white	I	
pink	I I I	

14. Write the totals in the table.

15. Which color was picked more often, red or white?

_____

16. Which color was picked more often, yellow or blue?

_____

17. How many times in all were cubes picked from the bag?

_____

1.

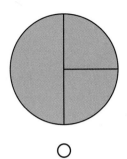 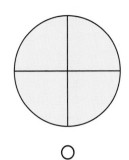 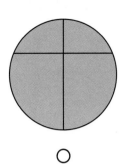

○   ○   ○   ○

2.

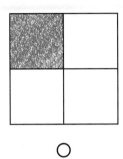 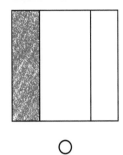 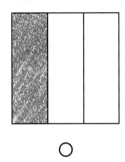

○   ○   ○   ○

3.

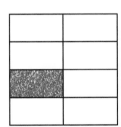

$\frac{1}{2}$ $\frac{1}{8}$ $\frac{1}{3}$ $\frac{1}{10}$

○   ○   ○   ○

4. $\frac{1}{2} > \frac{1}{4}$ $\frac{3}{8} < \frac{1}{12}$ $\frac{10}{10} = 1$ $\frac{1}{9} < \frac{1}{3}$

○   ○   ○   ○

5.

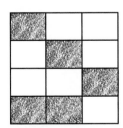

$\frac{5}{7}$ $\frac{5}{10}$ $\frac{5}{12}$ $\frac{6}{12}$

○   ○   ○   ○

Oral Directions *Mark the correct answer. NH means "Not here." Mark it whenever the answer is not given.*

#1. Which shape shows equal parts?
#2. Which shape shows $\frac{1}{3}$?
#3. What fraction of the shape at the left is shaded green?
#4. Mark the statement that is NOT true.
#5. What fraction of the rectangle is shaded blue?

6.

$\frac{3}{5}$	$\frac{3}{9}$	$\frac{4}{7}$	$\frac{3}{7}$
○	○	○	○

7.

$\frac{3}{3}$	$\frac{12}{12}$	$\frac{10}{10}$	$\frac{1}{2}$
○	○	○	○

8.

4 🥕	2 🥕	6	8
○	○	○	○

9.

$\frac{1}{12}$	$\frac{1}{7}$	$\frac{1}{6}$	$\frac{1}{10}$
○	○	○	○

Cube Color	Total
red	3
blue	10
green	4
yellow	5

10.

red	blue	green	yellow
○	○	○	○

11.

red	blue	green	yellow
○	○	○	○

12.

10	9	22	NH
○	○	○	○

Oral Directions *Mark the correct answer. NH means "Not here." Mark it whenever the answer is not given.*

#6. What fraction of the group is red?
#7. What fraction does not equal one whole?

#8. Tina had four carrots. She gave half of them to her brother. How many carrots did Tina give her brother?
#9. Mark the greatest fraction.
#10. Which cube color was picked most often?
#11. Which cube color was picked least often?
#12. How many times in all were cubes picked?

Multiplication

Diagnosing Readiness
for Chapter 11

2. Add.

   $3 + 3 + 3 =$ _____

1. Skip count by 2s.

   2, _____, 6, _____, 10

3. Skip count by 5s.

   5, 10, 15, _____, 25, _____

4. Look at the field above. Write an addition sentence to tell how many trees there are on both sides of the field.

   _____ _____ = ☐

5. Skip count by 10s.

   10, 20, _____, _____, 50

To the Family

Looking Back	Chapter 11	Looking Ahead
In Grade 1 children learned skip counting. In Chapter 1 children reviewed basic addition facts.	**Multiplication** Children model and solve simple problems involving multiplication using arrays, repeated addition, and counting by multiples. Children also memorize 2s, 5s, and 10s facts.	In Grade 3 children will memorize the multiplication table for numbers between 1 and 10 and multiply by one-digit numbers.

Page 343 Your child solved problems that review math skills from previous chapters and will help your child with the skills in Chapter 11.

Math at Home The chapter theme is equal groups. Help your child place small objects such as buttons or pennies in equal groups and then practice the corresponding multiplication facts.

Math Literature Read math or theme-related stories with your child. Look for the following books in your local library.
The Amazing Multiplication Pop-Up Book by Kate Petty (Dutton Children's Books, 1998)
Each Orange Had 8 Slices by Paul Gigant, Jr. (Mulberry Books, 1992)

California Content Standards in Chapter 11 Lessons*

	Teach and Practice	Practice		Teach and Practice	Practice
Number Sense			**2.1** Recognize, describe, and extend patterns and determine the next term in linear patterns (e.g., 4, 8, 12 . . . ; the number of ears on one horse, two horses, three horses, four horses).		5, 9
2.2 (🔑) Find the sum or difference of two whole numbers up to three digits long.		11			
3.1 (🔑) Use repeated addition, arrays, and counting by multiples to do multiplication.	1–7	11	**2.2** Solve problems involving simple number patterns.		10
3.3 (🔑) Know the multiplication tables of 2s, 5s, and 10s (to "times 10") and commit them to memory.	8–10		**Mathematical Reasoning**		
Algebra and Functions			**1.0** Students make decisions about how to set up a problem.		6
1.2 Relate problem situations to number sentences involving addition and subtraction.	2	4, 11	**1.1** Determine the approach, materials, and strategies to be used.	7	4, 8
1.5 (Gr. 3) Recognize and use the commutative and associative properites of multiplication.	5		**1.2** Use tools, such as manipulatives or sketches, to model problems.	6	1, 3, 7
Statistics, Data Analysis, and Probability			**2.1** Defend the reasoning used and justify the procedures selected.		7, 8
2.0 (🔑) Students demonstrate an understanding of patterns and how patterns grow and describe them in general ways.		5, 9, 10	**3.0** Students note connections between one problem and another.	11	9, 10

* The symbol (🔑) indicates a key standard as designated in the Mathematics Framework for California Public Schools.
Full statements of the California Content Standards are found at the beginning of this book following the Table of Contents.

Name_____

Modeling Multiplication

What you need

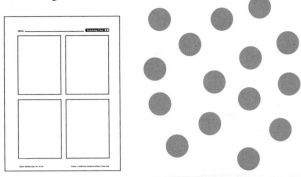

Workmat 6 and counters

3 groups of 4 . . . that's 12 in all.

Put counters in equal groups.
Complete the chart.

	Number of Groups	Number in Each Group	Number in All
1.	3	4	12
2.	3	5	
3.	2	3	
4.	4	3	
5.	2	2	
6.	4	1	
7.	3	2	
8.	2	5	
9.	1	4	
10.	4	2	

California Content Standards *Number Sense 3.1 (🔑)*
Use repeated addition, arrays, and counting by multiples to do
multiplication. Also Mathematical Reasoning 1.2.

Draw to show equal groups.
Write how many in all.

11. Make 3 groups of 2.

6
___

in all

12. Make 2 groups of 4.

___

in all

13. Make 4 groups of 4.

___

in all

14. Make 2 groups of 5.

___

in all

15. Make 3 groups of 4.

___

in all

16. Make 3 groups of 1.

___

in all

17. Make _____ groups of _____.

___

in all

346 three hundred forty-six

🏠 **Home Activity** Ask your child to use pennies to form equal groups and then find how many in all. Homework Workbook 11-1

Name_____ **Addition and Multiplication**

How many helicopters are there in all?   3 groups of 2

> You can add
> or multiply
> equal groups.

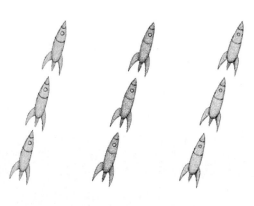

$$2 + 2 + 2 = 6$$

$$3 \times 2 = 6$$

times   product

Word Bank

times
product
multiply

Add. Then multiply.
Use counters if you like.

1.

    $$4 + 4 = \underline{\hspace{1cm}}$$

    $$2 \times 4 = \underline{\hspace{1cm}}$$

2.

    $$1 + 1 = \underline{\hspace{1cm}}$$

    $$2 \times 1 = \underline{\hspace{1cm}}$$

3.

    $$3 + 3 + 3 = \underline{\hspace{1cm}}$$

    $$3 \times 3 = \underline{\hspace{1cm}}$$

4.

    $$2 + 2 + 2 + 2 = \underline{\hspace{1cm}}$$

    $$4 \times 2 = \underline{\hspace{1cm}}$$

California Content Standards *Number Sense 3.1 (🗝)*
*Use repeated addition to do multilplication. Algebra and
Functions 1.2.*

Add. Then multiply.
Use counters if you like.

5.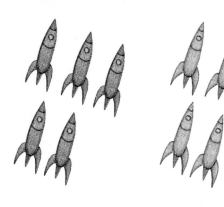

$5 + 5 =$ _____

$2 \times 5 =$ _____

6.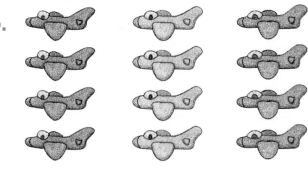

$4 + 4 + 4 =$ _____

$3 \times 4 =$ _____

7.

$2 + 2 =$ _____

$2 \times 2 =$ _____

8.

$5 + 5 + 5 =$ _____

$3 \times 5 =$ _____

Problem Solving

Visual Thinking

9. Look at the picture.
Complete each number sentence.

_____ $+$ _____ $=$ _____

_____ $\times$ _____ $=$ _____

Home Activity Ask your child to write addition and multiplication sentences about equal groups, such as 5 groups of 2.
Homework Workbook 11-2

Name_____ **Using Arrays**

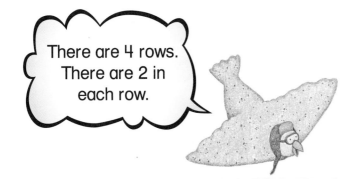

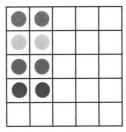

$4 \times 2 = 8$

rows   in each   in all
row

Use counters and the grid to show each fact.

1.   3   ×   2   = _____
   rows   in each   in all
   row

2.   3   ×   3   = _____
   rows   in each   in all
   row

3.   2   ×   5   = _____
   rows   in each   in all
   row

4.   4   ×   5   = _____
   rows   in each   in all
   row

California Content Standards *Number Sense 3.1 (⚷)*
Use arrays to do multiplication. Also Mathematical Reasoning 2.1.

Write each multiplication fact.

5.

$\underline{3} \times \underline{5} = \underline{15}$

rows   in each   in all
       row

6.

$\underline{\hphantom{00}} \times \underline{\hphantom{00}} = \underline{\hphantom{00}}$

rows   in each   in all
       row

7.

$\underline{\hphantom{00}} \times \underline{\hphantom{00}} = \underline{\hphantom{00}}$

rows   in each   in all
       row

8.

$\underline{\hphantom{00}} \times \underline{\hphantom{00}} = \underline{\hphantom{00}}$

rows   in each   in all
       row

9.

$\underline{\hphantom{00}} \times \underline{\hphantom{00}} = \underline{\hphantom{00}}$

rows   in each   in all
       row

10.

$\underline{\hphantom{00}} \times \underline{\hphantom{00}} = \underline{\hphantom{00}}$

rows   in each   in all
       row

 Home Activity Ask your child to place pennies on the grid on the front of this page to multiply numbers like 2 × 3 and 3 × 4. Homework Workbook 11-3

Name_____ **Multiplying Across and Down**

Asian Kites

You can multiply across or down.

2 groups of kites

5 kites in each group.

$2 \times 5 = \underline{10}$

$$\begin{array}{r} 5 \\ \times\ 2 \\ \hline 10 \end{array}$$

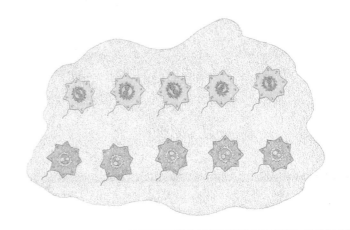

Find each product.

1.   4 groups of 2

$4 \times 2 = \underline{\hspace{1cm}}$ $\begin{array}{r} 2 \\ \times\ 4 \\ \hline \end{array}$

2.   1 group of 4

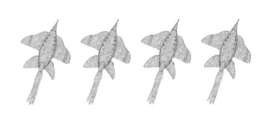

$1 \times 4 = \underline{\hspace{1cm}}$ $\begin{array}{r} 1 \\ \times\ 4 \\ \hline \end{array}$

3.   2 groups of 2

$2 \times 2 = \underline{\hspace{1cm}}$ $\begin{array}{r} 2 \\ \times\ 2 \\ \hline \end{array}$

4.   5 groups of 3

$5 \times 3 = \underline{\hspace{1cm}}$ $\begin{array}{r} 5 \\ \times\ 3 \\ \hline \end{array}$

California Content Standards Number Sense 3.1 (🔑)
*Use repeated addition, arrays, and counting by multiples to do
multiplication. Also Algebra and Functions 1.2, Mathematical
Reasoning 1.1.*

Multiply across and down. Write the number.

5.

$$\begin{array}{r} 3 \\ \times\ 2 \\ \hline 6 \end{array}$$

_2_ × _3_ = _6_

6.

$$\begin{array}{r} \Box \\ \times\ \Box \\ \hline \end{array}$$

___ × ___ = ___

7.

$$\begin{array}{r} \Box \\ \times\ \Box \\ \hline \end{array}$$

___ × ___ = ___

8.

$$\begin{array}{r} \Box \\ \times\ \Box \\ \hline \end{array}$$

___ × ___ = ___

9.

$$\begin{array}{r} \Box \\ \times\ \Box \\ \hline \end{array}$$

___ × ___ = ___

10.

$$\begin{array}{r} \Box \\ \times\ \Box \\ \hline \end{array}$$

___ × ___ = ___

Problem Solving

Algebra

Write the number sentence to solve.

11. There are 3 groups of kites. There are 2 kites in each group. How many kites are there in all?

___ ◯ ___ = ___

12. There are 3 kites in one group. There are 2 kites in the other group. How many kites are there in all?

___ ◯ ___ = ___

Home Activity Show your child 3 groups of 5 pennies. Ask him or her to write the multiplication fact both vertically and horizontally. Homework Workbook 11-4

Name_____ **Multiplying in Any Order**

You can multiply numbers in any order.
The answer stays the same.

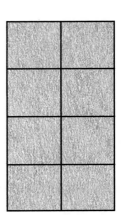

Algebra

2 Rows of 4

$2 \times 4 = \underline{8}$

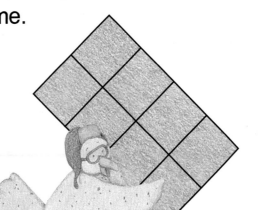

4 Rows of 2

$4 \times 2 = \underline{8}$

Use grid paper.
Color to show the number in each row.
Then turn the grid.
Write the multiplication sentences.

Word Bank

multiplication sentence

1. 5 rows of 2   or   2 rows of 5

   _____ $\times$ _____ = _____   _____ $\times$ _____ = _____

2. 4 rows of 3   or   3 rows of 4

   _____ $\times$ _____ = _____   _____ $\times$ _____ = _____

3. 1 row of 4   or   4 rows of 1

   _____ $\times$ _____ = _____   _____ $\times$ _____ = _____

4. 0 rows of 5   or   5 rows of 0

   _____ $\times$ _____ = _____   _____ $\times$ _____ = _____

California Content Standards Algebra and Functions 1.5
(Gr. 3) Recognize and use the commutative property of multiplication. Number Sense 3.1 (🖙). Also Statistics, Data Analysis,
and Probability 2.0 (🖙).

three hundred fifty-three **353**

Write the missing numbers. Multiply.

5. 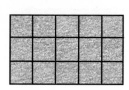 ⋯⋯3⋯⋯ rows of ⋯⋯5⋯⋯   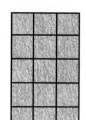 _____ rows of _____

3 × 5 = 15   5 × 3 = _____

6. _____ rows of _____   _____ rows of _____

2 × 3 = _____   3 × 2 = _____

7. _____ row of _____   _____ rows of _____

1 × 3 = _____   3 × 1 = _____

8. 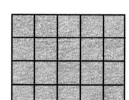 _____ rows of _____   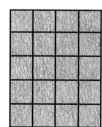 _____ rows of _____

4 × 5 = _____   5 × 4 = _____

 ## Math Reasoning

Number Sense

9. Draw the next larger square.
Write the number sentence.

    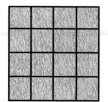

2 × 2 = 4   3 × 3 = 9   4 × 4 = 16   _____ × _____ = _____

Home Activity Ask your child to draw rows to show that order does not change the product of 2 × 4. Homework Workbook 11-5

Name_____ **Problem-Solving Strategy**

Draw a Picture

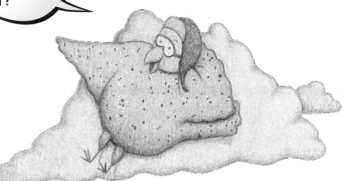

There are 3 leaves. There are 3 bugs on each leaf. How many bugs are there in all?

Understand

You need to find how many bugs in all.

Plan

You can draw a picture.
Then write a multiplication sentence.

Solve

$\underline{3} \times \underline{3} = \underline{9}$

Look Back

How did the picture help you know what numbers to multiply?

Draw a picture to solve.
Write a multiplication sentence.

1. There are 4 flowers. Each flower has 2 leaves. How many leaves are there?

   _____ × _____ = _____

 California Content Standards *Mathematical Reasoning 1.2 Use tools, such as sketches, to model problems. Number Sense 3.1 (🔑). Also Mathematical Reasoning 1.0.*

Draw a picture to solve.
Write a multiplication sentence.

2. There are 4 horses. Each
    horse has 4 legs. How
    many legs are there in all?

    _____ × _____ = _____

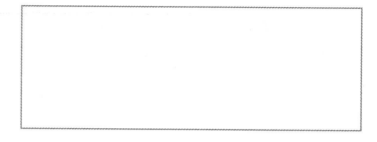

3. There are 6 legs on each
    ant. There are 3 ants.
    How many legs are there
    altogether?

    _____ × _____ = _____

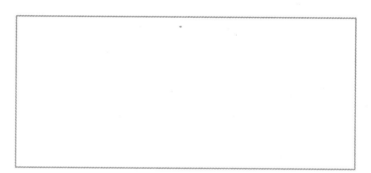

4. You want to make 5 cakes.
    You need 2 eggs for each
    cake. How many eggs do
    you need?

    _____ × _____ = _____

Math Reasoning

Draw a picture to solve.

5. There are 4 cats and
    2 ducks. How many legs
    are there on all the
    animals?

    _____ legs

Home Activity Ask your child to explain the picture he or
she drew to solve the problem on this page. Homework
Workbook 11-6

Name_____

Add or multiply.

1.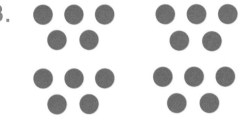

   $4 + 4 =$ _____

   $2 \times 4 =$ _____

2.

   $4 + 4 + 4 =$ _____

   $3 \times 4 =$ _____

3.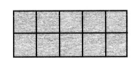

   $\begin{array}{r} 5 \\ \times\, 4 \\ \hline \end{array}$

   $4 \times 5 =$ _____

4.

   $\begin{array}{r} 2 \\ \times\, 3 \\ \hline \end{array}$

   $3 \times 2 =$ _____

Write the missing numbers. Multiply.

5.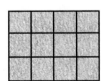

   _____ rows of _____

   $2 \times 5 =$ _____

   _____ rows of _____

   $5 \times 2 =$ _____

6.

   _____ rows of _____

   $3 \times 4 =$ _____

   _____ rows of _____

   $4 \times 3 =$ _____

Draw a picture to solve.
Write a multiplication sentence.

7. There are 3 triangles. Each triangle has 3 sides. How many sides are there?

   _____ $\times$ _____ = _____

Name_____

1. 200 + 30 + 4 | 432 ○   234 ○   200304 ○   NH ○

2.

4 × 5 = 20 ○   4 × 1 = 4 ○   5 × 3 = 15 ○   4 × 4 = 16 ○

3.

○   ○   ○   ○

4.  | $\frac{1}{3}$ ○ $\frac{3}{4}$ ○ $\frac{1}{4}$ ○   NH ○

5.

5 ○   10 ○   3 ○   15 ○

Oral Directions *Mark the correct answer. NH means "Not here." Mark it whenever the answer is not given.*

#1. Which number is the same as 200 + 30 + 4?
#2. Which multiplication sentence matches the picture?

#3. Solve the riddle. Which solid am I? I have two faces. I don't have any vertices.
#4. Which fraction is shown by the shaded part of the group?
#5. Diego counted the wheels on 5 tricycles at the park. How many wheels did he count?

Name_____
Ways to Multiply

Solve. Draw or write to show how.

1. There are 4 branches with 3 birds on each branch.
   How many birds are there in all? _____ birds

2. There are 5 posts with 2 birds on each post.
   How many birds are there in all? _____ birds

3. There are 3 puddles with 1 bird in each puddle.
   How many birds are there in all? _____ birds

California Content Standards *Mathematical Reasoning 1.1
Determine the approach, materials, and strategies to be used.
Number Sense 3.1 (⚬━). Also Mathematical Reasoning 1.2, 2.1.*

Choose a way to find each product.
Draw or write to show your choice.

> Use addition.
>
> Use counters.
>
> Draw a picture.

4. $4 \times 2 =$ _____

6. $5 \times 5 =$ _____

Math Reasoning

Number Sense

7. What patterns do you see when
   you multiply by 0 or 1?

> $5 \times 0 = 0.$
> $5 \times 1 = 5.$

Home Activity Ask your child how he or she would solve
5×4. Homework Workbook 11-7

Name_____ **Multiplying by 2**

How many ducks do you see?

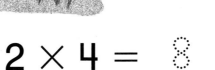

When I multiply by 2, I think of doubling. 2 × 4 is double 4.

$$2 \times 4 = \underset{\cdots}{8}$$

Find each product.
Think of doubling to help.

1. $2 \times 0 =$ _____ $2 \times 1 =$ _____ $2 \times 2 =$ _____

2. $2 \times 3 =$ _____ $2 \times 4 =$ _____ $2 \times 5 =$ _____

3. $2 \times 6 =$ _____ $2 \times 7 =$ _____ $2 \times 8 =$ _____

4. $2 \times 9 =$ _____ $2 \times 10 =$ _____ $0 \times 2 =$ _____

5. Could 11 ever be the product of 2 and another number?

   Explain. _____

   _____

California Content Standards *Number Sense 3.3 (🔑) Know the multiplication tables of 2s and commit them to memory. Also Mathematical Reasoning 1.1, 2.1.*

Find each product.
Think of doubling to help.

6.
$$\begin{array}{r} 9 \\ \times\ 2 \\ \hline 18 \end{array}$$
$$\begin{array}{r} 3 \\ \times\ 2 \\ \hline \end{array}$$
$$\begin{array}{r} 2 \\ \times\ 4 \\ \hline \end{array}$$
$$\begin{array}{r} 2 \\ \times\ 7 \\ \hline \end{array}$$
$$\begin{array}{r} 10 \\ \times\ 2 \\ \hline \end{array}$$
$$\begin{array}{r} 5 \\ \times\ 0 \\ \hline \end{array}$$

7.
$$\begin{array}{r} 2 \\ \times\ 2 \\ \hline \end{array}$$
$$\begin{array}{r} 2 \\ \times\ 6 \\ \hline \end{array}$$
$$\begin{array}{r} 2 \\ \times\ 9 \\ \hline \end{array}$$
$$\begin{array}{r} 8 \\ \times\ 2 \\ \hline \end{array}$$
$$\begin{array}{r} 2 \\ \times\ 1 \\ \hline \end{array}$$
$$\begin{array}{r} 2 \\ \times\ 5 \\ \hline \end{array}$$

Complete each fact.
Find the missing factor.

8. $2 \times \underline{\hspace{1cm}} = 16$

9. $2 \times \underline{\hspace{1cm}} = 8$

10. $2 \times \underline{\hspace{1cm}} = 6$

11. $\underline{\hspace{1cm}} \times 2 = 18$

12. $\underline{\hspace{1cm}} \times 2 = 14$

13. $2 \times \underline{\hspace{1cm}} = 10$

14. $2 \times \underline{\hspace{1cm}} = 20$

15. $\underline{\hspace{1cm}} \times 2 = 0$

 Problem Solving

Solve.

16. Mary wanted to put 2 rings on each of her 10 fingers. How many rings did she need in all? _____ rings

Home Activity Ask your child to recall 2s facts such as 2×3 and 9×2. Homework Workbook 11-8

Name_____ **Multiplying by 5**

6 children are playing marbles.
Each child has 5 marbles.
How many marbles do they
have in all?

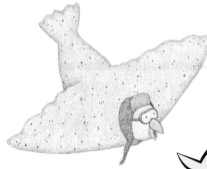

	5
	10
	15
	20
	25
	30

First, I'll make equal rows of five. Then, I'll count by fives to find the product.

There are 30 marbles in all.

$6 \times 5 = 30$

Find each product.

1. $5 \times 0 = \underline{\hspace{1cm}}$ $5 \times 1 = \underline{\hspace{1cm}}$ $5 \times 2 = \underline{\hspace{1cm}}$

2. $5 \times 3 = \underline{\hspace{1cm}}$ $5 \times 4 = \underline{\hspace{1cm}}$ $5 \times 5 = \underline{\hspace{1cm}}$

3. $5 \times 6 = \underline{\hspace{1cm}}$ $5 \times 7 = \underline{\hspace{1cm}}$ $5 \times 8 = \underline{\hspace{1cm}}$

4. $5 \times 9 = \underline{\hspace{1cm}}$ $5 \times 10 = \underline{\hspace{1cm}}$ $0 \times 5 = \underline{\hspace{1cm}}$

5.   What patterns do you see when you multiply by 5?

Explain. _____

_____

California Content Standards *Number Sense 3.3 (⚷) Know the multiplication tables of 5s and commit them to memory. Also Statistics, Data Analysis, and Probability 2.0 (⚷), 2.1, Mathematical Reasoning 3.0.*

Find each product.

6.
$$\begin{array}{r} 5 \\ \times\ 6 \\ \hline 30 \end{array}$$
$$\begin{array}{r} 5 \\ \times\ 7 \\ \hline \end{array}$$
$$\begin{array}{r} 9 \\ \times\ 5 \\ \hline \end{array}$$
$$\begin{array}{r} 2 \\ \times\ 5 \\ \hline \end{array}$$
$$\begin{array}{r} 1 \\ \times\ 5 \\ \hline \end{array}$$
$$\begin{array}{r} 5 \\ \times\ 5 \\ \hline \end{array}$$

7.
$$\begin{array}{r} 8 \\ \times\ 5 \\ \hline \end{array}$$
$$\begin{array}{r} 3 \\ \times\ 5 \\ \hline \end{array}$$
$$\begin{array}{r} 6 \\ \times\ 5 \\ \hline \end{array}$$
$$\begin{array}{r} 4 \\ \times\ 5 \\ \hline \end{array}$$
$$\begin{array}{r} 10 \\ \times\ 5 \\ \hline \end{array}$$
$$\begin{array}{r} 0 \\ \times\ 5 \\ \hline \end{array}$$

Complete each fact.
Find the missing factor.

8. $2 \times \rule{2cm}{0.4pt} = 10$

9. $5 \times \rule{2cm}{0.4pt} = 15$

10. $\rule{2cm}{0.4pt} \times 4 = 20$

11. $\rule{2cm}{0.4pt} \times 5 = 40$

12. $\rule{2cm}{0.4pt} \times 5 = 30$

13. $5 \times \rule{2cm}{0.4pt} = 45$

 Math Reasoning

Number Sense

14. How can you use 7×5 to help you find 8×5?

_____

_____

Home Activity Ask your child to recall 5s facts such as 3×5 and 8×5. Homework Workbook 11-9

Name_____ **Multiplying by 10**

Alex has 6 rows of plants with 10 in each row.
How many plants does he have?

You can skip count or use a fact you know to find the product.

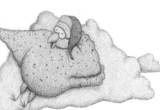

Skip Count by 10	**Use a Fact You Know**
10, 20, 30, 40, 50, 60	$6 \times 1 = 6$ 6×1 ten $= 6$ tens $6 \times 10 = 60$

Alex has 60 plants.

Find each product.

1. $10 \times 0 =$ _____ $10 \times 1 = 10$ $10 \times 2 =$ _____

2. $10 \times 3 =$ _____ $10 \times 4 =$ _____ $10 \times 5 =$ _____

3. $10 \times 6 =$ _____ $10 \times 7 =$ _____ $10 \times 8 =$ _____

4. $10 \times 9 =$ _____ $10 \times 10 =$ _____ $0 \times 10 =$ _____

5. What patterns do you see when you multiply by 10?

   Explain. _____

   _____

California Content Standards *Number Sense 3.3* (🔑) *Know the multiplication tables of 10s and commit them to memory. Also Statistics, Data Analysis, and Probability 2.0* (🔑)*, 2.2, Mathematical Reasoning 3.0.*

Find each product.

6.

9	10	10	10	10	5
× 10	× 2	× 4	× 7	× 9	× 10
90					

7.

10	10	10	8	10	10
× 3	× 0	× 10	× 10	× 1	× 6

Complete the table.
Follow the rule.

8.

Multiply by 5	
In	Out
5	
6	
	35
	40
9	

9.

Multiply by 10	
In	Out
5	
6	
	70
	80
9	

Math Reasoning

Number Sense

10. Look at the products in the two tables above.
    What patterns do you see?

_____

_____

Home Activity Ask your child to recall 10s facts such as
10 × 5 and 10 × 10. Homework Workbook 11-10

Name_____

Write a number sentence for each part
of the problem. Use counters if you wish.

Think: Do you need to add, subtract, or multiply?

1. Each roller coaster car holds
   2 children. How many children can
   ride on a roller coaster with 7 cars?

   $2 \times 7 = 14$ children

   Only 9 children get on the roller coaster.
   How many seats are not used?

   $14 - 9 = 5$ seats

2. Sue bought a soda for $1.25 and
   popcorn for $2.50. How much did
   she spend?   _____

   She paid for the soda and popcorn
   with a $5.00 bill. How much change
   should she get back?   _____

3. Jeff wants to go on 4 rides.
   Each ride costs 5 tickets. How
   many tickets does Jeff need?   _____ tickets

   Jeff only has 6 tickets.
   How many more tickets does he
   need to go on 4 rides?   _____ tickets

California Content Standards *Mathematical Reasoning 3.0
Students note connections between one problem and another. Also
Number Sense 2.2 (⟶), 3.1 (⟶), Algebra and Functions 1.2.*

Write a number sentence for each part
of the problem. Use counters if you wish.

4. Jared bought 35 tickets for rides.
   He used 20 tickets. How many
   tickets did he have left?   _____ tickets

   He then used 10 more tickets. How
   many tickets does Jared have now?   _____ tickets

5. Mary bought 7 pencils for 10¢ each.
   How much did she spend?   _____

   She paid for the pencils with 3 quarters.
   How much change should she get?   _____

6. Cecilia bought a book of animal
   stamps. The book had 5 rows with
   5 stamps in each row. How many
   stamps are in the stamp book?   _____ stamps

   She used 7 stamps for letters. How
   many stamps does she have left?   _____ stamps

 **Problem Solving**

Number Sense
The problem below has four steps.
Write the missing steps. $2 \times 8¢ = 16¢$

7. Steve bought 2 erasers for 8¢ each
   and 5 pencils for 10¢ each. He paid $16¢ + 50¢ = 66¢$
   with a $1.00 bill. How much
   change should he get back?   _____

Home Activity Ask your child to explain how he or she
solved Exercise 7. Homework Workbook 11-11

Name_____

Solve. Draw or write to show how.

1. There are 3 boxes with 5 marbles in each box.
   How many marbles are there in all?   _____ marbles

Multiply.

2. $\begin{array}{r} 9 \\ \times\,10 \\ \hline \end{array}$ $\begin{array}{r} 5 \\ \times\,2 \\ \hline \end{array}$ $\begin{array}{r} 2 \\ \times\,4 \\ \hline \end{array}$ $\begin{array}{r} 10 \\ \times\,7 \\ \hline \end{array}$ $\begin{array}{r} 8 \\ \times\,2 \\ \hline \end{array}$ $\begin{array}{r} 4 \\ \times\,10 \\ \hline \end{array}$

3. $\begin{array}{r} 8 \\ \times\,5 \\ \hline \end{array}$ $\begin{array}{r} 9 \\ \times\,2 \\ \hline \end{array}$ $\begin{array}{r} 5 \\ \times\,9 \\ \hline \end{array}$ $\begin{array}{r} 10 \\ \times\,10 \\ \hline \end{array}$ $\begin{array}{r} 10 \\ \times\,0 \\ \hline \end{array}$ $\begin{array}{r} 1 \\ \times\,2 \\ \hline \end{array}$

4. $\begin{array}{r} 6 \\ \times\,5 \\ \hline \end{array}$ $\begin{array}{r} 2 \\ \times\,7 \\ \hline \end{array}$ $\begin{array}{r} 5 \\ \times\,10 \\ \hline \end{array}$ $\begin{array}{r} 6 \\ \times\,2 \\ \hline \end{array}$ $\begin{array}{r} 7 \\ \times\,5 \\ \hline \end{array}$ $\begin{array}{r} 10 \\ \times\,3 \\ \hline \end{array}$

Write a number sentence for each part
of the problem. Use counters if you wish.

5. Sarah bought 4 packs of pencils.
   Each pack has 5 pencils. How many
   pencils did she get?   _____ pencils

   Sarah gave 6 pencils to friends. How
   many pencils does she have now?   _____ pencils

Name _____

1.
○
○
○
○

---

2. $9 \times 5 =$ ☐

45	14	46	NH
○	○	○	○

---

3. $379 <$ ☐

299	378	379	380
○	○	○	○

4.

○ 4 inches
○ 4 feet
○ 4 yards
○ NH

5.

○	○	○	○

Oral Directions *Mark the correct answer. NH means "Not here." Mark it whenever the answer is not given.*

#1. Use your inch ruler to solve the problem. Jon cut a ribbon that was 5 inches long. Which of these shows the ribbon he cut?

#2. Multiply.
#3. Which number makes the statement true?
#4. About how tall is a bookcase in real life?
#5. In which figure is the fraction of the shaded part not equal to 1?

Add. Then multiply.

1.

$4 + 4 =$ _____

$2 \times 4 =$ _____

2.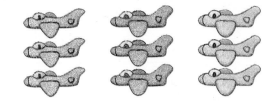

$3 + 3 + 3 =$ _____

$3 \times 3 =$ _____

Multiply across and down. Write the numbers

3.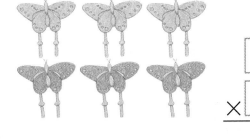

$\times$ ☐
☐

_____ $\times$ _____ $=$ _____

4.

$\times$ ☐
☐

_____ $\times$ _____ $=$ _____

Solve. Draw or write to show how.

5. There are 4 jars with 5 flowers in each jar.   _____ flowers
   How many flowers are there in all?

Draw a picture to solve.
Write a multiplication sentence.

6. There are 3 trees.
   Each tree has 4 birds.
   How many birds are there?

   _____ $\times$ _____ $=$ _____

Multiply.

7.

9	10	3	10	5	2
×5	×2	×6	×9	×8	×4

8.

1	6	2	5	10	3
×5	×10	×0	×5	×4	×2

9.

7	2	5	2	2	10
×10	×8	×3	×2	×5	×8

Write the missing numbers. Multiply.

10.

 _____ rows of _____

$2 \times 4 =$ _____

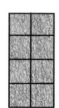 _____ rows of _____

$4 \times 2 =$ _____

11.

 _____ rows of _____

$3 \times 2 =$ _____

 _____ rows of _____

$2 \times 3 =$ _____

Write a number sentence for each part
of the problem. Use counters if you wish.

12. Maria had 25 ride tickets.
She used 10 tickets. How many
tickets did she have left?   _____ tickets

Maria bought 10 more tickets. How
many tickets does she have now?   _____ tickets

Name_____

1. $4 + 4 + 4$ | 3×4 4×4 3×3 NH

              ○   ○   ○   ○

2.

     $3 + 2 = 5$ $2 \times 2 = 4$ $2 \times 3 = 6$ $6 \times 2 = 12$

         ○   ○   ○   ○

---

3. $5 \times 8 = 40$ 3   13   40   NH

so $8 \times 5 = \boxed{}$ ○   ○   ○   ○

---

4.   6   16   60   61   600

    $\times 10$ ○   ○   ○   ○

---

5.   7   35   34   12   NH

    $\times 5$ ○   ○   ○   ○

---

6. 19 marbles   9 marbles   16 marbles   18 marbles

      ○   ○   ○   ○

Oral Directions *Mark the correct answer. NH means "Not here." Mark it whenever the answer is not given.*

#1. Which shows another way to find $4 + 4 + 4$?
#2. Which number sentence shows how many planes in all?

#3. If you know $5 \times 8 = 40$, what is 8×5?
#4–5. Find each product.
#6. Rosi has 3 bags of marbles. Each bag has 6 marbles in it. How many marbles does she have in all? Draw a picture to find the product if you wish.

7.

$2 \times 4 = 8$
○

$4 + 4 = 8$
○

$\begin{array}{r} 4 \\ \times\ 2 \\ \hline 8 \end{array}$
○

$\begin{array}{r} 4 \\ \times\ 4 \\ \hline 16 \end{array}$
○

8.

$\begin{array}{r} 9 \\ \times\ 2 \\ \hline \end{array}$

18
○

11
○

17
○

NH
○

9. 4×4

○

○

○

○

10.

○ $2 \times 3 = 6$ cards, $6 + 5 = 11$ cards

○ $2 \times 3 = 6$ cards, $6 - 5 = 1$ card

○ $2 + 3 = 5$ cards, $5 - 5 = 0$ cards

○ $2 + 3 = 5$ cards, $5 \times 5 = 25$ cards

Oral Directions *Mark the correct answer. NH means "Not here." Mark it whenever the answer is not given.*

#7. Which number sentence does NOT match the picture?
#8. Multiply.

#9. Which array shows 4×4?
#10. Joel had 2 packs of baseball cards. Each pack had 3 cards inside. He gave 5 cards to his friend Mary. How many cards does he have left? Which two number sentences could you use to solve the problem?

CHAPTER 12 Division

Diagnosing Readiness

for Chapter 12

1. 2 children share acorns.
    Circle each child's fair share.

2. Billy saw 2 groups of bees.
    How many bees are in each group?

    _____ bees in each group.

3. $2 \times 5 =$ _____

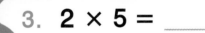

4. $7 - 3 =$ _____

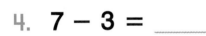

5. Mandy found 6 leaves.
    Ned found 2 leaves.
    How many leaves did they find in all?
    Write the number sentence.

    _____ ◯ _____ = _____ leaves

To the Family

Looking Back ◄	Chapter 12 ►	Looking Ahead
In Chapter 1 children reviewed basic subtraction facts. In Chapter 11 children solved problems involving multiplication facts and memorized 2s, 5s, and 10s facts.	**Division** Children use repeated subtraction, equal sharing, and equal groups with remainders to do division. Children write division sentences and connect multiplication and division.	In Grade 3 children will memorize basic division facts and divide numbers up to three digits by a one-digit number.

Page 375 Your child solved problems that review math skills from previous chapters and will help your child with the skills in Chapter 12.

Math at Home The chapter theme is sharing equal groups. Help your child divide small objects such as buttons or pennies into equal groups and then practice the corresponding division facts.

Math Literature Read math or theme-related stories with your child. Look for the following books in your local library.
One Hundred Hungry Ants by Eleanor J. Pinczes (Houghton Mifflin Company, 1993)
Divide and Ride by Stuart J. Murphy (HarperCollins Juvenile Books, 1997)

California Content Standards in Chapter 12 Lessons*

	Teach and Practice	Practice		Teach and Practice	Practice
Number Sense			**Mathematical Reasoning**		
3.1 (🔑) Use repeated addition, arrays, and counting by multiples to do multiplication.		2	1.1 Determine the approach, material, and strategies to be used.		1, 5
3.2 (🔑) Use repeated subtraction, equal sharing, and forming equal groups with remainders to do division.	1–7		1.2 Use tools, such as manipulatives or sketches, to model problems.		1–4
2.3 (🔑), Grade 3, Use the inverse relationship of multiplication and division to compute and check results.	7		2.0 Students solve problems and justify their reasoning.		8
Algebra and Functions			2.1 Defend the reasoning used and justify the procedures selected.		3, 6
1.2 Relate problem situations to number sentences involving addition and subtraction.	8		3.0 Students note connections between one problem and another.		3, 7
1.3, Grade 3, Select appropriate operational and relational symbols to make an expression true (e.g., if 4 _ 3 = 12, what operational symbol goes in the blank?).	8				

* The symbol (🔑) indicates a key standard as designated in the Mathematics Framework for California Public Schools.
  Full statements of the California Content Standards are found at the beginning of this book following the Table of Contents.

Name_____ **Modeling Division**

Three children are making 12 paper airplanes. They want to share the work equally. How many airplanes should each child make?

There are 3 children. Each child should make 4 airplanes.

Use counters and Workmat 6.
Use the chart to make equal groups.
Write the number in each group.

Word Bank

equal groups
divide

	Number in All	Number of Groups	Number in Each Group
1.	12	3	4
2.	8	4	
3.	15	3	
4.	20	4	
5.	9	3	
6.	10	2	
7.	16	4	

California Content Standards *Number Sense 3.2 (☎) Use repeated subtraction, equal sharing, and forming equal groups to do division. Also Mathematical Reasoning 1.1, 1.2.*

three hundred seventy-seven **377**

Circle equal groups.
Write the number in each group.

8.

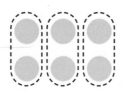

3 groups of _2_

9.

2 groups of _____

10.

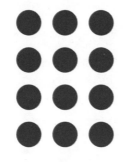

3 groups of _____

11.

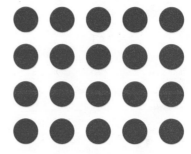

4 groups of _____

12.

3 groups of _____

13.

4 groups of _____

Make your own equal groups.

14.

_____ groups of _____

15.

_____ groups of _____

Home Activity Give your child 12 objects, such as pennies or markers. Have him or her make 2, 3, or 4 equal groups.
Homework Workbook 12-1

Name_____ **Division as Sharing**

Carlos, Lea, and Jon have 6 orange slices. If they share the orange equally, how many slices should each get?

Each group must have the same number.

Carlos, Lea, and Jon should each get 2 orange slices.

Make equal groups to solve.

1. Mia has 8 pineapples. She places an equal number of pineapples in 2 bags. How many pineapples are in each bag?

    There are __4__ pineapples in each bag.

---

2. Phil shared 12 pears with Sue, Bob, and Kim. If each person took the same number, how many pears did each person get?

    They each took _____ pears.

California Content Standards *Number Sense 3.2 (🔑) Use equal sharing and forming equal groups to do division. Also Number Sense 3.1 (🔑), Mathematical Reasoning 1.2.*

Use counters. Make equal groups to solve.
Draw to show what you did.

3. Ms. Jones has 14 markers to give to her 2 art groups. If she shares the markers equally, how many markers can she give each group?

She can give each group __7__ markers.

4. Mr. Lang put 10 new books on the bookshelf. He put the same number on each of the 5 shelves. How many new books did he put on each shelf?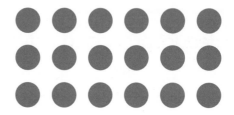

He put _____ new books on each shelf.

5. Antonio and Mike found 18¢ when they cleaned up their room. If they shared the money equally, how much money did each get?

They each got _____ ¢.

 Math Reasoning

Number Sense

6. Three friends shared some baseball cards. If they each got 3 cards, how many cards did they start with?

_____ cards

Home Activity Ask your child to tell you a story about when he or she shared something with a friend. Homework Workbook 12-2

Name_____ **Division as Repeated Subtraction**

Mel has 8 socks left in his sock drawer.
Each day he takes out 2 socks to wear.
How many days can he keep taking out socks?

Day 1	Day 2	Day 3	Day 4
$8 - 2 = 6$	$6 - 2 = 4$	$4 - 2 = 2$	$2 - 2 = 0$

Mel can take out socks for 4 days.

Subtract equal groups to solve.

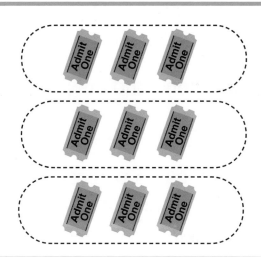

1. Pat has 9 tickets for rides at the park.
   Each ride costs 3 tickets.
   How many rides can Pat go on?

   Pat can go on __3__ rides.

---

2. 20 children are ready to eat lunch.
   4 children will fit at each picnic table.
   How many picnic tables do they need?

   They need _____ picnic tables.

3. How many picnic tables do
   they need if there are only
   19 children? Explain.

   They need _____ picnic tables.

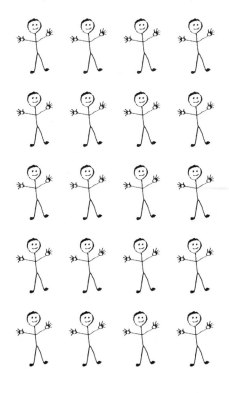

California Content Standards *Number Sense 3.2 (🔑) Use repeated subtraction to do division. Also Mathematical Reasoning 1.2, 3.0.*

three hundred eighty-one **381**

Use counters. Subtract equal groups to solve.
Draw to show what you did.

4. Mr. Jones buys 15 rings for the
    bottle toss game. Each player
    needs 5 rings to play.
    How many people can play?

    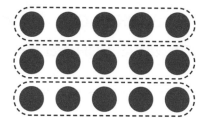

    _3_ people can play.

5. Mrs. Barrett has 12 pencils left.
    Each day she hands out 6 pencils.
    How many days can she hand
    out pencils?

    She can hand out pencils for _____ days.

6. Erin has 25 postcards. Each day
    she was on vacation, she mailed
    5 postcards to friends. How many
    days was she on vacation?

    She was on vacation for _____ days.

Math Reasoning

Number Sense

7. How are division and subtraction alike?
    How are they different?

Home Activity Ask your child to use pennies to find how
many groups of 5 there are in 15. (3 groups) Homework
Workbook 12-3

Name_____ **Division with Remainders**

Carlos and Marta are making puppets.
They have 14 buttons.
They need 3 buttons for each puppet.
How many puppets can they make?

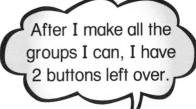

After I make all the groups I can, I have 2 buttons left over.

They can make 4 puppets. 2 buttons are left over.

Circle groups to solve. Write how many are left over.

1. Stan has 14 cloth triangles to make quilt squares.
   He uses 4 triangles for each square.
   How many quilt squares can he make?

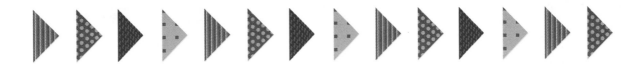

Stan can make ___3___ quilt squares.
How many triangles are left over?   ___2___ are left over.

2. Sara has 23 cotton balls for making caterpillars.
   It takes 5 cotton balls to make each caterpillar.
   How many caterpillars can she make?

Sara can make _____ caterpillars.
How many cotton balls are left over?   _____ are left over.

California Content Standards *Number Sense 3.2 (key) Use equal sharing and forming equal groups with remainders to do division. Also Mathematical Reasoning 1.2.*

three hundred eighty-three **383**

Use counters to solve. Draw to show what you did.

3. Ana has 20 beads to use for making necklaces. She puts 6 beads on each necklace. How many necklaces can Ana make?

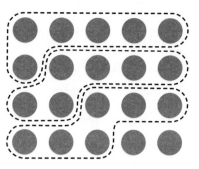

Ana can make __3__ necklaces.
How many beads are left over?

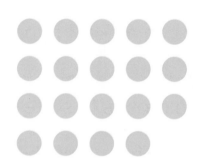

__2__ are left over.

4. Bill has 19 crayons in his desk. He can put 8 crayons in each crayon box. How many boxes can he fill?

Bill can fill _____ boxes.
How many crayons are left over?

_____ are left over.

5. Tara picked 16 apples. She can put 5 in each basket. How many baskets can she fill?

Tara can fill _____ baskets.
How many apples are left over?

_____ is left over.

 Math Reasoning

Solve. You can use counters to help.

6. Joe is putting his marbles in bags of 10 marbles each. He has 38 marbles. How many bags does he need?

Joe needs _____ bags.
How many bags will be full?

_____ bags will be full.

384 one hundred eighty-four

Home Activity Ask your child to use pennies to find how many groups of 4 there are in 10. Point out the ones left over and have your child count them. (2 groups of 4, 2 left over)
Homework Workbook 12-4

Name_____ **Diagnostic Checkpoint**

Circle equal groups.
Write the number in each group.

1.

    3 groups of _____

2. ● ● ● ● ●
   ● ● ● ● ●

    5 groups of _____

3. ● ● ● ● ● ● ● ● ● ●

    2 groups of _____

Solve. Use counters if you wish.

4. Allen picked 8 peaches.
   He wants to share them equally with his sister.
   How many peaches will each person get?

   Each person will get _____ peaches.

5. Jack wants to run 10 miles. Each day he
   runs 2 miles. How many days will it take him
   to reach his goal of 10 miles?

   It will take him _____ days.

6. Yuko has 13 party favors.
   She wants to give 2 to each party guest.
   How many guests can Yuko invite to her party?

   Yuko can invite _____ guests.
   How many party favors are left over?   _____ is left over.

Name _____

1.

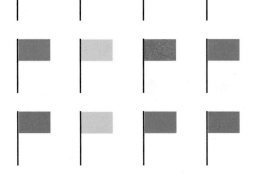

- ○ $4 \times 4 = 16$
- ○ $3 \times 4 = 12$
- ○ $3 \times 3 = 9$
- ○ $2 \times 4 = 8$

2. $\frac{1}{4} >$ ☐

$\frac{1}{3}$	$\frac{1}{2}$	$\frac{1}{8}$	NH
○	○	○	○

3. Jan has 53 books.

Sue has 34 books.

$53 - 34 = 19$	$53 + 34 = 87$	$87 - 34 = 53$	NH
○	○	○	○

4. $5 \times 6 =$ ☐

25	29	11	30
○	○	○	○

5.

Favorite Animal	Tally
Lion	ⅢⅢ IIII
Tiger	IIII
Bear	ⅢⅢ ⅢⅢ IIII

- ○ 9
- ○ 4
- ○ 5
- ○ 10

Oral Directions *Mark the correct answer. NH means "Not here." Mark it whenever the answer is not given.*

#1. Which number sentence shows how many flags in the three rows all together?
#2. Which fraction is less than one-fourth?

#3. Which number sentence tells how many more books Jan has than Sue?
#4. Multiply.
#5. How many more people chose Bears than Lions as their favorite amimal?

Name_____

Michelle and Diana have 4 apples.
If they share all the apples equally,
how many apples will each get?

Understand

You need to find how many
apples each girl will get.

Plan

You can write a division sentence.

Solve

$$4 \div 2 = 2 \text{ apples}$$

Look Back

Did you answer the question?

Word Bank

division sentence

Write a division sentence.
Use counters if you wish.

1. 12 people share 3 picnic blankets equally.
   How many people are on each blanket?

   _____ ÷ _____ = _____ people

---

2. 5 children share 15 water balloons equally.
   How many balloons does each child get?

   _____ ÷ _____ = _____ balloons

California Content Standards *Number Sense 3.2 (🔑) Use
repeated subtraction, equal sharing, and forming equal groups to
do division. Also Mathematical Reasoning 1.1.*

three hundred eighty-seven **387**

Write a division sentence to solve.
Use counters if you wish.

3. On their hike, 3 children picked 18 berries. They shared them equally. How many berries did each get?

$18 \div 3 = 6$ berries

4. Ms. Gish found 9 oak leaves. If she puts the same number in 3 bags, how many leaves can she put in each bag?

_____ $\div$ _____ = _____ leaves

5. Mr. Lyles separated his 14 students into 2 equal teams. How many students are on each team?

_____ $\div$ _____ = _____ students

6. Tanesha has 16 cookies. She gives the same number to 4 friends. How many cookies did each friend get?

_____ $\div$ _____ = _____ cookies

7. At the park, 20 children run relay races on 5 equal teams. How many children are on each team?

_____ children

8. At lunch, 12 children share 4 benches equally. How many children are sitting on each bench?

_____ children

Math Reasoning

Number Sense

9. Tell a story for this division sentence.

$10 \div 2 = 5$

three hundred eighty-eight

Home Activity Ask your child to divide 8 pennies into 2 equal groups. Then have him or her write a division sentence to show the problem. Homework Workbook 12-5

Name_____ **Practicing Division**

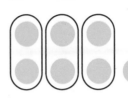

Divide.

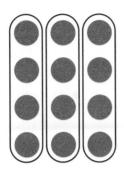

The R stands for the remainder or what's left over.

$12 \div 4 = \underline{3}$ R $\underline{0}$

12 divided by 4 equals 3.

$7 \div 2 = \underline{3}$ R $\underline{1}$

7 divided by 2 is 3 with 1 left over.

Divide.

Word Bank

remainder

1.
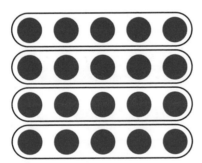

$20 \div 5 = \underline{\quad}$ R $\underline{\quad}$

2.
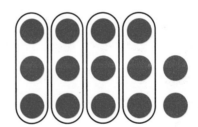

$14 \div 3 = \underline{\quad}$ R $\underline{\quad}$

3.
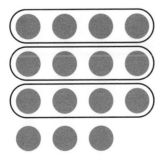

$15 \div 4 = \underline{\quad}$ R $\underline{\quad}$

4.
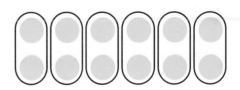

$12 \div 2 = \underline{\quad}$ R $\underline{\quad}$

California Content Standards *Number Sense 3.2 (🔑) Use repeated subtraction, equal sharing, and forming equal groups with remainders to do division. Also Mathematical Reasoning 2.1.*

three hundred eighty-nine **389**

Circle equal groups to divide.

5.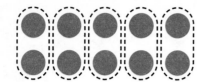

$10 \div 2 = \underline{5}$ R $\underline{0}$

6.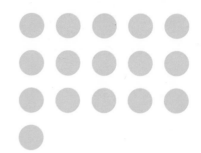

$16 \div 5 = \underline{}$ R $\underline{}$

7.

$9 \div 4 = \underline{}$ R $\underline{}$

8.

$18 \div 6 = \underline{}$ R $\underline{}$

9.

$8 \div 4 = \underline{}$ R $\underline{}$

10.

$11 \div 3 = \underline{}$ R $\underline{}$

Problem Solving

Solve. Use counters if you like.

11. You have 14 airplanes.
Can you give an equal number
to each of your 3 friends?
Tell why or why not.

390 three hundred ninety

Home Activity Ask your child to divide 8 pennies into 3 equal groups and count what's left over. Then have him or her write a division sentence to show the problem. Homework Workbook 12-6

Name_____ **Relating Multiplication and Division**

You can use multiplication
to help you divide.

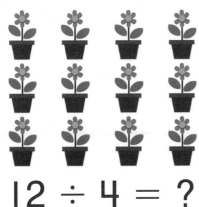

$12 \div 4 = ?$

Think: 4 times
what number
equals 12?

$4 \times \underline{3} = 12$

So, $12 \div 4 = \underline{3}$

Use the array to complete each sentence.

1.

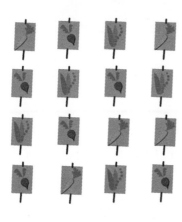

$3 \times \underline{\hspace{1cm}} = 6$

$6 \div 3 = \underline{\hspace{1cm}}$

2.

$2 \times \underline{\hspace{1cm}} = 10$

$10 \div 2 = \underline{\hspace{1cm}}$

3.

$4 \times \underline{\hspace{1cm}} = 16$

$16 \div 4 = \underline{\hspace{1cm}}$

4.

$5 \times \underline{\hspace{1cm}} = 15$

$15 \div 5 = \underline{\hspace{1cm}}$

California Content Standards *Number Sense 2.3 (🔑),
Grade 3, Use the inverse relationship of multiplication and division
to compute and check results. Number Sense 3.2 (🔑). Also
Mathematical Reasoning 3.0.*

Solve each problem.
Use counters if you wish.

5.

$5 \times \underline{\hspace{1cm}} = 5$

$5 \div 5 = \underline{\hspace{1cm}}$

6.

$4 \times \underline{\hspace{1cm}} = 8$

$8 \div 4 = \underline{\hspace{1cm}}$

7.

$3 \times \underline{\hspace{1cm}} = 9$

$9 \div 3 = \underline{\hspace{1cm}}$

8.

$4 \times \underline{\hspace{1cm}} = 20$

$20 \div 4 = \underline{\hspace{1cm}}$

9.

$2 \times \underline{\hspace{1cm}} = 12$

$12 \div 2 = \underline{\hspace{1cm}}$

10.

$1 \times \underline{\hspace{1cm}} = 4$

$4 \div 1 = \underline{\hspace{1cm}}$

11.

$6 \times \underline{\hspace{1cm}} = 18$

$18 \div 6 = \underline{\hspace{1cm}}$

12.

$3 \times \underline{\hspace{1cm}} = 12$

$12 \div 3 = \underline{\hspace{1cm}}$

 Problem Solving

Solve.
Write the number sentence.

13. Helena has 25 plants.
She can place 5 plants
on each shelf. How many
shelves can she fill?

_____

14. Look back at 13. Write
the multiplication sentence
you could use to help
solve the problem.

_____

Home Activity Ask your child to explain which
multiplication fact he or she could use to find $6 \div 3$.
Homework Workbook 12-7

Name_____ **Problem-Solving Application**

Choose the Operation

Write the number sentence.

Think: Do you add, subtract, multiply, or divide?

Algebra

1. Tony has 2 oranges.

    He cuts each orange into 4 pieces.

    How many pieces of orange does he have?

    add   subtract   (multiply)   divide

    2 (×) 4 = 8 pieces

    _____

2. Ana bought 5 bananas.

    She gave 3 of the bananas to Ted.

    How many bananas does she have left?

    add   subtract   multiply   divide

    _____ ( ) _____ = _____ bananas

    _____

3. Kevin picked 4 apples.

    Karen picked 5 apples.

    How many apples did they pick in all?

    add   subtract   multiply   divide

    _____ ( ) _____ = _____ apples

    _____

4. Kellie puts 9 melons in 3 bags.

    If she puts the same number in each bag,

    how many melons are in each bag?

    add   subtract   multiply   divide

    _____ ( ) _____ = _____ melons

California Content Standards *Algebra and Functions 1.2*
Relate problem situations to number sentences involving addition
and subtraction. Algebra and Functions 1.3, Grade 3. Also
Mathematical Reasoning. 2.0.

Circle **add**, **subtract**, **multiply**, or **divide**.
Write the number sentence.

5. Richard has 6 grapes.
   He eats 2 of the grapes.
   How many grapes does he have left?

   add   subtract   multiply   divide

   _____ ◯ _____ = _____ grapes

6. Alma wants to give her 4 friends an equal
   number of muffins. If she makes 8 muffins,
   how many muffins will each friend get?

   add   subtract   multiply   divide

   _____ ◯ _____ = _____ muffins

7. Yolanda has 3 berries.
   Mary has 4 times as many berries as Yolanda.
   How many berries does Mary have?

   add   subtract   multiply   divide

   _____ ◯ _____ = _____ berries

8. Lina hiked 5 miles on Friday.
   She hiked 3 miles on Saturday.
   How many miles did she hike in both days?

   add   subtract   multiply   divide

   _____ ◯ _____ = _____ miles

Home Activity Ask your child to explain how he or she
decided to add, subtract, multiply, or divide each problem.
Homework Workbook 12-8

Name_____ **Diagnostic Checkpoint**

Circle equal groups to divide.

1.

   $7 \div 3 =$ _____ R _____

2.

   $15 \div 5 =$ _____ R _____

Solve each problem.
Use counters if you wish.

3. $3 \times$ _____ $= 18$

   $18 \div 3 =$ _____

4. $7 \times$ _____ $= 14$

   $14 \div 7 =$ _____

Write a number sentence to solve.
Use counters if you wish.

5. Jeff cut a submarine sandwich into
   6 pieces. If each person gets 2 pieces,
   how many people can Jeff feed?

   _____ $\div$ _____ $=$ _____ people

Circle **add, subtract, multiply,** or **divide.**
Write the number sentence.

6. Sara wants to make 2 apple pies.
   She needs 6 apples for each pie.
   How many apples does she need to buy?

   add   subtract   multiply   divide

   _____ $\bigcirc$ _____ $=$ _____ apples

1.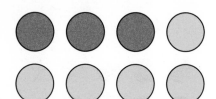

$\frac{3}{5}$ ○ $\frac{3}{8}$ ○ $\frac{5}{3}$ ○   NH ○

2.

○ 3 berries   ○ 5 berries

○ 4 berries   ○ 6 berries

3. 319 + 51 = ☐

829 ○   360 ○   370 ○   380 ○

4.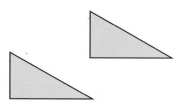

○   ○   ○   NH ○

5.

○ about 1    ○ about 3

○ about 2    ○ about 4

Oral Directions *Mark the correct answer. NH means "Not here." Mark it whenever the answer is not given.*

#1. What fraction of the group is red?
#2. 6 children share 18 berries equally. How many berries does each child get?

#3. Add.
#4. Which shape could you make by putting the two triangles together?
#5. About how many paper clips long is the crayon?

Circle equal groups.
Write the number in each group.

1. ● ● ● ●
   ● ● ● ●

   2 groups of _____

2. ● ● ●
   ● ● ●
   ● ● ●

   3 groups of _____

Write a number sentence to solve.
Use counters if you wish.

3. Ted has 8 pieces of bread.
   If he needs 2 pieces for
   each sandwich, how many
   sandwiches can Ted make?

   _____ ÷ _____ = _____ sandwiches

4. Jill has 12 ice cubes. She
   wants to put 4 ice cubes in
   each glass. How many glasses
   can she fill with ice cubes?

   _____ ÷ _____ = _____ glasses

Solve. Use counters if you wish.

5. Becky's book has 16 pages. She reads
   4 pages each day. How many days will
   it take her to finish reading the book?

   It will take her _____ days.

6. Sam has 11 water slide tickets. Each ride
   costs 4 tickets. How many times can he
   ride the water slide?

   Sam can ride the slide _____ times.

   How many tickets are left over? _____ are left over.

Circle equal groups to divide.

7.

$18 \div 6 =$ _____ R _____

8.

$14 \div 3 =$ _____ R _____

Solve each problem.
Use counters if you wish.

9. $2 \times$ _____ $= 12$

   $12 \div 2 =$ _____

10. $3 \times$ _____ $= 6$

    $6 \div 3 =$ _____

Circle add, subtract, multiply, or divide.
Write the number sentence.

11. Tiana had 6 tickets to a concert.
    She gave 2 tickets to Robert.
    How many tickets does she have left?

    add   subtract   multiply   divide

    _____ ◯ _____ $=$ _____ tickets

12. Wanda earns 5 dollars each hour working
    at the pet store. If she works for 8 hours,
    how much money will she earn?

    add   subtract   multiply   divide

    _____ ◯ _____ $=$ _____ dollars

Name_____

1.

- ○ 4 cookies
- ○ 5 cookies
- ○ 6 cookies
- ○ 7 cookies

2.

$9 \div 3 = \boxed{} R \boxed{}$

3	6	3 R 1	NH
○	○	○	○

3.

$6 \div 2 = 3$	$6 \times 4 = 24$	$18 + 6 = 24$	$18 \div 6 = 3$
○	○	○	○

4.

$8 - 2 = 6$	$8 \div 2 = 4$	$8 + 2 = 10$	$8 \times 2 = 16$
○	○	○	○

5.

- ○ 1 marble
- ○ 2 marbles
- ○ 3 marble
- ○ NH

Oral Directions *Mark the correct answer. NH means "Not here." Mark it whenever the answer is not given.*

#1. 3 children share 15 cookies equally. How many cookies does each child get?
#2. Divide.

#3. Eighteen people ride in six cars, with the same number of people in each car. Which number sentence shows how to find the number of people in each car?
#4. Marvin had 8 apples. He buys 2 more apples. Which number sentence show how many apples Marvin has now?
#5. Bill has 11 marbles. He wants to share them equally among 3 friends. How many marbles will he have left over?

6.

$14 \div 4 =$ ☐ **R** ☐

3	3 R1	3 R2	NH
○	○	○	○

7. $16 \div 2 =$ ☐

$16 \times 2 = 32$	$2 \times 6 = 12$	$2 \times 8 = 16$	$2 \times 3 = 6$
○	○	○	○

8.

4 groups of ☐

20	4	10	5
○	○	○	○

9.

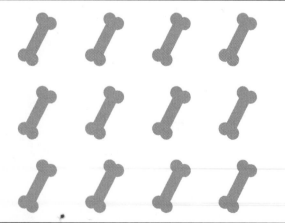

○ 2 bones

○ 3 bones

○ 4 bones

○ 5 bones

Oral Directions *Mark the correct answer. NH means "Not here." Mark it whenever the answer is not given.*

#6. Divide.
#7. Which multiplication sentence could help you find $16 \div 2$?
#8. How many dots are in each of the 4 groups?
#9. 4 dogs share 12 bones equally. How many bones does each dog get?

add

$$7 + 2 = 9$$

between

$$20, 21, 22$$

21 is between 20 and 22.

addend

$$4 + 3 = 7$$

addends

calendar

October						
S	M	T	W	T	F	S
			1	2	3	4
5	6	7	8	9	10	11
12	13	14	15	16	17	18
19	20	21	22	23	24	25
26	27	28	29	30	31	

addition sentence

$$7 + 3 = 10$$

cent

 or

1 ¢   1 cent

after

$$21, 22$$

22 is just after 21.

centimeter (cm)

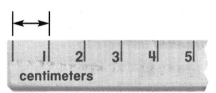

before

$$20, 21$$

20 is just before 21.

circle

Picture Glossary

cone 	difference $8 - 3 = 5$ $\begin{array}{r} 8 \\ -\ 3 \\ \hline 5 \end{array}$ difference
corner (vertex) vertex 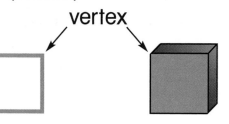	digit digit ↓ 32 ↑ digit 32 has two digits.
cube A cube is a rectangular prism with 6 equal faces. 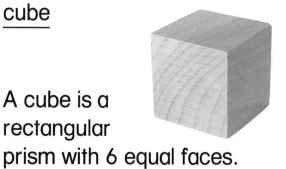	dime or 10¢ 10 cents
cup (c) 	divide 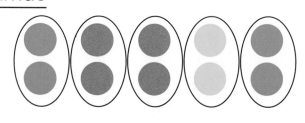 $10 \div 2 = 5$
cylinder 	division sentence $12 \div 3 = 4$

dollar

100¢ or $1.00

fact family

$$9 + 1 = 10 \qquad 10 - 9 = 1$$

$$1 + 9 = 10 \qquad 10 - 1 = 9$$

double

$$5 + 5 = 10$$

foot (ft)

12 inches = 1 foot

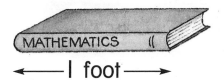

←—— 1 foot ——→

Your math book is 1 **foot** long.

eighths

$\frac{1}{8}$	$\frac{1}{8}$	$\frac{1}{8}$	$\frac{1}{8}$	$\frac{1}{8}$	$\frac{1}{8}$	$\frac{1}{8}$	$\frac{1}{8}$

fourths

$\frac{1}{4}$	$\frac{1}{4}$	$\frac{1}{4}$	$\frac{1}{4}$

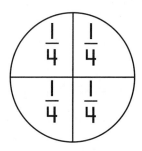

equals

$$7 \overset{\downarrow}{+} 2 = 9$$

fraction

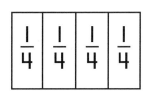

one half   one third   one fourth

estimate

about 30 berries

gram (g)

A sheet of paper
is about 1 gram.

Picture Glossary

greater than

$$52 > 48$$

52 is greater than 48.

hour hand

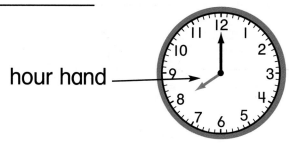

hour hand

half dollar

50¢ or 50 cents

hundreds

2 hundreds

halves

 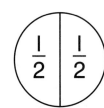 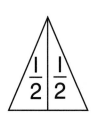

inch (in.)

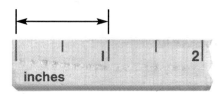

inches

height

kilogram (kg)

It measures about 1 kilogram.

hour

It takes about an hour.

length

less than $$47 < 48$$ 47 is less than 48.	**minute**  It takes about a minute.
line of symmetry 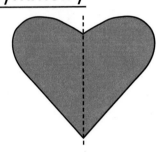	**minute hand** minute hand 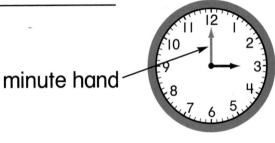
liter (L) 	**multiplication sentence** $$4 \times 3 = 12$$
meter (m) 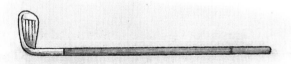 A golf club is about 1 **meter** long.	**multiply**  $$3 \times 2 = 6$$
minus $$10 \overset{\downarrow}{-} 2 = 8$$	**nickel**  or 5¢ 5 cents

Picture Glossary

number line

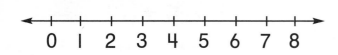

pint (pt)

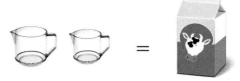

ones

4 ones

plus

$$8 + 1 = 9$$

pattern

pound (lb)

The butter weighs about 1 pound.

penny

 or

1¢   1 cent

product

$$3 \times 2 = 6$$

$$\begin{array}{r} 3 \\ \times\ 2 \\ \hline 6 \end{array}$$

product

perimeter

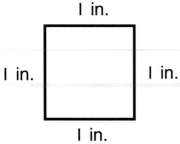

perimeter = 4 inches

pyramid

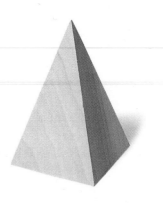

quart (qt)

related facts

$$7 + 5 = 12$$

$$12 - 5 = 7$$

quarter

 or

25¢   25 cents

skip count

2   4   6   8   10

rectangle

sphere

rectangular prism

square

A square is a rectangle
with 4 equal sides.

regroup

10 ones = 1 ten

subtract

$$6 - 3 = 3$$

Picture Glossary

subtraction sentence

$$12 - 6 = 6$$

times

$$2 \times 5 = 10$$

sum

$$10 + 3 = 13$$

$$\begin{array}{r} 10 \\ + \ 3 \\ \hline 13 \end{array}$$

sum → 13

triangle

ten-frame

twelfths

$\frac{1}{12}$	$\frac{1}{12}$	$\frac{1}{12}$	$\frac{1}{12}$	$\frac{1}{12}$	$\frac{1}{12}$
$\frac{1}{12}$	$\frac{1}{12}$	$\frac{1}{12}$	$\frac{1}{12}$	$\frac{1}{12}$	$\frac{1}{12}$

tens

3 tens

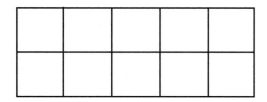

weight

thirds

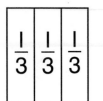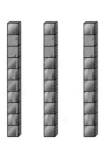

yard (yd)

$$36 \text{ inches} = 1 \text{ yard}$$

A baseball bat is about 1 **yard** long.

+	**=**	
add	equals	5:00
—	**>**	
subtract	greater than	10:30
×	**<**	
multiply	less than	square

rectangle	sphere	cone
triangle	cylinder	pyramid
circle	cube	rectangular prism

penny	quarter	one half $\dfrac{1}{2}$
or	or	
nickel	half dollar	one third $\dfrac{1}{3}$
or		
dime	dollar	one fourth $\dfrac{1}{4}$
or		

Credits

PHOTOGRAPHS

All photographs by Scott Foresman unless otherwise noted.

Front Cover and Back Inset: Carr Clifton; Front and Back Cover Background: PhotoDisc

page x: bottom left, Uniphoto; center, John Reis/The Stock Market; right, Chromosohm/Joe Sohm/Photo Researchers, Inc. 52: Ann Summa for Scott Foresman. 210: John Reis/The Stock Market. 219: Uniphoto. 221: Uniphoto. 231: top left, Fred George/Tony Stone Images; top right, © Rafael Macia/ Photo Researchers, Inc.; center, Chuck Place Photography; bottom, © Adam Jones/Photo Researchers, Inc. 232: top, David R. Frazier/Photo Researchers, Inc.; bottom, © Scott Berner/The Stockhouse, Inc. 235: © Chromosohm/Joe Sohm/Photo Researchers, Inc. 265: top left, Darren Maybury/Corbis; bottom left, Randall Hyman; right, Paul Souders/Corbis. 266: top left, © Tom McCarthy/The Stockhouse, Inc.; bottom left, Jan Reynolds. 332: © Tim Davis/Photo Researchers, Inc.

ILLUSTRATIONS

Chapter 1 Sharon Hawkins Vargo. Chapter 2 Nathan Young Jarvis. Chapter 3 Susan Lexa. Chapter 4 Brian Karas. Chapter 5 Jackie Urbanovic, April Hartmann, Dartmouth Publishing. Chapter 6 Amy Wummer. Chapter 7 Darcia Labrosse. Chapter 8 Chi Chung, Art Thompson. Chapter 9 Jerry Zimmerman. Chapter 10 Bernard Adnet. Chapter 11 Paul Yalowitz. Chapter 12 Lehner & White, Toby Williams.